THE FAMILY TREE

ITALIAN

GENEALOGY GUIDE

Terni
Narni
Rieti
Bracciano
ROME
Frascati
Albano
Roma
Velletri
Frosinone
Nettuno
C. Circello
Terracina
Gaeta
C. of Gaeta
Ischia
Portici
B. of Naples
Castellamare
Sorrento
Amalfi
Salerno
G. of Salerno
P. Licosa
NAPLES
Aversa
Avellino
Vesuvius
Nocera
ABRUZZO CITRA
Gran Sasso
M. Corno
Aquila
Chieti
M. Velino
L. Celano
Pescara R.
Sangro R.
Termoli
MOLISE
Capua
Benevento
Voltarno R.
PRINCIPATO ULTRA
PRINCIPATO CITRA
Sala
Laugenegro
M. Gargano
Manfredonia
G. of Manfredonie
Foggia
Barletta
Trani
Bitonti
Bari
T. di Bari
Venosa
Altamira
Bradano R.
Potenza
Basenta R.
BASILICATA

C. of Policastro
P. Palinuro
Paola
Cosenza
Castrovillari
Grati B.
CALABRIA CITRA
CALABRIA ULTRA
G. of St. Eufemia
Stromboli
C. Vaticano
Maida G.
Squillac
Cotr
Catanz
Lipari Isles
Lipari
Vulcano
G. of Castel a Mare
B. of Palermo
Messina
Aspromonte
Reggio
C. Spartivento
Strait of Messina
Trapani
Monreale
Palermo
Cefalu
Patti
M. Madonia
Mt. Etna
Catonia
Marsala
Mazara
Aspromonte

Tiber R.
Teverone R.
Tivoli
M. Velino

T y r r h e n i a n S e a

THE FAMILY TREE
ITALIAN
GENEALOGY GUIDE

How to Trace Your Family Tree in Italy

MELANIE D. HOLTZ

FAMILY
TREE
BOOKS

CINCINNATI, OHIO
familytreemagazine.com/store

Contents

PART FOUR: ADVANCED SOURCES AND STRATEGIES

Introduction

The writing of this book brings me great joy. With it, I honor the sacrifices my ancestors made when they left Italy and created a life for us here in the United States. We have opportunities they could only have dreamed of and were not possible in the Italy they knew. They left behind all they knew and people they held dear to provide us with a better life. And they succeeded. Our children can go to school and have enough food on the table, and there is extra money in the budget for extracurricular activities. *Mille grazie per tutti, Antonino Lo Schiavo, Giuseppa Catanese, Maria Di Domenico, e Matteo Catanese....*

After growing up in Pennsylvania, I came to know the Italian side of my family in my early twenties. In some ways, this was fortuitous because—when my Italian relatives told me the stories, passed down the recipes, and relayed the diverse history of our ancestors—I was ready and old enough to know the value of what was being conveyed. I listened, recorded the stories, copied photos, and traced our family history. I went to Italy, saw the houses where my great-grandparents were born, explored the parishes where they were baptized, reconnected with Italian cousins, and embraced this part of my history.

Through reconnecting with this side of my family, I came to understand some puzzling things about myself. I had always favored Italian foods, tried to take Italian in high school, and chosen to do my senior paper on famous Italians. I was so excited about the homemade stromboli my friend's mother served for dinner one night that my mother prepared it for my sixteenth birthday party. Something in my DNA knew I was Italian before I did. Now, more than twenty years later, my Italian history is ingrained in my very being.

As I began researching my Italian ancestors, I fell in love with Italian research, language, and culture. It speaks to me as nothing ever has before. On my first trip to Italy, I stood on the roof of my Palermo hotel and looked out over the mountains that had fed and sheltered my ancestors for centuries, and I felt like I had come home. It was an indescribable feeling and unlike anything I had ever experienced before. I'm sure others have had similar experiences upon returning to their Italian hometowns.

I soon became the local expert in Italian genealogy, and before long decided to make this my vocation. I began to prepare myself to offer research services to clients, educating myself in Italian records, history, and language. I submitted a portfolio of work to the Board for Certification of Genealogists and had my work vetted by the top genealogists in the field. My work passed muster, and I became a board-certified genealogist. I've now been a professional genealogist for fifteen years. I travel regularly to Italy, maintain an office there, and continue to grow my Italian research and language skills.

Genealogy, like everything, is constantly changing. New resources are being found or becoming available in different formats. FamilySearch's Italian digitization initiative **<www.familysearch.org/wiki/en/Italian_Records_Available_Through_FamilySearch>** is making it easier to research Italian civil and military records from home. Italian archives and libraries have taken up the baton and continued (or have begun) their own digitization projects. The Italian archival website, Portale Antenati **<www.antenati.san. beniculturali.it>**, will eventually make all civil records and military conscription records held in Italy's provincial/state archives available on the Internet for all to access.

I've tried hard to make this book of great value to the twenty-first century researcher. This includes, but is not limited to, detailing useful record types, discussing recent changes to conservation, and identifying upcoming trends that might affect where you find records. In the Internet age, more and more resources can be mined online for information about your ancestors, their society, or the historical time period they lived within. These resources are constantly changing and expanding, allowing easier access to more resources.

Cordiali Saluti,

Melanie D. Holtz
July 2017
Lo Schiavo Genealogica

PART 1

LINKING YOUR FAMILY TREE TO ITALY

1

Discovering Your Italian Heritage

When asked what they remember most about their upbringing, most Italian-Americans will talk about food, family, and community. Family members lived in close proximity to each other and were an important part of each other's lives. You had Sunday dinner at Nonno (Grandpa) and Nonna's (Grandma's) house every week—if they didn't live with you already. If you got in trouble at school, your cousin Giovanni had already told your mother by the time you got home. You learned to respect your parents and grandparents and took care of them in their old age. Dinner conversation was lively and accompanied by shoving and teasing from your siblings and cousins. Your *nonno* took great pleasure in secretly giving you more almond cookies than your mother would allow.

Italian customs and holidays often evolved so they were part Italian, part American. A turkey may have appeared on the Christmas table, but so did your *nonna*'s octopus pasta with gravy (spaghetti sauce), Zia (Aunt) Lucia's *panella* (a type of fried polenta), *pannetoni* (a sweet bread), and the chicken your *zio* (uncle) Batta brought to the back door of your grandparents' home a few hours before the meal. Maybe you celebrated the Feast of the Seven Fishes, a Christmas Eve tradition brought over from the old country. Or perhaps your ancestors crossed themselves repeatedly to ward off the *malocchio* (the

A

We owe a lot to our Italian immigrant ancestors. My great-grandfather, Antonino Lo Schiavo (pictured here in 1930), came to Pennsylvania from Termini Imerese, Palermo province.

evil eye), a superstition that a jealous or envious look from another person could cause physical harm.

All of this is part of Italian-American history, tradition, and culture. The sense of family and tradition is what we hope to keep alive for our children and grandchildren.

Our Italian ancestors often sacrificed a lot to immigrate to the United States, leaving behind their families and a life they would always miss. They (like my great-grandfather, Antonino Lo Schiavo in image **A**) worked hard, focused on their families, pressed onward when life presented difficulties, and made a better life for themselves and their descendants. All of this should make us proud of where we come from and truly grateful to those who came before.

This guide is designed to help you honor and celebrate your ancestors' legacy. While this book is not exhaustive, it will cover key resources and information you need to research your Italian ancestors. Through your research, you will learn more about Italian

Famous Italian-Americans

The list of Italian-Americans who have contributed to life here in the United States is truly endless. In fact, the European credited with founding America, Christopher Columbus, was Italian-born. One has only to listen to the music of Frank Sinatra, Perry Como, or Dean Martin to understand the impact Italian-Americans have made in the entertainment industry. Italian-Americans have also had a lasting effect on the country's laws and politics. Supreme Court Justice Antonin Scalia served in our highest court for many years, and William Paca signed the Declaration of Independence and was a member of the Continental Congress (showing that Italian-American influence extends much further back in time than is commonly understood). Joseph Alioto, Rudolph Giuliani, and Fiorello La Guardia all served as mayors to large US cities, while Anthony Joseph Bevilacqua, Justin Francis Rigali, and Joseph Louis Bernardin all became archbishops in the Catholic Church and served large Italian-American communities.

history, genealogy, and your cultural legacy than you ever believed possible. By the end of this book, I believe your Italian blood will be "singing in your veins."

In this chapter, we'll discuss some of the important facets of Italian-American culture, plus the major immigration trends you can expect to see.

Andiamo! (Let's go! Let's get started!)

ITALIAN IMMIGRATION AND SETTLEMENT PATTERNS

Italian immigrants have always been part of the United States' ethnic makeup, but Italians didn't arrive in large numbers until the 1850s. The earliest immigrants were often artisans or laborers recruited by US railroads, mining companies, and other large manufacturers for a certain job as the western part of the United States was settled. Most of these emigrants came from northern areas of Italy, and they sought opportunities to open businesses and own land in the United States and Latin American countries.

The major wave of Italian immigration to the United States occurred between 1880 and 1924, when the United States accepted nearly four million immigrants from Italy. Most came in through the ports of New York, Boston, Philadelphia, and New Orleans, although you will find significant Italian immigration into other US ports, such as Baltimore and Los Angeles. Many of these immigrants settled in large cities, where jobs were plentiful and living conditions, less costly, particularly after 1890. Others intimidated by the hustle and bustle of city life moved to outlying towns after a few years of city living. Some were even bound for jobs in Montana or California, depending on where other immigrants from their town or province had already settled.

International Italian Immigration

Between 1880 and 1924, more than eight million Italians left Italy for life in another country, but only about half of them immigrated to the United States. As a result, your Italian ancestors may have first immigrated to Argentina, then followed a cousin down to Uruguay before immigrating to the United States to take a job as a tailor in their brother's business. The path to their life in the United States was often circuitous.

Here are some other major primary destinations for Italian emigrants. If you can't find your ancestor in US arrival records (or suspect he might have come to the United States via another country), consider researching records from these countries.

Argentina

The Spanish began colonizing Argentina in the sixteenth century, and European immigration began there in the nineteenth century and consisted mainly of Italians, Jews, Spaniards, Frenchmen, and Germans. By 1913, nearly three million Europeans had settled in Argentina.

The Argentinian government at this time encouraged European immigration to bring in more people from what they felt were more "cultured" populations to settle and develop the sparsely populated country. Immigration laws in the 1800s were not as strict as those in the United States, offering free land to new arrivals—an especially attractive offer to southern Italians, many of whom were forbidden by law from holding land in their home country.

Most Italian immigrants came in through Buenos Aires and settled nearby. Just like in other areas of the world, Italian immigrants clustered in communities. However, in Argentina their clusters were smaller, usually consisting of those from the same town or group of towns within an Italian province. (In other countries, Italian immigrants clustered more into provincial or regional groups.)

Australia

Italians are the third-largest ethnic group (and Italian the third most spoken language) in Australia. While a few Italians trickled in between 1770 and 1850, the majority of immigrants did not come until the 1850s, when gold rushes in Victoria and Western Australia enticed Italian immigrants seeking fortune. Victoria saw the first Italian community spring up due to this influx of immigrants. However, the number of immigrants was small compared to the number of Italians immigrating to other countries.

The British shipped convicts to Australia in the early 1800s, and some Italians came as indentured servants to serve in the cane fields in the northern part of Queensland. There were also immigration surges after both World Wars due to poor living conditions in Italy, particularly after World War II when the composition of Australia began to change and Italians became a leading ethnic group.

Most Italian immigrants came from rural communities and worked in agriculture, growing bananas, tobacco, and other crops. Australia also offered work for those in other industries:

Fishermen found work off the large coastline of the island, and miners found work in the country's interior.

Brazil

After the end of Portuguese rule in 1822, the government created immigration laws designed to draw immigrants to settle in the forested areas of Brazil. Between 1880 and 1930, nearly 1.5 million Italians immigrated to Brazil, mainly settling in Italian communities in or near São Paulo. By 1950, over ninety percent of all rural land was owned by families of Italian descent. The immigrants were required to take on a Portuguese version of their surname, which now makes it difficult to find their original Italian surname.

Brazil was thought to be a country where an immigrant who had a little money could settle in an area and prosper. This was especially true after World War I, when immigration to other European countries was difficult because of the ravages of war. A predetermined system of land division enabled communities steeped in Italian culture to grow rapidly. Because newly developed communities had to border existing ones, immigrants didn't live far from their families. These communities were arranged around a *praça*, or square, reminiscent of an Italian *piazza*.

Canada

Statistics disagree about whether Canada or the United States received the most Italian immigrants, but the majority suggest Canada did. Many Italian immigrants settled in the provinces of Quebec or Ontario, where they maintain a large presence today. Pier 21 in Nova Scotia was often their point of immigration, though some immigrants came into US ports and entered Canada from the United States (or vice versa).

Italian immigration to Canada began in the early 1800s, but the majority came post-1860. Immigration increased in the 1920s, and there was a large influx after World War II as Italians sought post-war job opportunities. Italians viewed immigration during this time period as permanent, unlike immigration in earlier years when they entertained the idea of going home.

Like US laws, Canadian immigration laws of this time period required an immigrant to be sponsored by a relative or friend. Sometimes a future boss or landlord, called a *padrone* (plural: *padroni*), would sponsor the immigrant. This type of sponsorship also occurred in the United States, and some *padroni* cheated Italian immigrants out of their savings, leaving them destitute. However, there were good *padroni*, as well as fraternal organizations and mutual aid societies, available to help.

Uruguay

Second only to Canada, Uruguay saw a large number of Italians immigrate, beginning around 1870. Nearly fifty percent of all modern-day Uruguayans claim Italian descent, most from the Italian regions of Genoa, Piemonte, Napoli, Veneto, and Sicilia.

Some say that the Uruguayan immigration numbers are skewed because it was perceived to be a way station for immigrants who would later move on to Argentina where there were large tracts of land to be settled. But the large Italian-Uruguayan population seems to undermine that theory.

AUSTRALIA

Most Italian emigrants from 1880 to 1910 were driven from their homeland by poverty and lack of jobs. Changes in property and inheritance laws and the entrenched feudalism in many areas of the country prompted the lower classes to emigrate. With no possibilities of getting a job, they had to find a way to put food on the table and provide for their families.

Some countries (like Argentina) needed settlers to colonize the vast amount of unsettled land and sent representatives to Italy to recruit immigrants with the promise of free land, an attractive offer considering nearly 80 percent of nineteenth-century Italians worked in the agricultural industry. The ability to own land—especially enough to support your family—was a key factor in many immigrants' decision to leave their home country.

Some Italian immigrants intended their stays to be temporary, either for a season or for a particular job. Their plans were then to return to Italy, often with enough money to support their families and perhaps buy a little plot of land. These men were called "birds of passage," many going back and forth across the Atlantic Ocean several times over the years.

While most left the homeland for economic reasons, other Italians emigrated to avoid mandatory military conscription. Those from the southern areas of the mainland and Sicilia (Sicily), especially, felt little loyalty to the national government, which continued some of the same policies after Italian Unification (see chapter 4) that had kept the working class in poverty for many years.

Prior to 1880, more immigrants came from the northern provinces, usually emigrating through the ports of Genoa, Italy, or Le Havre, France (image **B**), but the bulk of Italian immigrants were southern Italians seeking economic opportunities. After 1880, most Italian immigrants came from southern Italy and Sicilia (historically the poorest regions of modern Italy), emigrating from the port of Napoli. In fact, statistics show that eighty percent of the United States' total Italian immigration came from southern Italy and Sicilia.

At the time, US lawmakers were concerned that immigrants, Italian or otherwise, would become public charges immediately upon entering the United States. As a result, they crafted immigration law that attempted to ensure Italian immigrants were financially soluble. Immigrants were required to state the amount of money in their possession, the name of the person they were going to stay with, and where that person resided. Each immigrant also needed a sponsor, someone willing to support them financially until they were able to find jobs and support themselves. This was often a family member, be it a sibling or distant cousin. This helped ensure the immigrant had sufficient financial means or support.

Immigrants also received a thorough physical at their port of entry, and those who didn't pass because of a physical ailment were sent back on the next ship heading to Italy.

Your Italian ancestors may have come through Le Havre, France, like these folks did aboard the *S.S. La Champagne*.

Others were detained until the ailment had abated. Records of those detained can be found amongst the immigration manifests, usually at the end of each ship's passenger list.

The immigrants' life experiences and where in Italy they originated influenced their decisions about how to live in the new country. According to historian Edward C. Stibili in a 1987 article for the *U.S. Catholic Historian*:

> The culture of the southern Italian peasant has been described by scholars as characterized by religious syncretism, *campanilismo* (village-mindedness), and amoral familialism…Loyalty to the *paese* (country) and local saints were overshadowed by loyalty to the peasant's immediate family. The family gave the individual both status and a measure of security.

It wasn't until 1869 that Italy began to record the numbers of emigrating Italians. Initially, most were headed for temporary employment in other parts of Europe and South America, where they did not intend to settle permanently. (See the International Italian Immigration sidebar for more.) Their focus shifted to the United States around 1880. J.T. Senner wrote in an 1896 article for the *North American Review*:

> As long as the migration to and from was entirely unrestricted [by the Italian government], Italians in large numbers were in the habit of crossing and recrossing the ocean, some as many as ten times, as so called "birds of passage" and taking out of the United States, or other countries of [North] America, the

gains which their standard of living, far below that of an American wage earner, made it easy for them to accumulate.

Initially, living conditions for immigrants were poor, but they quickly improved so much that they exceeded what the immigrant had left behind. Italian immigrants often lived quite modestly during the first few years, as they saved enough money to support their families back home or for purchasing tickets so the rest of their family could join them in America. Even some immigrants who didn't originally intend to stay in the Americas wound up sending for family members to permanently join them. According to Senner:

> Quite a large proportion of those who originally came to the United States with no intention of acquiring residence, found the country so advantageous and congenial to them that they changed their minds, sent for their families, and settled permanently within the United States, acquiring, in time, rights of citizenship.

Unlike records from some European ports, Italian emigration resources (except for passenger lists, which came with immigrants and are held at American repositories) were largely destroyed. Italian officials felt they had no historical value, and thus the passenger lists, passports (or documents needed to get them), and ship passenger tickets found in a family's possession are the only likely source of emigration information on an Italian ancestor. We'll talk more about these resources in chapter 2.

ITALIAN-AMERICAN LIFE: *LA FAMIGLIA* (THE FAMILY)

For Italians and those of Italian descent, *la famiglia,* or "the family," has always been the most important social unit, putting focus on family, church, and community. Immigration to other countries was often the only means of providing for and protecting their families when jobs and opportunities were lacking. Starvation was a reality in the lives of many Italians prior to emigration, and it was a powerful motivator when it came time to decide whether or not to emigrate. They made great sacrifices so we could have the lives we enjoy now. America, after all, is the land of opportunity, and a gift we often take for granted.

While some Italian immigrants knew they were immigrating permanently, others intended their time in America to be temporary. These immigrants were called "birds of passage," hard-working Italians who immigrated with the season or for a particular job and intended to return home to Italy. They moved back and forth between countries with the seasons, as new opportunities arose, or as more money was needed to support their families, buy land, pay taxes, etc.

Antonino Lo Schiavo (front) drinks homemade wine with sons-in-law, Earl Ripper (back left) and Tom Fasso (back right) in Evans City, Pennsylvania, in 1940.

Similarly, many immigrants practiced chain migration, a system of sponsorship amongst family and friends. The father of a family usually came first, followed by an eldest son and (eventually) the rest of the family. However, if an immigration was intended to be temporary, the father and eldest son might immigrate at the same time, enabling them to save double the money.

Some immigrants eventually became disillusioned with America. In his book *La Merica* (Temple University, 2003), Michael La Sorte writes:

> Disillusionment could come in a variety of forms. Many Italians demanded more of America than America was willing or able to give. Men came to America under the impression that they would be employed in a job of their own choosing the day they landed. Farmers who sought to manage a farm were informed that Italian farm managers simply did not exist. Those with training from technical schools in Italy did not find jobs commensurate with their talents. Others had great difficulty making the necessary adjustments to American culture.

Family and cultural heritage were central to Italian-American life. Even in the new country, many Italian immigrant families would still marry people from their region in Italy. My grandmother, Josephine Lo Schiavo, is seen here sitting to the bride's left in 1935.

However, despite the difficulties, what immigrants found in the New World was usually far better then what they left behind in the old country. Those who chose to settle permanently in the United States worked hard to create lives for themselves (image **C**).

In many Italian immigrant families, it was common for couples to speak Italian (or their local dialect) amongst themselves at home but to insist their American-born children speak and learn only English. This was their way of ensuring that their American-born children would have as many advantages as possible, many of which were not possible for the average person in Italy.

Extended family members settled close to each other or remained close despite their town of residence within the United States. Cousins of all levels (first, second, third) knew each other and grew up knowing they had an extended family unit to rely on when things got tough. Reliance on public charity was considered disgraceful unless there were absolutely no family members left to depend on.

Fraternal organizations dedicated to helping Italian-Americans begin their lives in the United States began to appear in the mid- to late nineteenth century. Membership dues supported these organizations, which provided help to new immigrants and served as a connection to their homeland. Many Italian immigrants purchased life insurance policies through their fraternal organizations, as an assurance that their families would receive some sort of financial assistance were they to pass away. The Order Sons of Italy in America and the Sons of Columbus were two such organizations. However, smaller groups more specific to an Italian region or town also existed. For example, a Sicilian living in Pittsburgh in the early twentieth century could join the Unione Frattelanza Siciliana, or the Fraternal Sicilian Union, through which they enjoyed many benefits and could socialize with those from their area of the country.

Many of our ancestors married someone from the same town or region, even after immigrating to the United States (image **D**). This concept, known as *campanilismo* (or regionalism), was common because of the prevalent opinion that the bride's and groom's families should be well acquainted with one another. This practice served to strengthen family ties by expanding that all-important family unit who supported you in times of trouble.

KEYS TO SUCCESS

Learn the basics of Italian-American immigration. Knowing the broader cultural context surrounding your ancestor's decision to leave the country—and researching the immigrant experience—can inform and enrich your family stories, plus give you a greater appreciation for the hardships your ancestors experienced.

Consider searching for your immigrant ancestor in other countries that were popular destinations for Italian emigrants. Many emigrants who ended up in the United States first came through countries such as Canada, Brazil, and Argentina, chasing job opportunities.

Find clues to your Italian ancestry by asking questions about their everyday lives here in the United States. What foods did they eat? Did several generations live together? What Italian traditions did your family celebrate?

Research their lives after they arrived in the United States. What challenges did they face? Did they belong to a fraternal organization? Did they go back and forth to Italy several times before settling permanently in the United States?

2

Jump-Starting Your Italian Research

enealogical research is a lot like using blocks to build a tower. Each piece of information or evidence about an ancestor provides a portion of the foundation for additional research. To put it another way: The evidence in one document can lead you to the next genealogical discovery. And by carefully tracing your steps and learning about the sources you're researching, you can make the most of your research time and dig deep roots for your family tree.

While you might be chomping at the bit to research your Italian ancestors, it's important to remind yourself of some key genealogical principles before you dive into records. This chapter will walk you through the basics of genealogy.

FIRST STEPS

Rome wasn't built in a day, and neither will your family tree. Genealogy research requires patient, methodical work. For example, we could use one ancestor's record to discover the names and birth information of their parents, then find the parents' marriage record to learn the names and birth information of *their* parents (and so on). We'll outline some of the first steps you should take in your research.

Start With Home Sources

Italian-Americans are all about family, and that's exactly where Italian genealogy begins. Begin your research by taking stock of what information and records have already been preserved by family members.

We all have someone in our family who keeps photos, letters, documents, and other mementos, and these family files are where you should start your research. Determine what you have and evaluate them for genealogical clues. Ask your cousin, your second cousin, and your *zie e zii* (aunts and uncles). You may find photos, passports, letters to and from Italy, steamship tickets, military papers, journals, Italian birth records, bank books (many Italian immigrants kept a bank account back home), membership cards for fraternal organizations or unions, recipes, and other valuable clues about your ancestors. We'll discuss how to best obtain and use this information in chapter 3.

If someone else in your family has done some genealogical research, ask if they will share their findings and digitized copies of the documents and photographs in their collection. This is a great way to jump-start your ancestral research (though, of course, the relative's research might not be totally accurate). You don't need to "recreate the wheel" if some of the work has already been done, but you do want to verify the accuracy of their findings.

Determine Your Research Goals

Once you've established what you already know, you'll need to decide upon some concrete goals for your research. What do you want to accomplish? Do you want to know everything about your ancestors back to the start of written records, or do you simply want to see if a long-told family story is true? Do you seek your ancestor's hometown in Italy, or are you striving to find the documents necessary to reclaim Italian citizenship? Knowing what your goals are will help you build a clear research plan to achieve them.

Once you've defined your goals, break them down into smaller chunks. By having more easily achievable goals, you can allow your research to gain momentum while you reap the rewards of having made concrete accomplishments. A few examples of your subgoals might be:

- Find my great-grandfather's US death certificate to see the names of his parents and if his Italian town of birth is listed.

- Learn what year my great-great-grandmother immigrated to the United States.

- Have a student in the Italian studies program at the university translate the letters found in Mom's cabinet that were sent from Giuseppa Moretti in Genoa, Italy.

- Determine what documents are needed for me to apply at an Italian consulate to reclaim my Italian citizenship.

Don't be too broad in your initial research goals. A research goal of "trace the families of all Russo immigrants to the United States between 1880 and 1910 to determine whether any of them were relatives" is too broad of a research objective or goal. A more defined goal might be "research the family of Eduardo Russo, who lived two houses away from grandmother Russo on the 1910 US census, and determine whether the two families were relatives."

Build a Family Tree

As you evaluate what you find and start accomplishing your research goals, record your information in a family tree. By graphically displaying your findings, you'll be able to more easily track your progress and identify areas needing future research. Family trees also make your research easier to share with family members and other researchers.

Being in the twenty-first century, you'll likely want to take advantage of digital family-tree making software or online programs. Ancestry.com **<www.ancestry.com>**, FamilySearch.org **<www.familysearch.org>**, and MyHeritage **<www.myheritage.com>** are the three most prominent family-tree building sites, as they allow you to sync digitized documents from each website's respective records databases. Online family trees like these also allow you to make connections with users who might be distant cousins, opening up new collaboration opportunities. Other services, such as software programs RootsMagic **<www.rootsmagic.com>** and Family Tree Maker **<www.mackiev.com/ftm>**, allow you to take your family trees offline, plus each program has syncing options with Ancestry.com's family tree function.

UNDERSTANDING GENEALOGICAL SOURCES

Not all genealogical sources are created equal, and it's important to know what kind of resource you're using. In this section, we'll discuss the different kinds of genealogical sources, information, and evidence.

AUTHORED WORKS VS. RECORDS

Most resources are **records**, documents created during or shortly after an event for administrative purposes, such as *battesimi* (baptismal records), *nati* (birth records), *censimenti* (census records), and *atti di matrimonio* (marriage records). You'll spend most of your time—particularly on the Italian side of the Atlantic—researching records.

Authored works, also known as published sources, are collections of already completed research. These could be formally published histories of a family or town, or an Excel spreadsheet with extracted information from a town's civil records. In general,

authored works are less trustworthy than records, as the person publishing the document may have made mistakes or even intentionally introduced errors.

ORIGINAL VS. DERIVATIVE RECORDS

Records are further classified based on how the information was obtained. An **original record** is created at the time of the event or close to it, and the person providing information for the record is usually a direct participant in the event. Some examples include birth records and marriage certificates. Could these records still err? Of course. Humans with inherent flaws created all records, and information may have been given incorrectly (either by accident or on purpose). However, original records are still the preferred type due to their proximity to important events.

On the other hand, a **derivative record** is a resource created from a prior record, after the event. These resources were not created by people directly involved in an event, so are more prone to contain errors. For example, a marriage certificate is an original record, but an extract from an Italian town hall (whether an *estratto*, an internationally friendly extract, or a certificate) is a derivative record. However, a photocopy of the original record—or an image uploaded to FamilySearch.org—is not considered derivative as long as no changes appear to have been made to the record. All translated records are considered derivative, which is important to consider when working with Italian records.

PRIMARY VS. SECONDARY VS. INDETERMINABLE INFORMATION

Similar to how genealogy records can be original or derivative, the information contained in those records can vary in trustworthiness.

Primary information is data reported by an eyewitness to the event, either at the time of the event or many years later. For example, the death date in a death record created four days later by two neighbors of the deceased is likely primary information. Even if the neighbors didn't directly see the person slip from life's grasp, then they likely saw the priest arrive to give the final sacraments, heard the weeping, or saw the civil official come to verify the death.

Secondary information, on the other hand, is hearsay, noted by people who didn't personally witness an event. While this kind of data may still be true, you should trace it back to more reliable, primary information. This includes all oral history, plus individuals' memories, as these can err or change over time. Someone who says the Mafia killed his great-grandfather, for example, likely heard that story passed down through his relatives. Unless he has a death record providing evidence of the ancestor's violent death or some Italian court records documenting the murder and the Mafia's involvement, it's secondary information that shouldn't be trusted until backed up by primary information.

If you're not sure where a piece of data comes from, it could be considered **indeterminable information**. This means that the data's accuracy, for the moment, is impossible to gauge. In the death record example from earlier, would a neighbor have primary information of the deceased's parent's names? Maybe or maybe not, making this information indeterminable or (at best) secondary if it can be determined that she was told the information by someone else or knew the parents personally.

Note that a single record can contain different kinds of information, so it's important to keep in mind how these records were created and to critically evaluate each piece of data in a record. For example, a burial record may contain a person's burial and death dates (primary information), his birth information as provided by next of kin (secondary information), and the name of his spouse (indeterminable information, as the person providing the information may or may not have personally known the deceased's spouse).

DIRECT VS. INDIRECT VS. NEGATIVE EVIDENCE

The information you find can affect your genealogy questions in different ways, and being able to parse out the ways these various resources affect your hypotheses is crucial to successfully applying evidence to your biggest research problems.

Specifically, information in your research can either directly or indirectly inform your research question. **Direct evidence** is any piece of information that can stand alone and answer a research question. For example, a civil birth record that states the child was born on 2 March 1856 at 10:00 a.m. in the city of Trieste gives direct evidence about said child's birthdate, place, and time. Meanwhile, **indirect evidence** is any piece of information that, by itself, does *not* answer the research question and needs correlation with other evidence. For example, a US census record may list Simone Mattei as widowed, providing indirect evidence that he was previously married. If you wanted to learn about Simone's wife, you would need to do further research to establish (1) that he was, in fact, married and (2) to whom he was married.

Sometimes information can even support a research claim by its absence. **Negative evidence** is information that should be in a record but isn't, allowing us to infer a genealogical conclusion based on a lack of clearly stated evidence. For example, the Italian death record of Attilio Catanese may give his parents' names as Simone Catanese and Maria Abbate, and the section for Simone's occupation and residence may be crossed out. While no word precedes Simone's name to indicate he was deceased, the fact that they did not insert an occupation and residence implies he was indeed deceased and provides negative evidence of this conclusion. In this situation, you should research Simone Catanese's death record.

For more on how to analyze genealogical evidence, consult *Evidence Explained: Citing History Sources from Artifacts to Cyberspace* by Elizabeth Shown Mills (Genealogical Publishing Co., 2015), which discusses how to interpret sources and provides citation examples for nearly any type of record you may encounter within genealogy. The examples for Italian records are limited, but the book does cover the basics of citing civil records and some censuses. Dr. Thomas W. Jones' *Mastering Genealogical Proof* (National Genealogical Society, 2013) will also help you understand the sometimes complicated subject **<www.ngsgenealogy.org/cs/mastering_genealogical_proof>**.

THE GENEALOGICAL PROOF STANDARD

How can you tell "good" research from "bad" research? And how can you be confident that your own research can pass muster? Genealogists have put together proof standards that answer those questions and hold researchers accountable. These best practices—which apply to any kind of research, whether you're pulling information from Italian- or English-language records—provide guidance on how we should conduct, analyze, and record our research.

Genealogical standards are not often taught in Italian genealogy. But why not? Beginners, professionals, and genealogists in between can all benefit from careful, methodical approaches to genealogy that hold their research to a set of criteria. After all, we all want our genealogy to be well researched, to consult all available resources, and to understand what the documents are telling us about our ancestors in their historical and social context.

The Board for Certification of Genealogists' book, *Genealogy Standards*, available online **<www.bcgcertification.org/catalog/index.html>**, can provide guidance on genealogical standards and is a "must have" for any genealogist. The group's website also contains many educational resources, including links to free and for-pay webinars that will help you improve your genealogical skills.

The Genealogical Proof Standard (GPS) provides a measuring stick by which we can evaluate whether our research and genealogical conclusions are sound. There are five parts to the GPS, all of which must be met when we make genealogical conclusions:

1. **The research must have been reasonably exhaustive.** Please note that the standard says *reasonably* exhaustive research. Obviously, you can never truly exhaust possibilities in your research. Rather, the GPS requires you to pursue all probable sources before drawing conclusions about your ancestors.

So what are the practical applications of the *reasonably* exhausted principle? Let's look at an example. You're trying to determine the birth date of Lucia Parotta, who was born in the town of Termini Imerese, Palermo province, Sicily, about 1850. Since Sicily's civil registration began in 1820, you determine a civil record of her birth will provide the most accurate information because it was created near the time of the event (see the earlier sections on genealogy sources and information for more). You find it and—*voila!*—discover her birth record. Has your research been reasonably exhaustive?

The answer is no. Any record can err, so you should always back up your research with other sources. Therefore, "reasonably exhaustive" research has sought out these other records. Civil marriage supplements (documents that were to be attached to a marriage record, called *allegati* or *processetti*) often contained extracted birth or baptismal records of the bride and groom. Additionally, the marriage announcements (banns) and marriage record would give the couple's ages, providing evidence of her year of birth. The birth records of her children might also provide evidence of her year of birth, but these records do not always give the mother's age. Another important record would be her baptismal record—even if it doesn't list a specific birth date, you can safely assume that Lucia's baptism happened shortly after her birth. Once you've considered these possibilities—and pursued them to the best of your ability—your research could be considered "reasonably exhaustive."

2. **Your work must contain complete and accurate citations for all sources that provide evidence toward your conclusion.** Noting from where (and when) you found information is nearly as important as (if not more important than) the information itself. Always cite your sources, as this will allow you to revisit them at any time and give credence to your work when others view it. Citation programs like EasyBib **<www.easybib.com>** make formatting your citation a breeze, and many software programs will even create citations for you.

3. **All evidence pertaining to the genealogical question or problem must be analyzed and correlated with other evidence and information relevant to the research problem.** In other words: Put the pieces of your research together, and do your best to understand how they all fit. Consider how the information in records affects your research question and what (if any) insight it provides. You may need to branch out and extend your research to other members of the family or acquaintances in order to find the needed evidence.

4. **All conflicts of evidence have been analyzed and resolved, and the proposed answer to the problem is still sound.** You can't ignore the evidence in one record just because it doesn't agree with what other records are saying. Any record can err, and you'll need to evaluate all sources that provide information on the genealogical question and determine which are the strongest. Could a recordkeeper have misheard a name when writing it down, or have you found an incorrect transcription? Resolve any

such conflicts in your research, and make sure the conclusions to your research can still stand after settling those issues.

5. **Your results are presented in a "soundly reasoned, coherently written conclusion."** This may mean writing a report to your personal files or typing it into the notes section of your genealogy software program. By writing our conclusions in narrative form, we can see the strength of our research and whether other records may need to be mined for clues. If you're working with Latin or Italian-language documents, be sure to include translations.

KEYS TO SUCCESS

☘ Study and incorporate key genealogical principles, such as the differences between direct and indirect sources and primary and secondary information, as these best practices will give your research a strong foundation.

☘ Begin with what you already know about your ancestors through family files, then methodically build your research off of this research baseline.

☘ Define realistic research goals. Evolve them as your research progresses and you find more information.

☘ Evaluate each document carefully to get the most (and most accurate) information.

☘ Consult published resources on genealogical documentation. Understand the Genealogical Proof Standard (GPS) and how to apply it to your research.

3

Identifying Your Immigrant Ancestors

While researching records from the old country can be fun and exciting, Italian genealogy research doesn't begin in Italy. Before your research jumps across the Atlantic, you'll need to learn all you can about your immigrant ancestor *after* he came to the United States. By learning who your immigrant ancestor was and when he left his homeland, you'll set concrete dates for your research and (hopefully) minimize the chance that you'll waste time looking for records of the wrong person.

In this chapter, we'll discuss how to discover your immigrant ancestor and his town of origin in US records using various resources.

GATHERING WHAT YOU ALREADY KNOW

Gathering and recording the information you already know about your ancestors is key to having a solid foundation for your research, allowing you to focus your efforts on the type of records most likely to provide information on your ancestors. This will make your research more efficient.

You should begin the research on your Italian ancestors in three main ways: collecting oral histories/interviewing your Italian relatives, searching family documents and records, and documenting data you already know.

Interviewing Your Italian Relatives

Your oldest Italian relatives are some of the best sources for information about your ancestors, and their stories can jump-start your research when you're just getting started or have hit a roadblock. Information gained through oral history is often key to creating a solid foundation for your genealogical research. With today's technological advances, you don't even have to take written notes, as you can simply turn on a digital tape recorder and allow relatives to talk. Nowadays, distant relatives are just a click away through technology like Skype <www.skype.com/en> or FaceTime <www.facetime.com>. And the number of potential cousins you can connect with continues to grow as genealogy becomes more popular.

Write your questions down ahead of time so you don't forget to ask something important. *Family Tree Magazine* has some great interview questions and tips at <www.familytreemagazine.com/premium/oral-history-interview-question-lists>. I often like to ask specific questions that are designed to prompt memories, such as:

- What was their Italian name?
- Do you remember what town in Italy your ancestors came from?
- When did they marry?
- Where did they reside after they immigrated to the United States?
- What challenges did they face?

Make sure you transcribe your interview once you've finished. You can choose from a variety of oral interview transcription software, including Express Scribe <www.nch.com.au/scribe> and Stories Matter <storytelling.concordia.ca/storiesmatter>, software built by and for oral historians. Also be sure to take notes about how your relative responded to various questions. For example, you might note that "Aunt Nel really didn't want to talk about her grandfather; she said he was a hard man to love." Your impressions of the conversation can have great value in your research, providing clues to genealogical mysteries yet to be solved.

Once, before the advent of digital recorders, I surreptitiously turned on a tape recorder that was hidden in my purse when my grandmother and her sister began to talk about their parents and grandparents. My grandmother was a first-generation Italian-American and was too self-conscious to answer my questions when she knew the tape recorder was on. Now that both my grandmother and great-aunt have passed away, those thirty minutes or so of conversation between them are priceless. Their conversation revealed many pieces of information I had never heard before, including the name of our Italian immigrants' grandfather (their great-grandfather) and details about the passing of their mother in the 1918 influenza epidemic.

Don't limit yourself to direct-line ancestors. It is surprising how much a second cousin might remember and how key documents and photographs tend to end up in the possession of the relatives you least expect. Stories and memories of more-distant relatives can add flavor and meat to your family history and may provide key pieces of information that will allow you to turn the research to the Italian records. Also schedule more than one interview with each relative. The first interview will prompt more memories they can share with you during the second go-around.

Searching Family Documents and Records

We often have documents or records within our families' files that can provide key information on immigrant ancestors, before and after immigration. Recently, after nearly twenty years of researching my Italian family, I discovered a newspaper article in my grandmother's files, detailing my great-grandfather and great-aunt's near fatal exposure to carbon monoxide in the 1930s. The article triggered my living relatives' memories, providing me with new stories and life details. That memory was followed by other memories that gave me a unique glimpse into the personalities and lives of my Italian ancestors.

Don't limit your research to the files of your immediate family group. Ask your cousins what pictures, documents, or information they have. A cousin, a great aunt, or even a nephew three times removed may have a better picture of your immigrant Italian ancestors or perhaps an original document they brought with them from Italy. Records in the possession of extended family can be valuable.

For example, if you know the birthdate of your great-uncle but not the birthdate of your great-grandfather, you can feasibly search in the military conscription or extraction lists for your great-uncle within the Italian province they came from. In this way, you will likely discover the names of your great-grandfather's parents, plus maybe his town of origin.

RESEARCH TIP

Think Broadly

Consider a variety of possibilities as you research your family history. Approaching a genealogical problem from all possible angles can increase your chances of success.

A

TRANSLATION:

[Number 19077]

Casellario Giudiziale

Penal Certificate

District Court of Caltanissetta

In the name of Giuseppe Picceri, son of the deceased Saverio [Picceri] and Giuseppa D'Antona, born on 26 November 1879 in Riesi, Province (or State) of Caltanissetta, by request of the same for immigration....

Even if your ancestor didn't carry a passport, he might have carried a penal certificate, which a person needed to acquire a passport. A translation is indicated above.

Some of the most commonly found documents in Italian American families' files are:

- **Italian birth records** (*certificati di nascita* or *certificati di nati*): Many immigrants brought a copy of their birth records as proof they were old enough to be employed in their job of choice or to marry.

- **Italian passports** (*passaporti*): Immigrants needed to provide some documentation showing they had met qualifications to emigrate, and these could include either a passport or documents required for receiving a passport. For example, an Italian citizen applying for a passport had to submit a copy of his birth record and a penal certificate showing that he was in good standing with Italian law enforcement when he applied for his passport. Copies of documents presented when applying for a passport (image **A**) were often brought with the emigrant. The United States did not require Italian immigrants to have passports until after 1900. Therefore, if your ancestor came before that year, you might find that he was never issued a passport.

Italian identification booklets (*carte d'identitá*), required by the Italian government, can unlock a variety of information about your Italian-American ancestors.

- **Italian identification booklets** (*carta d'identitá*): Italian identification booklets were required since the mid-twentieth century. These booklets often give an individual's full name, parents' names, birth date and birthplace, civil status (married or single), town and address of residence, occupation, and physical description (which can be hard to come by in other genealogical resources). See image **B** for one such document.

- **Military discharge papers**: Many Italian immigrants brought their military discharge papers as proof they had served their designated time in the Italian military. It was often the only proof they needed to show when Italian draft notices arrived during World War I and World War II. Immigrants would go to the nearest Italian consulate to have a letter drafted to the military command containing the details of their service and subsequent discharge. See chapter 11 for more on military records.

- **Family correspondence**: Family correspondence often contained addresses of relatives back in Italy. Surprisingly, people didn't move as frequently as they do here in the United States, and you may find that a distant cousin or aunt still resides at

C

Ancestors carried photographs, like this one of my great-grandfather's sister Giuseppa (Lo Schiavo) Guercio from Caltavuturo in the Palermo province.

the address on family letters. In researching my Italian family, I found an address on letters between the daughter of the Italian immigrant and an Italian cousin in the 1950s was still valid. In fact, the daughter of the Italian cousin still resided in that home and was very excited to receive a phone call from her American cousins. I've even been able to visit these distant cousins several times!

- **Family photographs or memorial cards**: Photographs of the ancestors, such as this one of Giuseppa (Lo Schiavo) Guercio (image **C**), often have names and other notes written on the back of the photo, which may help in your genealogical research. Additionally, memorial cards (a somewhat unlikely resource) picked up at wakes and funerals may contain information on the ancestor such as name, birth date, birthplace, and date of death.

- **Original marriage certificates**: If your ancestors immigrated separately and married in the United States, you may find the document from the stateside ceremony. Look for the priest's signature as well, as this can help you determine the parish where your ancestors were married. For example, my immigrant ancestors married in downtown Pittsburgh, and the original marriage certificate (which was passed down through the generations) has the signature of a man named Father Lagorio, who served all three of Pittsburgh's Italian parishes at the time.

- **Original certificates of naturalization**: The original certificate of naturalization, given to an immigrant upon his naturalization, is often found in family papers and can serve as proof of naturalization when you are applying for Italian-American dual citizenship.

Documenting Data

It's essential that you record each piece of information you find about your ancestors and where you found it. Build your family tree as you go along. Otherwise, the next time you sit down to work on your family research, you may end up duplicating the work you did before. There are family tree software programs available, such as Family Tree Maker **<www.mackiev.com/ftm>** and RootsMagic **<www.rootsmagic.com>**, that allow you to more easily record your research and print out family tree charts and reports on your ancestral families. You can also build online family trees on sites such as Ancestry.com **<www.ancestry.com>** and MyHeritage **<www.myheritage.com>**. This can make the research easier and more enjoyable.

Additionally, understanding the source of the information can help when you have two or more documents providing conflicting evidence on the same genealogical fact (which happens more often than you might realize). For example, let's look at three records that conflict regarding the birth year of Maria Bigotti:

- The 1940 US federal census lists Maria Bigotti's age as seventy-two (born about 1868).

- The Italian birth record of her eldest son from 1890 says she was twenty-four at that time (born about 1866).

- Maria Bigotti's baptismal record dated 7 June 1867 states she was born "yesterday" (i.e., 6 June 1867) to Giovanni Bigotti and Maria Virga.

Of the three documents providing evidence on Maria Bigotti's birth year, her baptismal record would be the strongest form of evidence. This document was created at the time of her baptism—the day after her birth—likely with her father or the midwife in attendance, as was customary. Therefore, a person who had firsthand knowledge of her birth provided the information to the parish priest.

US SOURCES TO CONSULT FOR IMMIGRATION CLUES

Before turning to the Italian records, you should exhaust what records can be found in the United States. This heavy lifting in the beginning of your research will provide a solid base for your research when it eventually turns to Italian records, allowing you to establish the year your ancestor came to the United States. The *Family Tree Magazine* Records Checklist, downloadable from **<www.familytreemagazine.com/cheatsheet/recordreferences>**, can guide you in finding US sources.

This section will discuss the three most common US records for researching immigrant ancestors: census records, passenger lists, and naturalization records.

Federal and State Censuses

US federal censuses have been conducted every ten years since 1790, but due to privacy restrictions only records that are at least seventy-two years old are released to the public. At print time, all the US censuses from 1790 to 1940 have been made available, with the only notable exception being the 1890 census (which was destroyed by fire and flood). Federal census records between 1790 and 1940 are some of the most widely available records, with indexes and images of census records on websites like Ancestry.com **<www.ancestry.com>**, FamilySearch.org **<www.familysearch.org>**, and MyHeritage **<www.myheritage.com>**.

Federal census records have recorded various information throughout the years, and each enumeration had slightly different questions. Notably, census records provided a year of immigration (1900–1930) and whether an ancestor was a naturalized US citizen or resident alien (1900–1940). Census records also play a key role in determining relationships and occupations, and they can reveal children who passed away before reaching maturity.

PLACE OF ABODE				NAME	RELATION	HOME DATA				PERSONAL DESCRIPTION					EDUCATION		PLACE OF BIRTH	
				of each person whose place of abode on April 1, 1930, was in this family	Relationship of this person to the head of the family						Color or race	Age at last birthday	Marital condition	Age at first marriage			PERSON	FATHER
28				Yacona	Daughter				✓	F	W	10	S		Yes		Pennsylvania	Italy
29				Antonio	Son				✓	M	W	8	S				Pennsylvania	Italy
30				Paul	Daughter				✓	F	W	6	S				Pennsylvania	Italy
31				Vincenzo	Brother				✓	M	W	43	S		No	Yes	Italy	Italy
32	6	6		Martino Joe	Head	O	2000		No	M	W	74	M		Yes	Yes	Italy	Italy
33				Mary	Wife-H				✓	F	W	71	M	26	No	No	Italy	Italy
34				Camille	Daughter				✓	F	W	42	S		No	Yes	Italy	Italy
35	7	7		Crossini Paul	Head	O	2000		Yes	M	W	38	M	27	No	Yes	Russia	Russia
36				Georgie	Wife-H				✓	F	W	37	M	24	No	No	West Virginia	Austria
37				Julia	Daughter				✓	F	W	11	S		Yes	Yes	Pennsylvania	Russia
38				Mary	Daughter				✓	F	W	9	S				Pennsylvania	Russia
39				Paul	Son				✓	M	W	7	S				Pennsylvania	Russia

This 1930 federal census record shows that Joe and Mary Martino (lines 32 and 33) emigrated from Italy but does not list a town, a common occurrence on census records.

State censuses can also provide clues to an immigrant's birth year, relationships to other members of the household, and many other types of information useful to building your Italian family tree. They can often be used to supplement federal censuses that are missing or have been destroyed. Check the websites of your state library to see what censuses it conserves. You can find out what years state censuses were taken for your state of interest through the U.S. Census Bureau's website <www.census.gov/history/www/genealogy/other_resources/state_censuses.html>. Note that state censuses were often made in duplicate, so you may find an additional copy in another archive.

In general, censuses only provide a country of birth, though you'll occasionally see a region listed along with the country. Some Italians actively avoided the census enumerator, as interaction with authorities in the old country was usually not pleasant. Sometimes they would give fictitious names. In the 1930 federal census record (image D), the Martino family is likely the Catanese family. Further research on this family revealed that Matteo Catanese used the Martino surname and four others during the course of his life. (Read this family's story in chapter 13.)

As the majority of Italian emigration post-1880 came from southern Italy and Sicily, the historically poorer regions of the country, many Italian emigrants were not literate. This often caused misunderstandings when a census enumerator asked their designated questions (and, of course, an illiterate respondent couldn't check the document to make sure the information was recorded correctly). Therefore, information on census records should be supported by other evidence. In particular, an ancestor's age and year of immigration are often estimated and may change from one census to the next. Fading memories and multiple informants compounded this problem.

Playing the Name Game

While you may think you know what name your ancestor went by, knowing your ancestor's original name—as well as any potential spelling variants or nicknames—is essential for research in both the United States and Italy. We'll discuss Italian naming conventions in more detail in chapter 6.

Your ancestor's "original" surname (i.e., before any potential Americanization) will be listed on passenger lists and often in US records created during the first five to seven years in the new country. After that, Italians began to evolve their given names and surnames, often due to social pressure to have a more "American" name or to apply for jobs that weren't given to Italians because of their ethnicity. Some immigrants changed their names for other, more dramatic reasons: escaping military conscription, hiding from family they left behind, or shielding themselves from criminal elements such as the Black Hand.

These name changes can create problems for researchers. For example, one family I researched entered the United States using *De Botta* and are found in the first federal census after their arrival with this surname. However, by the time their third child was born in the United States, their surname had become the less-Italian *Bott*, and later *Brown*. This can create difficulties when researching Italian families, especially when the final surname is in no way similar to their original Italian surname. Brown didn't strike me as a natural transliteration/corruption of De Botta, and so I never would have thought to search for it in US census records.

Given names were also commonly changed after immigration to sound more American. Even first-generation Italian-Americans were born with one given name but used another. Check out this online resource of Italian given names and their English equivalents **<www.oocities.org/irishkenj/givename.html>**. A list like this is especially useful when you encounter unusual Italian given names like *Timoteo* (Timothy), *Gervazio* (Gervase), or *Durante* (Durand). Determining the English version of an Italian name could be key to finding these ancestors within US records.

Passenger Lists

Italian immigrants entered the United States through various ports, and all ships carried lists of their passengers and crew members. The National Archives and Records Administration (NARA) has microfilmed passenger lists in their collection for the major US ports as well as many smaller ones. A complete listing of their holdings can be found at **<www.archives.gov/research/immigration/passenger-arrival.html#film>**. As briefly discussed in chapter 1, the six major ports of entry for Italians were Baltimore (1820–1952), Boston (1821–1850), New Orleans (1820–1945), New York (1820–1957), Philadelphia (1800–1845), and Los Angeles (1907–1949).

Called a customs list prior to 1891, a passenger list can provide a lot of information about an immigrant. The list that follows demonstrates the wealth of information one might find on a passenger list, though what information you actually see will depend on when and from where your ancestors left:

- age and marital status
- relationship (listed as relatives)
- date of immigration and emigration
- name of ship
- place of last residence
- amount of ticket and who paid passage
- whether ever in United States before
- name of relatives/destination in the United States
- physical characteristics and condition of health
- nationality and place (town)/country of birth
- country of birth for father and mother

Note that, after 1900, Italians were usually designated as *South Italian* or *North Italian*, an important distinction because the United States had different quotas for the two regions. This distinction can be a clue to your ancestor's town of origin. For example, if your ancestor's passenger manifest says he was born in San Pietro and was northern Italian, this could help you narrow down the list of possible towns of birth when there are multiple towns by the same name in Italy.

Immigrants purchased their departure tickets at the shipping line's main office (or one of its satellite offices) before traveling to the point of departure. For example, most Sicilian immigrants did not travel to the port city of Napoli to buy their ticket, then go home for a few weeks, then return to Napoli to board the ship to America. Rather, they purchased their ticket at a satellite office in a closer town (usually in Palermo) several weeks or months in advance. Occasionally, you will find an Italian ancestor who purchased a ticket but did not get on the ship; these "passengers" were then crossed out on the passenger list.

Even if you already know the name of your immigrant ancestors and where they came from, an approximate birth year, and when they immigrated, your ancestor's passenger list will provide an age and maybe even a place of birth, last place of residence, and the name and town of residence of the closest relative back in Italy.

Naturalization Records

Just like today's immigrants, your ancestors had the opportunity to become full US citizens by going through the naturalization process. While the process changed throughout the years, finding your ancestor's naturalization records (if he was naturalized) has been made easier in recent years with the digitization of many naturalization record collections by commercial organizations like Ancestry.com and Fold3 **<www.fold3.com>**. FamilySearch International also has microfilmed and digitized many naturalization records, available online or at the main Family History Library in Salt Lake City. You can search FamilySearch's online catalog to see whether they have naturalization records available for a location of interest **<www.familysearch.org/catalog/search>**.

But large online databases aren't the only place to find these records—state libraries, county courthouses, and local historical societies have begun to microfilm or digitize the naturalization records in their collections. NARA has created indexes to the naturalization records in its collection, as the requests for these records have expanded exponentially in the last ten to fifteen years due, in part, to the increasing interest in dual citizenship from Italian-Americans seeking to reclaim the citizenship of their ancestors. US and Italian archives are struggling to keep up with the demand for documents like naturalization records that are needed not only for genealogical research but also for requests for dual citizenship.

So what, exactly, are naturalization records? These were documents used by the government in assessing and either approving or denying an immigrant's application for citizenship. Prior to 1906, these documents may simply give the ancestor's name, his present country of citizenship (prior to naturalization), the court of naturalization, and the date of naturalization. After 1906, the federal government standardized the naturalization process, requiring two kinds of documents that are more informative for genealogists:

- **Declaration of Intention:** Also known as "first papers," this document (image **E**) has key information such as the immigrant's full name (often indicating any subsequent names or aliases), when and where she immigrated, place of last residence in her country of origin, which port she emigrated from, and what country she currently held citizenship in, plus her birth date and place.

- **Petition for Naturalization:** Also known as "final papers," these documents (image **F**) contain the immigrant's full name (again with any subsequent name changes, formal or otherwise), the date/ship/port of emigration, his current residence, and the names/birth dates/residences of the immigrant's spouse and children. This document includes a section for when he took his oath of allegiance at

E

ORIGINAL

Form 2202—L
U. S. DEPARTMENT OF LABOR
NATURALIZATION SERVICE

No. 125713

UNITED STATES OF AMERICA

DECLARATION OF INTENTION

☞ Invalid for all purposes seven years after the date hereof

State of Pennsylvania,
Western District of Pennsylvania, } ss:

In the District Court of the United States.

I, _____ Mrs. Carmela Catanese _____, aged __46__ years, occupation _____ Housewife _____, do declare on oath that my personal description is: Color _White_, complexion ____Dark____, height _4_ feet _7_ inches, weight _145_ pounds, color of hair ____Grey____, color of eyes ___Brown___ other visible distinctive marks _____ None _____

I was born in ____Isuello, Italy____

on the __16th__ day of ___July___, anno Domini 1_862_; I now reside at ____Box 54, Haffey,____, Pennsylvania.
(Give number, street, and city or town.)

I emigrated to the United States of America from ____Palermo, Italy____ on the vessel _____ Unkown _____; my last
(If the alien arrived otherwise than by vessel, the character of conveyance or name of transportation company should be given.)

foreign residence was _Isuello, Italy_____; I am _____married; the name of my { wife / husband } is _____ Giuseppe _____; { she / ~~he~~ } was born at ____Italy____ and now resides at _____ Italy _____

It is my bona fide intention to renounce forever all allegiance and fidelity to any foreign prince, potentate, state, or sovereignty, and particularly to _____

_____ Victor Emmanuel lll, King Of Italy _____

of whom I am now a subject; I arrived at the port of ____New York____ in the State of ____New York____, on or about the ____28th__ day of____December____, anno Domini 1_919_; I am not an anarchist; I am not a polygamist nor a believer in the practice of polygamy; and it is my intention in good faith to become a citizen of the United States of America and to permanently reside therein:
SO HELP ME GOD.

Mrs. Carmela Catanese
(Original signature of declarant.)

Subscribed and sworn to before me in the office of the Clerk of said Court at Pittsburgh, Pa., this __6th__ day of __September__ anno Domini 19 28

[SEAL]

_____ J. Wood Clark _____,
Clerk of the District Court of the United States.

By __M. D. Cline__, Deputy Clerk.

14—711   GOVERNMENT PRINTING OFFICE

Declarations of Intention, the first documents created during the naturalization process, can provide a wealth of information about immigrant ancestors, such as this document for Mrs. Carmela Catanese. Though her town of birth is given as "Isuello," further research suggests the correct town of origin is Isnello in the Palermo province.

the end of the process and often contained a place to write the number of his final citizenship certificate.

An ancestor's naturalization could have occurred in any federal, state, or county court, and (unhelpfully) individuals didn't have to file their first and final papers at the same court. Therefore, researchers are often confused about where to research for their ancestor's naturalization record.

You can request a search for your ancestor's pre-1906 naturalization record from the U.S. Citizenship and Immigration Services (USCIS) <www.uscis.gov/genealogy>. However, be prepared for a long delay in their response; at publication, the average person can expect to wait eight months to get a response to a USCIS naturalization record request. The USCIS may still conserve post-1906 naturalization records if the application was filed in a federal court. However, you will also want to research at NARA, which conserves some federal and state naturalization records after 1906, records from the county where the ancestor lived, and sometimes records from the municipal (town) level. Explore the website of your local historical society to see where the naturalization records of that county are conserved.

F

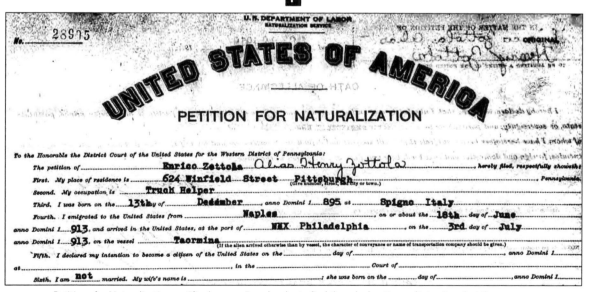

Petitions for Naturalization, or "final papers," are harder to find than declarations of intention, but they can provide valuable information nonetheless. The above—part of a Petition for Naturalization's first page—lists Enrico (Henry) Zottola's name, address, occupation, birth date and place, and more.

If an individual was mobile, you may have to research in all counties and towns that he resided in. For example, someone could conceivably file his Declaration of Intention in Allegheny County, Pennsylvania, then move to New York City and file his Petition for Naturalization there once the designated wait time has elapsed.

Fraternal Organizations

Italian immigrants often relied on fraternal organizations during their first few years in this country. These groups provided a way to stay connected with people from the same town, province, or region, even offering life insurance that provided some assurance that immigrants' families would have help were something bad to happen to them. Immigrants usually paid a small monthly fee that was used to help others within the organization.

There are hundreds of Italian fraternal organizations, cultural societies, and clubs still in operation today. A simple Google search will reveal what's available where your ancestor resided in the United States. Ancestry.com has digitized some records from one large group, the Order Sons of Italy in America <www.osia.org/about/who-we-are.php>; records include mortuary fund claims, enrollment and death benefit records, membership applications, and lodge records.

Some resources for fraternal organizations can be found at local historical societies and in the collections of cultural organizations. For example, the Western Reserve Historical Society in Cleveland <www.wrhs.org/research/library/significant-collections/italian-american> contains old lodge records for the Order Sons of Italy (which included membership rolls and a few vital records), information about this city's Little Italy, and charitable organizations that served the needy within the Italian community. This information could go a long way towards helping you understand the life of an Italian immigrant in Cleveland in the early twentieth century. Take the time to explore such resources.

RECORDS FOR FINDING TOWN OF ORIGIN

When beginning your research in Italian records, it's not enough to simply know your ancestors came from Italy. In fact, nearly all Italian records useful for genealogical research were (and still are) created at the municipal or *comune* (town) level. Therefore, you won't know in which town to research if you haven't first done some other research, making the search for your ancestors very difficult.

If an immigrant ancestor's place of origin has been passed down in family lore, congratulations! You've made a great first step in identifying your town of origin. But if you don't know a town of origin (or if you want to verify the family stories you've heard), you've got some work ahead of you.

You can determine your ancestor's place of origin in a variety of records. In this section, we'll discuss some common (and some not-so-common) resources that can reveal your ancestor's town of origin or (at least) point your research in the right direction.

Passenger Lists

Many researchers assume their ancestors were born in the town named on their ancestor's passenger list, but this may or may not be true. In addition to lacking specificity (many immigrants were listed simply as being born in Italy), passenger lists can also misrepresent a person's origin. For instance, your immigrant ancestor may have said he was from "Napoli" when he really came from the nearby city of Aversa, similar to how someone from Yonkers, New York (a city just north of New York City), may say he hails from New York City for simplicity's sake. This kind of generalization can throw off your research, so you'll sometimes need to think beyond the obvious to discover their true town of origin. See the Common Problems When Determining Towns of Origin sidebar for more potential passenger list pitfalls.

In addition, passenger lists may not always list the correct town—but what port your ancestor left Italy from may give you a clue about what region he came from. Nearly all emigrants from the northern provinces left from ports of Genova (Genoa), Italy, or Le Havre, France, while those in central and southern Italy typically left from Napoli (Naples) and those from Sicilia (Sicily) generally left from Palermo (sometimes by way of Naples).

One important thing to remember is that the official in Italy, who created the immigration manifest that came with the ship and your ancestor to the United States, was usually a native Italian, which lessens the chance of misspellings due to language issues. Misspellings happened, but not as often as people might think. Italian names were not deliberately changed at Ellis Island, despite this common misconception. Any changes to names were likely simply misunderstood, and you may need to think phonetically if you feel your ancestor's name might be misspelled.

Naturalization Records

Some naturalization documents provide the town of an ancestor's birth, depending on the year of the document and the laws in place at that time. Naturalization records after 1906 are more likely to have this information, and a town of birth can appear on either (or both, or neither) the Petition for Naturalization and the Declaration of Intention. Given that, make sure you research all parts of the naturalization file. See the section on naturalization records earlier in this chapter for more.

Common Problems When Determining Town of Origin

In my experience, researchers have trouble determining their Italian ancestor's place of origin using passenger lists for three main reasons:

- **The town name is abbreviated or illegible:** The box on a passenger manifest, used to insert the town name, was often not large enough for those long Italian town names. And even if the whole town name is printed, you may not be able to decipher the official's messy or archaic handwriting. Our guide on deciphering old handwriting (see chapter 6) may be able to help.
- **Multiple towns have the same name:** Great! Your ancestor is from Santa Maria. But which of the 120 Italian towns and hamlets that began with those two words did he call home? Some town names are based around their patron saint, so multiple towns could have the same names. You'll have to use clues from other records to help narrow down the list of possible matches for popular place names. We'll discuss this issue more in chapter 5.
- **Immediate family members have different towns of origin:** This problem likely has an interesting backstory that will explain the inconsistencies. For example, a husband often immigrated first to find work and then, if he intended to stay in America, would send for his family later. Between his departure from Italy and the rest of the family's emigration, his wife and children may have moved in with other relatives and so listed this new locale—which may or may not be the place where the wife and children were born or lived previously.

Vital Records

Depending on the year and place (as well as the recordkeeper's attention to detail), documents created during the major life events (birth/baptism, marriage, and death/burial) of your ancestors and their descendants often contain information about place of birth. For example, baptismal records of the first few American-born children of an Italian couple may note where the parents came from, particularly for those who didn't intend to stay in the United States and asked their parish priest to send a copy of the child's baptismal record back to the home parish in Italy. Likewise, couples may have noted their town or province of origin on marriage documents—more likely in parish marriage records, though both civil and parish are worth researching.

Date and places of birth are often given on an Italian immigrant's death certificate. However, remember this information was generally recorded many years after the event, and the reporting party may not remember the facts correctly. I once found a Pennsylvania death record for a Matteo Catanese that contained multiple changes on it—including to his birthdate and place of birth—that his wife and daughter had filed in the first few months following his death.

Legal Records

Records of various legal procedures can contain place-of-origin information as well. While most people don't consider property records a viable resource for finding an ancestor's town of origin, for example, I've found multiple Italian ancestors whose place of origin is given in some, if not all, property transfers they filed throughout their lives.

Likewise, the wills of Italian immigrants often show money or property being left to relatives who remained behind in Italy. In these cases, you can find an Italian town of origin, home parish, or address within the probate papers. Even the probate file of someone who died without a will can provide a clue as to that place of origin. In one case I researched, a couple whose only clues to their place of origin were her will and his intestate probate papers, which both showed a sum of money being sent back to birth parishes so that masses could be said for them upon their deaths. For example, these paragraphs from Maria (Di Domenico) Catanese's will specified that two hundred dollars would be paid to the Catholic Church in Isnello, partially to pay for a mass for the soul of her husband.

Cultural Clues

When records can't provide you with a town of origin, you may be able to turn to family stories or traditions for clues; see chapter 2 for more on evaluating what you already know about your family. Most people have some idea about what province or region of Italy their ancestors might have come from, and these leads (while not foolproof) can be extremely helpful.

Some questions to ask yourself and family members include:

- **Where did they first reside in the United States?** To help smooth their transition to the new country, people who moved to big cities often clumped together to form Italian enclaves, distinct communities with denizens who came from a particular town, province, or region. Because of this, you'll want to study the neighborhood your ancestor lived in to determine if it was one of these niche immigrant communities (Little Sicily, Little Calabria, Little Napoli, etc.).

- **Did they speak a dialect or different language?** As we'll discuss in chapter 6, Italians spoke in a variety of dialects based on where they came from, and these language variations can be informative. If your ancestors spoke the Napolitano dialect, for example, they were not from Milano, nor were Sicilian speakers from Abruzzo.

- **What were their favorite foods?** No, not all Italians favored pasta. Different areas of Italy favored different kinds of cuisine, and noting your ancestors' culinary habits can provide clues to where your family came from. Some parts of Italy used polenta

Case Study: Finding a Place of Origin

Emilio Antonio Martino immigrated to the United States in 1912 aboard the *S.S. America*. His port of embarkation was Napoli, suggesting he lived in a central, southern, or Sicilian town. His US immigration manifest said he last resided in *Valley Ariana* and that his father, Domenico Martino, was his closest relative in this town.

So how could I learn more? I turned to other US records. Emilio Antonio's WWI draft registration card clarified his birthdate was 5 May 1894, and stated that he was born in Frosinone, Italy. From researching Italian geography (see chapter 5), I knew Frosinone is both a province and a town so—while I was getting closer—I still had more research to do. No will or probate records were found for this ancestor in the town of death, and the 1920, 1930, and 1940 US federal censuses all give his place of birth as Italy. However, his US death certificate provided the key information that he was born in *Bov. Ernica*.

Bov. Ernica? From the Comuni-Italiani.it website **<www.comuni-italiani.it>**, I learned *Boville Ernica* in the Frosinone province is the only current town in Italy that ends in *Ernica*. Well, if he was born in Boville Ernica, why did his immigration manifest say he last resided in "Valley Adriana?" Comuni-Italiani.it lists the following hamlets or neighborhoods for the town of Boville Ernica: Area Castello, Casavitola, Colle Piscioso, Panicelli, San Lucio, Santa Liberata, and Scrima. None of these sound like "Valley Adriana."

I turned to other sources to learn more about this "Valley Adriana." The Family History Library has microfilmed civil records between 1871 and 1899, and Emilio's birth falls within this time frame. I found an Emilio Antonio Martino who was born on 5 May 1894 in the *contrada* (countryside neighborhood) of Valeriana, which was under the jurisdiction of Boville Ernica at that time. Close enough? It certainly seems possible that *Valeriana* was mistaken for "Valley Ariana" when this ancestor immigrated to the United States. Plus the parents listed on this Italian birth record (with some minor spelling differences) were the same as those listed on Emilio's US death record and WWI draft registration card. And, since Boville Ernica is in central Italy in the Frosinone province, we seem to have a match!

much more heavily than pasta, for example. Or if your *nonno* (grandfather) cooked *arancini* (stuffed rice balls—a Sicilian "poor man's" dish) on Saturday evenings to take to work the coming week, he likely had Sicilian blood coursing through his veins.

- **Whom did they marry?** While immigration provided access to a wider range of possible marriage partners, the majority of first-generation Italian-Americans still married someone from their region or province of origin. According to social historian Phyllis H. Williams in her book *South Italian Folkways in Europe and America: A Handbook for Social Workers, Visiting Nurses, School Teachers, and Physicians* (Yale University Press, 1938):

...The family functioned as the chief and sometimes the only means of transmitting culture. The intense regionalism called *campanilismo*...strengthened family ties and rendered adherence to its group objectives all the more expedient to individual members. It found particular expression in the strong societal taboo placed on marrying outside the immediate community. This in practice meant that the contracting parties should at least be known to each other's relatives...

As of 1900, this practice was still widespread, and it was common for the young couple's parents to arrange their marriage. It was part of every Italian mother's role within the family to do two things: (1) to find marriage partners for her children when the time came and (2) to save money so a bridal gift could be given to each son and a dowry to each daughter.

KEYS TO SUCCESS

Begin by inventorying what you already know. While family stories and documents you find around the home aren't foolproof, they can still provide a useful foundation for your research and provide valuable leads.

Be flexible with names. Spelling hasn't always been standardized like it is today—especially considering how your ancestors may have "Americanized" their names over the years. Keep a list of spelling variants for given names, surnames, and place names. Think phonetically. Consider that your ancestors may have also used nicknames.

Research a variety of US records. Identifying your immigrant ancestor is your first step in researching Italian ancestors, as an immigration date will determine when you should begin looking for your ancestors in Italian (rather than US) records.

Pinpoint your ancestor's town of origin—not just his province or region of origin—as most Italian records were created at the town level, and this piece of information will guide your research for most kinds of Italian records.

Listen to your family stories. Often, cultural traditions (such as what foods your ancestors liked to cook and what dialect they spoke at home) and your relatives' anecdotes can provide clues about where in Italy your family came from.

PART 2

GETTING TO KNOW THE OLD COUNTRY

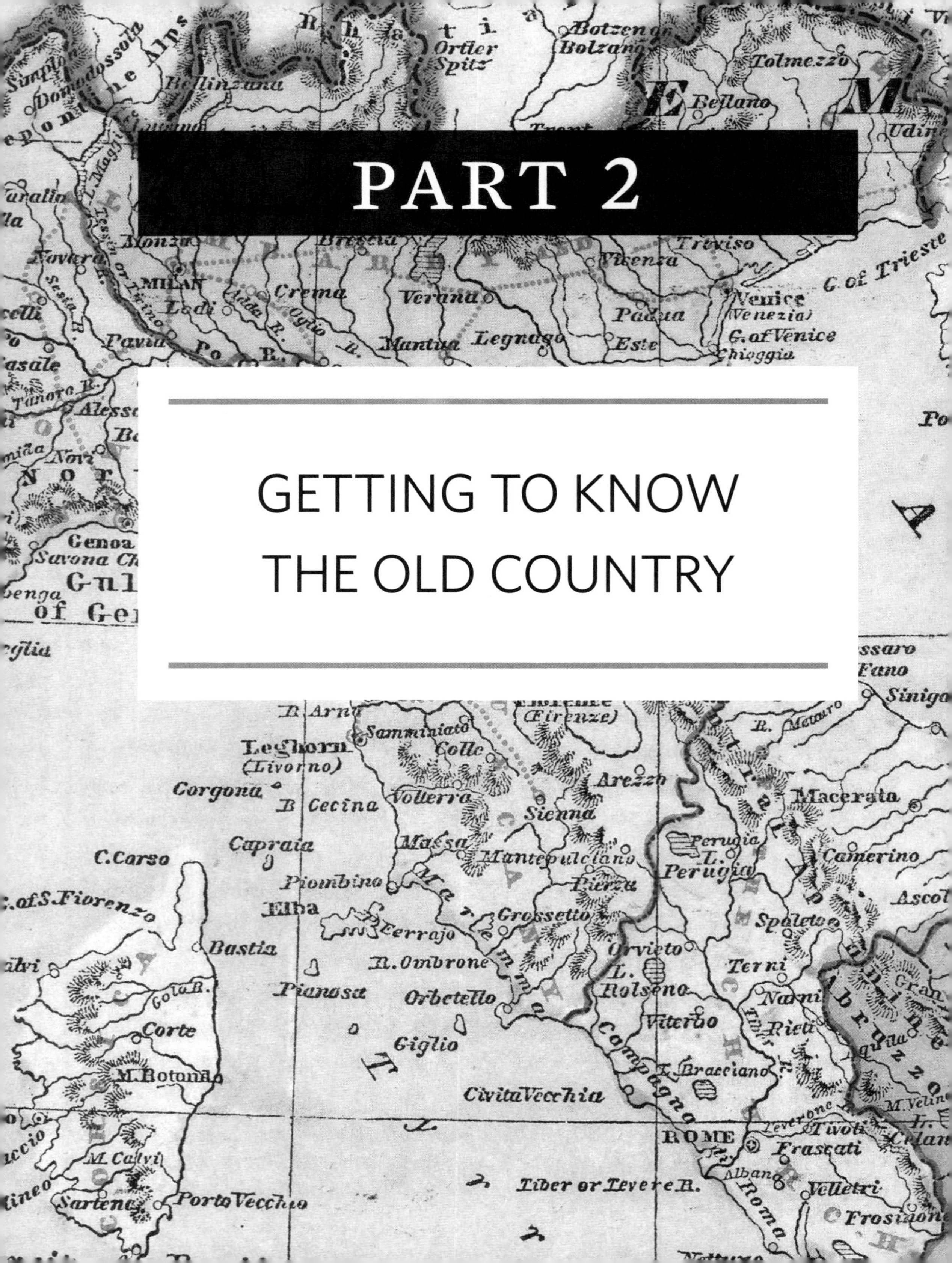

Understanding Italian History

nderstanding the basics of Italian history is important as you dig into your Italian ancestry, as knowing the wider historical trends can clue you into why your ancestors emigrated and made the decisions they did. Learning about your ancestors' historical era can also provide a glimpse at what everyday life may have been like for your relatives, coloring your research and filling in rich detail. In this chapter, we'll discuss the history of the region now known as Italy.

HISTORICAL OVERVIEW

La famiglia (the family) was the central force in Italian life (as it is today), with the actions of each family member reverberating throughout the whole family. But the macrohistory (historical events like wars, epidemics, feudalism, and revolutions) also make up the complicated and fascinating timeline of Italian history.

On the world stage, Italy is considered a rather young country. It was formed from multiple city-states around 1865 during a time period and process known as Italian Unification. Written records useful for genealogical research began in the mid-sixteenth century (with some notarial and university records beginning earlier). For the purposes of genealogy, Italian history can be divided into two main time periods: pre-Unification and post-Unification.

TIMELINE Italian History

753 BCE Rome is founded.

509 BCE Rome becomes a republic.

44 BCE Julius Caesar is assassinated.

27 BCE The Roman Empire is established; Augustus is crowned its first emperor.

476 CE Visigoths conquer Rome, ending the Roman Empire.

1054 The Roman Catholic and Eastern Orthodox churches split.

1096 The world's first university is founded at Salerno.

1321 Dante Alighieri completes *The Divine Comedy*.

1340 The Italian Renaissance begins.

1492 Italian-born Christopher Columbus lands in the West Indies.

1512 Michelangelo finishes the Sistine Chapel ceiling.

1524 Giovanni da Verrazzano is the first European to sight New York.

1563 The Council of Trent's decision begins Roman Catholic recordkeeping.

1582 The Gregorian calendar is introduced to Italy.

1796 Napoleon invades Italy.

1806 Napoleon begins civil registration in most areas of mainland Italy.

1816 The Kingdom of Sicily and the Kingdom of Naples unite to form the Kingdom of the Two Sicilies.

1861 The Kingdom of Italy is declared after years of war and conquest.

1865 The Italian capital moves from Turin to Florence, then to Rome five years later.

1895 Guglielmo Marconi invents the telegraph.

1900 Giacomo Puccini's opera *Tosca* is first performed.

1905 The first US pizzeria (Lombardi's Pizza) is established in New York City.

1908 A 7.1-magnitude earthquake (and the tsunami that follows) kills as many as 200,000 people in Sicily and southern Italy.

1915 Italy enters World War I aligned with the Allies.

1922 Benito Mussolini becomes prime minister of Italy.

1940 Italy invades Greece, entering World War II.

1943 Nazi troops occupy northern Italy.

1946 Italy becomes a republic.

1955 Italy joins the United Nations.

1960 Rome hosts the Summer Olympics.

1965 Luciano Pavarotti debuts in the United States.

1972 Francis Ford Coppola films *The Godfather*.

1998 The restoration of Leonardo da Vinci's *Last Supper* is completed.

Pre-Unification Italy (1300–1869)

Medieval Italy (and other areas of Europe) saw the development of communes, religious and political entities based around a town or city that historians say are the foundation of Italy's modern regionalism. Communes were governed with the town's needs and security in mind, especially important as the population increased, agriculture production changed, and people moved en masse to cities to find jobs. The communes became city-states, and the cities built walls surrounding them to defend against bandits and other criminals (many, like those in the north, still standing today). Religion was important to these towns' governments and people, aided by a city's proximity to the theocratic Papal States.

City-states were more common in northern and central Italy, but the Papal States south of Rome were a kind of city-state themselves. These states began in the ninth century and continued being founded through the fifteenth century (although some historians say they were still being founded in the sixteenth century). See the sidebar for a list of city-states.

Between the fourteenth and fifteenth centuries, industrious city-states expanded their power through military might, making them more regional than municipal (image **A**). They waged battles with each other to control key infrastructure needed for trade both on the peninsula and throughout the world, including ports, bridges, and mountain passes. Despite their differences, the city-states often shared commonalities in religion, language, culture, and law—aiding the growth and expansion of these states and the trade between them.

The Republic of Venice (Venezia), once part of the Byzantine Empire, is considered the first city-state. Another early city-state, the Republic of Ragusa, came under the Kingdom of Italy's control in 1808, and it consisted of Dalmatia (the southern part of today's Croatia).

Italian City-States

Northern City-States		Central City-States		Papal States
• Bergamo	• Padua	• Ancona	• Pisa	• Amalfi
• Bologna	• Parma	• Ascoli Piceno	• Siena	• Bari
• Brescia	• Piacenza	• Firenze	• Spoleto	• Naples
• Crema	• Reggio Emilia	• Lucca	• Terni	• Salerno
• Cremona	• Treviso	• Narni	• Todi	• Trani
• Genova	• Torino	• Perugia		
• Lodi	• Verona			
• Mantua	• Venezia			
• Milan	• Vicenza			

This map of Italy shows the Italian city-states in 1494.

While city-states were self-governing, they sometimes came together to form alliances. Once such partnership, the Lombard League, began in the twelfth century and initially included all northern city-states except for Venezia. The league fought against the land-hungry Holy Roman Emperors and later became known as the Veronese League. The league's city-state lineup varied throughout time, and it even eventually gained political support from the Republic of Venezia. Here we see the many layers of history, war, and politics play out on the national stage long before Italy became a republic. The laws of these city-states laid the foundation for regional statutes and civil law across the country.

Historians and others interested in Italian history often romanticize this period before the Spanish dominated Italy, as it laid the foundation for modern Italian culture and produced some of the world's greatest advancements. Called the Renaissance (literally meaning "rebirth"), this golden age of artistic, scientific, musical, literary, and intellectual awakening extended from the fourteenth through sixteenth centuries across Europe. Galileo Galilei, Michelangelo Buonarroti, Girolamo Fracastoro, Leonardo da Vinci, and Sofonisba Anguissola are just a few Italians whose work greatly influenced the renaissance. Firenze (Florence) and Venezia (Venice), in particular, were centers of art and culture during the Renaissance, dominating many of the historical texts about this time period. To learn more about the Renaissance, check out the following resources: Italian Renaissance Resources <www.italianrenaissanceresources.com>, Italian Renaissance Art.com <www.italian-renaissance-art.com/Italian-renaissance.html>, Artsy.net <www.artsy.net/article/artsy-editorial-these-women-artists-influenced-the-renaissance-and-baroque>, and LiveScience <www.livescience.com/55230-renaissance.html>.

Perhaps the first major event relevant to Italian genealogists was the Council of Trent, when a body of Catholic Church leaders met in the city of Trent to reform various policies of the church beginning in 1545. After the Council's adjournment in 1563, priests and bishops were required to begin to maintain baptismal, marriage, and death/burial records (image **B**). More reforms came to Roman Catholic parishes when, in 1614, *status animarum* (state of the souls) records were mandated. These records (such as the one in image **C**) can be used to track the vital statistics of parishioners and the sacraments they received. The canon and decrees of the Council of Trent can be found (in English) on the website of Hanover University <history.hanover.edu/texts/trent/trentall.html>.

You might be surprised to learn that Italy was under foreign rule at different points throughout history. The Hapsburg monarchy dominated western and central Europe for centuries, including portions of Italy. In 1494, France invaded Naples, leading to a bloody conflict between Spain and France, each of which dominated Italy at different points in time.

Between 1559 and 1713, Spain ruled most of present-day Italy, including Sicily and its valuable resources and key Mediterranean ports. Some records in this time period were

The Council of Trent, which met between 1545 and 1563, mandated that Catholic churches keep records of baptisms, marriages, and deaths/burials.

After 1614, the Church required Roman Catholic parishes to keep *status animarum* records of their parishioners' vital statistics and taking of the sacraments.

written in Spanish, mainly those created in the Kingdom of Naples (later the Kingdom of the Two Sicilies), which extended from southern Italy to the island of Sicilia (Sicily).

After a brief foray into self-governance, Sicily was transferred to the Austrian Hapsburgs in 1714 after the War of the Spanish Succession, and Austria was able to defend Italy against Spain in the War of the Quadruple Alliance a few years later. As such, you'll find German-language records from this time period mainly in northern Italy—though most genealogically useful resources were parish records, written in Latin.

Despite this setback, Spain reclaimed Sicily in 1734, when Charles III conquered Naples and proclaimed himself the ruler of Spain and Sicily. Charles III established the Sicilian Parliament and ruled until 1759, when he turned the rule of the island over to his nine-year-old son Ferdinand (who ruled as either "King of Naples and Sicily" or "King of the Two Sicilies" from 1759 to 1825).

By the end of the eighteenth century, many European monarchies were struggling to maintain power and order in their kingdoms. Various wars, efforts at reform, and conflicts with the noble classes had been costly in terms of both money and in the noble classes' prestige. This prompted revolutions and strife amongst the classes, as the poor became poorer and the rich became richer, widening the gap between the upper class and the common people.

For example, the island of Sicily was in a terrible famine in 1863. People were starving, and rioters who dared demand food for their families were summarily executed. Uprisings were frequent and the government's response to them brutal. Roving bands of bandits began to terrorize the countryside in an attempt to "redistribute the wealth." Banditry became a form of "upward mobility" and came to be seen by some as the only means of self improvement and justice for the common people. Some historians feel that these bandits—who some argue are precursors to the Mafia—were used to settle disagreements among the rural nobility.

Enter Napoleon Bonaparte, Emperor of France (image ). In 1796, Napoleon conquered Austria and gained control of Italian lands in one of his first major land grabs. In 1806, he implemented civil registration in northern Italy, and these valuable records were more detailed and included more information than ecclesiastical records. The king of Naples at the time, Gioacchino Napoleone Murat, followed Napoleon's lead and intro-

D

Napoleon Bonaparte (in addition to shaping European history) was central to beginning Italian civil registration.

duced civil registration—known as *stato civile napoleonico* (Napoleonic civil registration)—to the his kingdom in 1808, making the practice more widespread. You'll see some towns in this region begin civil registration in 1809, depending on how quickly a town could get the process in place.

Napoleonic influence also brought mandatory military conscription to Italy between 1802 and 1814. Conscription was not popular amongst the commonfolk, especially since those from the peasant class who did the brunt of fighting had little at stake in the war. Still, service in a united "Italian" army or navy during this period brought together people from diverse regions of the kingdom in new ways.

After Napoleon was defeated in 1815, most of the regions in modern-day Italy were returned to their former rulers after the Congress of Vienna. Northern Italian states (including the previously autonomous Venezia) came under Austrian rule (image **E**), while the Kingdom of Sardinia (now including Genoa) and the Kingdom of the Two Sicilies regained their independence. The Papal States, Toscana (Tuscany), and Piedmont became independent of foreign rule. At this time, civil registration ended in most areas of northern Italy, and the parishes were once again required to keep the vital records of the Italian people.

Despite changes to Italy's political situation, conditions remained bleak for many Italians. Significant peasant rebellions occurred in 1820–1822, 1848–1849, and 1859–1860, and the cholera epidemic of 1836–1837 made a bad situation worse. Sicily was hit especially hard. Not only was the loss of life tragic for the island's people, but the public uprisings and subsequent executions of participants added to the devastation and hatred of those in power.

Amidst this turmoil, the decades that follow are known as the *Risorgimento* ("resurgence" or "revival") and saw popular uprisings against former rulers throughout Italy. Some years of civil registration in Sicilia were destroyed during these revolts, most especially in the early 1820s and late 1840s. Lucy Riall, a renowned historian on the *Risorgimento*, details the historical considerations of this time period in her book, *Risorgimento: The History of Italy from Napoleon to Nation State* (Palgrave Macmillan, 2009):

> In Italian history, as in Italian politics, the *Risorgimento* has played a central role...the *Risorgimento* is thought to be a turning-point for Italy, the start of its present history and the source of its shared identity...Indeed the concept of '*Risorgimento*' has structured our knowledge of Italian history in several ways.
>
> First, Risorgimento denotes a period: traditionally 1815–1860, although many historians now trace the beginnings of the period to the reforms of the late eighteenth century, and extend its conclusion to the seizure of Rome from the Pope

Northern Italy was once part of the large, multi-ethnic Austrian Empire, shown here in 1860.

in 1870 and the rise to power of the Historic Left government in 1876. Risorgimento also describes a process of reorganization.

Indeed, the *Risorgimento* was critical for Italy's development, as residents of once-independent and distinct regions shook off foreign rule and began thinking of themselves as members of a larger, Italian state. Bloody revolts against Austrian rule in most major northern Italian cities in 1848 led to new regional governments and the Pope's restoration to power in Roma (Rome), while nationalist movements began to grow throughout the peninsula.

Through political maneuvering (and a brief military conflict with Austria), Sardinian leaders in northern Italy (including King Victor Emmanuel II of Piedmont and his chief minister, Camillo Benso, Count of Cavour) drove out foreign occupiers and convinced voters in northern and central Italy to unite under a large Kingdom of Sardinia-Piedmont.

Forces under General Giuseppe Garibaldi campaigned throughout southern Italy and Sicilia, promising land to any Sicilian who was willing to join the fight for independence. Sicilians donned their signature red shirts and fought alongside Garibaldi's forces, driving the Spanish Bourbons from the island and bringing the Kingdom of the Two Sicilies into the fold of a united Italy.

The first newly created Kingdom of Italy included all of modern Italy, with a few exceptions that would be acquired later: Venezia/Venice (annexed in 1866 after another war with Austria), the Papal States surrounding Rome (seized in 1870 during the Franco-Prussian War), Trieste (annexed after World War I), and Trentino (annexed after World War I).

After this point, civil registration became known as *stato civile italiano* (Italian civil records).

Post-Unification (1870–present)

Now united, Italy began to expand. The kingdom annexed Venezia (Venice) in 1866 through another war with Austria and ousted the French from Roma (Rome), taking control of the whole city except for the Vatican. At this time, Italy's capital city changed from Torino to Roma.

In the latter half of the nineteenth century, Italy began to hemorrhage people. Hunger, poverty, and forced military conscription featured strongly in many Italians' decisions to emigrate. Large concentrations of Italians emigrated to North and South America, Canada, and Northern Africa. In the last quarter of the nineteenth century, nearly half of all Sicilian immigrants came from the Palermo province. This mass immigration forever changed the dynamics of many Italian families and had broad consequences in the Italian labor force and economics of the country.

At the dawn of the twentieth century, Italy (like other European powers) had many colonial possessions, a fact not many Italian-Americans realize. In 1912, the Kingdom of Italy formed the Ministry of the Colonies to help govern its colonies around the world: Egypt, Somalia, Ethiopia, Rhodes (in modern Greece), Libya, and Eritrea, amongst others.

War shook Europe in 1914, and Italy initially remained neutral. Originally a member of the Triple Alliance (a pact with Germany and Austria-Hungary), Italy signed the Treaty of London with the Allied Powers in 1915 and agreed to join the war against its former allies in exchange for postwar territorial gains. The Allies won, but Italy gained only some of the territories it was promised (the formerly Austro-Hungarian regions of Trentino and Trieste through the Treaty of Saint-Germain-en-Laye), and this slight weighed heavily on the minds of Italian nationalists. Economic conditions in Italy continued to decline during and after World War I, and unemployment and inflation rates climbed.

Amidst the financial and political turmoil, political radical and WWI veteran Benito Mussolini formed the National Fascist Party and began a violent anti-socialism campaign that made him popular among the middle classes who feared the growing Marxist influence. The government collapsed, and Mussolini marched on Rome to demand the prime minister's resignation. He seized power in 1922, choking out political opposition and abolishing civil liberties over the next several years (image ). In fact, Italy's civil registration in this time period notes what year it was in the Fascist rule of the country.

Mussolini's government invaded Ethiopia and Albania, and Italy entered World War II as a member of the Axis Powers in 1940. Italy did not fair well during the war. Mussolini enforced some of the same laws against Jews as his Nazi allies, and military campaigns in Egypt and Greece stalled. The Allies invaded Sicily in 1943. By the end of that year, Mussolini was ousted and forced into exile. Italy officially joined the Allies, but a civil war between republicans/the Allies and German/Fascist forces continued until 1945. After the war, King Victor Emmanuel III abdicated, and Italians voted to establish a republican constitution.

Wars and political oppression were potent factors in many Italians' decision to emigrate. This passenger ship ticket from the port of Napoli documents one family's flight after Mussolini came to power.

So how did all of these historical events affect the records our ancestors left behind? Understanding the history behind the records is important not only to understand your ancestors' choices but also when seeking to determine what types of records may be found. Historical events—such as the ravages of war—also created record loss.

For example, you are not going to find a civil birth record for a Sicilian ancestor in 1808 because civil registration began in Sicilia in 1820. However, you will find a baptismal record because parish records can be found from the end of the Council of Trent in 1583 or from the creation of the parish in which you are researching. If you wish to learn more about Italian history, Spencer di Scala's book *Italy: From Revolution to Republic, 1700 to the Present* (Westview Press, 2008) is a comprehensive and moderately in-depth look at this complicated subject.

REGIONAL/PROVINCIAL IDENTITIES

Where in Italy our ancestors came from played a huge role in their lives before and after emigration. Understanding the history of the town, province, or region your ancestors came from can help you understand the choices they made, including why they emigrated, where they decided to settle, and whether they ever returned home to Italy. Those

Reference Books

Studying up on the history that affected our ancestor's lives, before and after immigration, is crucial to Italian genealogy. Here's a list of just some of the reference books I consulted when writing this book:

- *Costumi e Usanze dei Contadini di Sicilia (Customs and Habits of the Sicilian Peasants)* by Salvatore Salmonoe-Marino, translated by Rosalie N. Norris (Associated University Presses, 1981)
- *Economic Development and Social Change in Sicily* by Jane Hilowitz (Transaction Publishers, 1976)
- *Immigrants in the Lands of Promise: Italians in Buenos Aires and New York City, 1870–1914* by Samuel L. Baily (Cornell University Press, 1999)
- *The Italian Emigration of Our Times* by Robert Franz Foerster (Harvard University Press, 1919)
- *The Italians* by Luigi Barzini (Touchstone, 1996)
- *The Italians in America, 1492–1972* by Anthony F. LoGatto (Oceana Publications, 1972)
- *Italy: From Revolution to Republic, 1700 to the Present*, third edition by Spencer di Scala (Westview Press, 2004)
- *Lives of Their Own: Blacks, Italians, and Poles in Pittsburgh, 1900–1960* by John Bodner, Roger Simon, and Michael P. Weber (University of Illinois Press, 1982)
- *Risorgimento: The History of Italy from Napoleon to Nation State* by Lucy Riall (Palgrave MacMillan, 2009)
- *La Storia: Five Generations of the Italian American Experience* by Jerre Mangione and Ben Morreale (Harper Collins Publishing, 1993)
- *South Italian Folkways in Europe and America: A Handbook for Social Workers, Visiting Nurses, School Teachers, and Physicians* by Phyllis H. Williams (Yale University, 1938)
- *Understanding Western Society: A Brief History, Volume 2: From the Age of Exploration to the Present* by John P. McKay, et al. (Bedford/St. Martin's, 2014)

See appendix A or the worksheet at the end of this chapter for more great resources.

researching ancestors from larger cities, they may want to seek resources about the specific neighborhood that ancestors came from. Neighborhoods were often distinctly different from each other and may have traditions specific to that micro-locality.

As a result, look for resources that discuss the histories of your ancestor's region in detail. Many town and provincial histories (as well as published family histories) can be found on Amazon Italy **<www.amazon.it>** and are normally in Italian or French. However, you can occasionally find one that has been translated into English. Google Books **<books.google.com>** has an amazing collection of older Italian books thanks to an agreement with the Italian Ministry of Culture. Through this partnership, Google has digitized thousands of Italian books, making these resources much more easily available.

Cultural studies can help you get a sense for your region's character. For example, while somewhat generalizing, this paragraph from historian and writer André Vieusseux's book *Italy and the Italians in the Nineteenth Century* (Charles Knight Pall-Mall East, 1824) pretty accurately describes my Sicilian ancestors:

> The Sicilians are a race very distinct from those who inhabit the kingdom of Naples...they are warm and high-minded, shrewd and quick-sighted, but irritable and tenacious...Sicilian women are generally handsome and very fascinating; they are fond of music and pleasure, but they are also spirited and intelligent, and susceptible of high feelings.

Below is part of a history of Sicily that I wrote a few years ago. This portion of the history helps one understand what life was like for Sicilians (and others in lower classes throughout Italy) and what might have influenced their decisions in life, including their decision to emigrate:

"Life was hard in eighteenth- and nineteenth-century Sicily. Sicily has a long and bitter history with rulers whose feudalistic social and governmental policies were designed to enrich the coffers of the landowners. With the landowners almost solely comprising of the ruling government, the nobility, and the Catholic Church, average people faced great challenges. The majority of Sicilians were *contadini,* or peasant farmers who received little to no formal education outside the home. Occupations were often passed down from generation to generation within the same family, parents teaching their children what skills they knew in order to help them survive. Class distinctions were wide and practically unbridgeable. There were the rich, the ecclesiastical, and the poor, with precious few opportunities to earn a living that was somewhere in between.

The entrenched feudalistic social and governmental systems made poverty the norm. Inherent in such poverty is the struggle to provide even the most basic necessities of

Emigration Factors

So why did they leave? The answer to that question is as complicated as Italy's history. In the later half of the nineteenth century, Italians (especially southern Italians and Sicilians in the area known as the Mezzogiorno) were considered "wed to the soil," meaning having very little desire to leave their *comune* and *famiglia*. Sicilians, in particular, were thought to be the least entrepreneurial (though, of course, the thousands of Sicilians who owned grocery stores, produce stands, restaurants, and other businesses would disagree). In reality, these generalities don't coincide with historical reality.

The five decades following Italian Unification saw the most emigration (temporary and permanent) of the Italian people. This was often due to poverty, large gaps between the social classes, forced military conscription, and an overly large labor force. There was also a lack of arable land for the common people, due to large tracks of land being owned by foreigners, the Church, and the municipalities.

In other words, people often emigrated out of necessity, in order to provide for their families, which often extended to their parents, grandparents, and siblings' families. They fled military conscription or trouble with the Mafia. Oftentimes, it was the promise of free land that tipped the scales in favor of emigration. No matter what the reason, their choices did provide a better life, not only for the Italian immigrant and the families they left behind, but also for the generations that followed them and carry their blood.

Mille grazie per tutti, miei nonni...

life for one's family. With hunger so common, no part of an animal would go to waste. Meat was often consumed only on Sundays, if at all, with the breadwinner(s) getting the greater portion. Yet, even when a family was very poor, they took care of their own. Reliance on public charity was considered disgraceful unless there were absolutely no family members left to depend on."

KEYS TO SUCCESS

✔ Understand the history of the Italian town, province, and region you are researching, particularly as it relates to recordkeeping. Historical references can give you great insight into the day-to-day lives of your ancestors.

✔ Determine the years of civil registration, church records, and other genealogical sources for the area of Italy your ancestors hail from.

✔ Understand Italian emigration, as it provides a look at the historical, social, and cultural events that formed our immigrant ancestors and played a large part in their decision-making.

ITALIAN HISTORY BOOKS BY REGION

Region	Resources
Abruzzo	*From Prehistory to History Abruzzo and its Cultural Heritage: History, Art, Literature* by Sandro Sticca (Global Academic Publishing, 2013)
	Suffer the Children—Growing Up in Italy During World War II by Donato De Simone (Xlibris, 2008)
Aosta Valley	*Discover the Aosta Valley* edited by Giacomo Sardo (Musumeci Editore, 1992)
	Italian Folktales by Italo Calvino (Mariner Books, 1992)
Apulia	*Old Puglia: A Portrait of South Eastern Italy* by Desmond Seward and Susan Mountgarret (Haus Publishing, 2009)
	Venturing In Italy: Travels in Puglia, Land Between Two Seas edited by Barbara J. Euser and Connie Burke (Travelers' Tales, 2009)
Basilicata	*Christ Stopped at Eboli* by Carlo Levi (Farrar, Straus and Giroux, 2006)
	Women of the Shadows: Wives and Mothers of Southern Italy, second edition by Ann Cornelisen (Steerforth Press, 2001)
Calabria	*Old Calabria* by Norman Douglas (Cosimo Classics, 2007)
	The Other Italy by Karen Haid (Mill City Press, 2015)
Campania	*The Ancient Shore: Dispatches from Naples* by Shirley Hazzard and Francis Steegmuller (University of Chicago Press, 2009)
	Naples '44: A World War II Diary of Occupied Italy by Norman Lewis (Da Capo Press, 2005)
	Siren Land: A Celebration of Life in Southern Italy by Norman Douglas (Tauris Parke Paperbacks, 2010)
Emilia-Romagna	*Across the Ocean to the Land of Mines: Five Thousand Stories of Italian Migration from the Mountains of Bologna and Modena to America at the Turn of the Century* by Prof. Pier Giorgio Ardeni (Edizioni Pendragon, 2015)
	The Garden of the Finzi-Continis by Giorgio Bassani and William Weaver (Harcourt Brace Jovanovich, 1977)
	The Kidnapping of Edgardo Mortara by David I. Kertzer (Vintage, 1998)
Friuli-Venezia Giulio	*A Tragedy Revealed: The Story of Italians from Istria, Dalmatia, and Venezia Giulia, 1943–1956, second edition* by Arrigo Petacco (University of Toronto Press, 2005)
	Trieste and the Meaning of Nowhere by Jan Morris (Da Capo Press, 2002)
Lazio	*The Agony and the Ecstasy* by Irving Stone (Berkley, 1987)
	Rome: The Biography of a City by Christopher Hibbert (Penguin UK, 1987)
Liguria	*Genoa, 'La Superba': The Rise and Fall of a Merchant Pirate Superpower* by Nicholas Walton (Hurst, 2015)
	A House Near Luccoli by DM Denton (All Things that Matter Press, 2012)
Lombardia	*Milan Since the Miracle* by John Foot (Bloomsbury Academic, 2001)
	Twilight in Italy: Sketches from Etruscan Places, Sea and Sardinia by D.H. Lawrence (Penguin Classics, 2008)

Region	Resources
Marche	*The Dragon's Trail: The Biography of Raphael's Masterpiece* by Joanna Pitman (Touchstone, 2008)
	Urbino: The Story of a Renaissance City by June Osborne (University of Chicago Press, 2003)
Molise	*The Generosity of Strangers: When War Came to Fornelli* by Thomas Antonaccio (Create Space, 2012)
	The Women of Molise: An Italian Village, 1950 by Frank Monaco (Thomas Dunne, 2001)
Piemonte	*Barolo and Barbaresco: The King and Queen of Italian Wine* by Kerin O'Keefe (University of California Press, 2014)
	A Thread of Grace by Mary Doria Russell (Random House, 2005)
Sardegna	*Accabadora* by Michela Murgia (Counterpoint Press, 2012)
	Legacies of Violence: History, Society, and the State in Sardinia (Anthropological Horizons) by Antonio Sorge (University of Toronto Press, 2015)
	The Two Madonnas: The Politics of Festival in a Sardinian Community, second edition by Sabina Magliocco (Waveland Press Inc., 2005)
Sicilia	*The Peoples of Sicily: A Multicultural Legacy* by Louis Mendola and Jacqueline Alio (Trinacria Editions, 2014)
	Sacrificed for Honor: Italian Infant Abandonment and the Politics of Reproductive Control by David I. Kertzer (Beacon Press, 1994)
	Seeking Sicily: A Cultural Journey Through Myth and Reality in the Heart of the Mediterranean by John Keahey (Thomas Dunne, 2011)
	Sicily: An Island at the Crossroads of History by John Julius Norwich (Random House, 2015)
Toscana	*Brunelleschi's Dome: How a Renaissance Genius Reinvented Architecture* by Ross King (Bloomsbury, 2013)
	Mona Lisa: A Life Discovered by Dianne Hales (Simon & Schuster, 2015)
	Saving Italy: The Race to Rescue a Nation's Treasures from the Nazis by Robert M. Edsel (W.W. Norton & Company, 2014)
Trentino Alto Adige	*The Hidden Frontier: Ecology and Ethnicity in an Alpine Valley* by John W. Cole (Academic Press, 1974)
	South Tyrol: A Minority Conflict of the Twentieth Century by Rolf Steininger (Routledge, 2003)
Umbria	*On the Road with Francis of Assisi: A Timeless Journey Through Umbria and Tuscany, and Beyond* by Linda Bird Francke (Random House, 2006)
	Umbria: Italy's Timeless Heart by Paul Hoffman (Henry Holt, 1999)
Veneto	*City of Fortune: How Venice Ruled the Seas* by Roger Crowley (Random House, 2013)
	A History of Venice by John Julius Norwich (Vintage, 1989)
	Venice: A New History by Thomas F. Madden (Penguin Books, 2013)

5

Understanding Italian Geography

I n chapter 3, we discussed how to determine your immigrant ancestor's town of origin, but sometimes having a town name isn't enough. For example, fifty towns or hamlets in Italy start with *Santa Maria*, so you would need to do more research if Santa Maria was the only clue you had to your ancestor's town of origin. Having multiple towns with the same name is a common problem, as many surviving immigration manifests have limited space for the "last town of residence" or "town of birth."

So how can you overcome this obstacle? This chapter will cover Italy's geography and administrative systems, plus discuss how tools like maps and gazetteers can help you distinguish your Santa Maria from another.

Since Italy is a relatively new country that was formed from multiple city-states that each had its own collections of laws, it would take books to describe all the territorial and jurisdictional changes that occurred throughout Italy's history. Suffice it to say there were many city-states that comprise modern Italy, and you can see some of these divisions reflected within surviving records. For example, as you delve into older (i.e., pre-Unification) civil records, you'll notice that many provinces and regions had different names. Additionally, municipalities were sometimes called *universitarias* instead of *comunes*.

As we've briefly discussed in previous chapters, Italian records were administered via various jurisdictions, and knowing why records were created and which jurisdiction your ancestor lived in is crucial in your genealogy quest. In this section, we'll discuss the major political divisions used in Italy, what records were kept in them, and what archives have the records today.

ITALIAN POLITICAL JURISDICTIONS

Genealogists should be concerned with five primary political jurisdictions, organized here from smallest to largest. We'll discuss the fourth and fifth units (the ecclesiastical parish and the diocese) in chapter 8.

Town (*Comune*)/City (*Cittá*)

As in the United States today, towns (*comune*, plural: *comuni*) and cities (*cittá*) were the administrative divisions that most impacted an individual's life. These locales are classified as either towns or cities based on their size and population. In addition, towns and cities may contain one or many *frazione* (plural: *frazioni*) or *quartiere* (plural: *quartieri*), which are hamlets or neighborhoods, or *contrada* (plural: *contrade*), which are similar to US townships and found in areas of the countryside surrounding a town. Occasionally, you may see a *frazione* called *ld.*, or *localitá distraccata* (local district).

Cities can have several subdivisions, making research tricky. For example, the town of Lucca currently has more than ninety *frazioni*, *quartieri*, or *contrade*, a fact I became painfully aware of while trying to trace a family whose descendants only knew that their ancestors had lived outside the Lucca city walls. Therefore, to narrow down where this family resided, I consulted a state of the family record (*stato di famiglia storico*) from the municipal archives. At the time this family resided there, they lived in the *frazione* of San Pancrazio, which had its own town hall where civil records were recorded.

San Pancrazio is now under the jurisdiction of the city of Lucca. However, because this hamlet's records were sent to the provincial archives instead of the town of Lucca when the jurisdiction changed, my search of the civil records in Lucca came back negative. The repository referred me to the provincial archives, and only there could I find a copy of the record. I paid 12,5 euro ($14 US) per person on the record—a costly record considering there were just ten people on it, but it was worth the money. This is a good example of how understanding the jurisdictions, as well as how and when records are sent to the provincial archives, can aid in your research. Sometimes the location of the records you need is not obvious, and you have to dig a little deeper to find them. Contacting the provincial archives and asking for help locating San Pancrazio's civil records solved this problem.

A noteworthy up-and-coming trend regarding city jurisdictions is the formation of town unions (*unioni comuni*). Towns in these unions are usually near each other and combine to share common infrastructure, tourism goals, ease costs, etc. As part of these unions, towns are beginning to merge their municipal archives, affecting where you can find records. Many of these unions have their own homepage, and you can view one such page at **<www.unionepresolana.gov.it/servizi/notizie/notizie_homepage.aspx>**.

Another administrative unit, the metropolitan city, can also affect where records from your ancestor's town are found. Between 2014 and 2016, the Italian government created a handful of metropolitan cities that absorbed surrounding communities that were once independent: Roma, Milano, Napoli, Torino, Palermo, Bari, Catania, Firenze, Bologna, Genoa, Venezia, Messina, Reggio Calabria, and Cagliari. If your ancestor lived near one of these cities, records of him may now reside with the metropolitan city's records.

Province (*Provincia*)

Italy's provinces are similar to US counties. As of 2016, Italy contained 109 provinces, plus one northwestern region (Aosta) organized without provinces (image **A**). However, Italy is in the midst of a massive restructuring of its provinces and regions, and the provincial

RESEARCH TIP

Find Your Town on FamilySearch

The records that have been microfilmed or digitized by FamilySearch International, and made available through the Family History Library in Salt Lake City, are currently labeled based on the jurisdictions in a 1954 gazetteer. However, in the future, the plans are to label them according to their original province or name. The description in the FamilySearch online catalog often notes any name changes, provincial changes, or unusual aspects of a set of records. While not totally inclusive of all changes, this is a valuable first resource when you are looking for missing records or suspect a town may have changed its name. You could also e-mail the state/provincial archives (*archivio di stato*) for guidance if you feel this may be the situation with your ancestor's records.

ITALY

— International boundary

— Regional boundary

— Provincial boundary

⊛ National capital

Regions of Italy

1	Abruzzo	**11**	Lombardy
2	Aosta Valley	**12**	Marche
3	Apulia	**13**	Molise
4	Basilicata	**14**	Piedmont
5	Calabria	**15**	Sardinia
6	Campania	**16**	Sicily
7	Emilia-Romagna	**17**	Trentino-Alto Adige
8	Friuli-Venezia Giulia	**18**	Tuscany

Italy is divided into twenty regions (similar to US states), which in turn are made up of 109 provinces (similar to counties).

designation will be phased out in coming years. While it's not likely to significantly affect where and how genealogical records are conserved, it is something to be aware of since records could be transferred between provincial archives (e.g., when provinces are combined or phased out).

It is important to remember that the province a town resides in today is not necessarily the same as when your ancestors resided there. Towns near current provincial borders may have changed provincial jurisdictions multiple times over the years. In this instance, records of your ancestors would normally be found in the provincial archives of the province they belonged to at that time. Each province has a capital city (*capoluogo*) that has the same name (e.g., the city of Genova is the *capoluogo* for the province of Genova).

Region (*Regione*)

Italy's largest political division is the region (singular: *regione*, plural: *regioni*), similar to a US state. While all twenty regions are considered part of the country of Italy, five regions are semi-autonomous and have different legal statutes: Sardinia, Sicilia (Sicily), Trentino-South Tyrol (Trentino-Alto Adige/Südtirol), Aosta Valley, and Fruili-Venezia Giulia (image **B**). The Italian government created these semi-autonomous regions to protect their unique cultural and linguistic history. For example, the majority of people in the region of Aosta Valley speak a version of French on an everyday basis. While Italian and French are the official languages of this region, the majority of residents can also speak a French dialect called Valdôtain.

ITALIAN ARCHIVES

You now know how Italy is and was organized, but where are Italian records now? Five main types of archives conserve the majority of records useful for genealogical and historical research (and are accessible to researchers), and they somewhat mirror Italy's political structure.

Municipal Archives (*Archivio Municipale/Archivio Comunale*)

The municipal archives holds records at the town (*comune*, pl. *comuni*) and city (*cittá*) level. At these local-level archives, you can find a variety of records. Birth, marriage, and death records are held in the civil records office (called the *ufficio di stato civile*) and are available by postal inquiry. Likewise, population registers, family sheets, and census information can be found in the Ufficio di Anagrafe e Demografico (Population Statistics and Demographic Office) and may or may not be available for research, depending on the town and what type of record you wish to access. Note that older forms of municipal censuses may or may not survive, as many were destroyed with the onset of federal censuses,

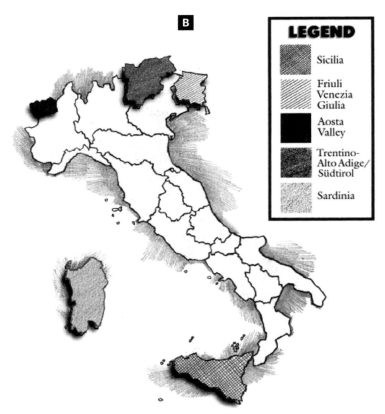

LEGEND

- Sicilia
- Friuli Venezia Giulia
- Aosta Valley
- Trentino-Alto Adige/Südtirol
- Sardinia

The Italian government has created five semi-autonomous regions, listed in the map above (illustrated by Cuccia Creative).

including records like: *registri di popolazione* (population registers), *foglio di famiglia* (family sheet), and *scheda individuale* (individual schedule).

These offices are often very busy, so be polite and appreciative of the official's time and effort. The Italian civil code says that only archival employees may consult the registers. However, you may run into a helpful official who will allow you to do the research yourself. (For more on the municipal and other government offices in Italy, consult *Guida Monaci, Annuario Generale Italiano*, an annual guide.)

Municipio (town hall) offices are typically open 9 a.m. to 1 p.m., Monday through Friday, but the hours vary by town. Additionally, if you visit the town of your ancestors, you must make an appointment at the *municipio* to request records. Send a letter or e-mail ahead of time asking for permission, as the office will want to have the appropriate staff on hand when you arrive. If you show respect for the officials' time in this way, you have a better chance of a positive research experience. (See appendix C for more on writing letters to Italian archives.)

This is a lesson I learned the hard way, before I started working as a professional genealogist. As I passed the town hall in Caltavuturo during my first trip to Italy, I decided to stop in and ask for my great-great-grandparent's death records. After waiting in line for twenty minutes, I was able to speak to the director of the archives and request photocopies of their death records. What followed was a diatribe of displeasure because I had not made an appointment. The director refused to get the records for me or allow me access (and said a few rude things about Americans that I won't repeat here). After discussing the situation with my travel companion, we were about to leave when another employee silently motioned me into a side office and showed me the register I needed. The employee was embarrassed by the behavior of her boss and apologized that she could not give me copies. Long story short: Show archival staff respect by making an appointment ahead of time.

A copy of each civil register is also held in another district-level government building, called the *Tribunale* or *Procura della Repubblica* (district court), for seventy years for use in court cases and other legal purposes, but registers from these repositories are not typically available for research. However, if you can prove a valid legal purpose (such as record loss at other repositories or a requirement for a dual citizenship application) and you can't acquire the record elsewhere, they may send you the record you need. These situations are evaluated on an individual basis.

Each year, the civil records at the *Tribunale* that have become more than seventy years old are sent to the provincial archives (see the next section) for preservation and made available for research, unless their physical condition prohibits it. However, not all *Tribunale* archives follow this rule consistently, and whether or not records are transferred on time may depend on the provincial archive's ability (or lack thereof) to house incoming

Knowing the Lingo
- *Municipio* or *casa comunale*, town hall
- *Comune* or *università*, comune or university
- *Ufficio di stato civile*, civil records office
- *Frazione* or *quartiere*, hamlet or neighborhood
- *Contrada*, township or countryside neighborhood
- *Localitá distraccata*, local district
- *Archivio di stato*, provincial/state archive
- *Capoluogo*, capital city (of a province)
- *Tribunale* or *Procura della Repubblica*, district court

records. (Note: Registers containing marriage banns and marriage supplements are not made in duplicate, and the original of these registers are transferred to the *Tribunale* at the end of the year. Therefore, you won't find them in a municipal archive, but they are available for research once they are transferred to the provincial archives.)

FamilySearch International is digitizing civil records from some of the *Tribunali* (plural), as not all of the district court archives have followed procedure and transferred the records to the provincial archives after seventy years.

You might, however, encounter unusual situations. For example, the town hall of Agrigento has both original sets of the civil records of its hamlet, Montaperto, within its collection. The second set of civil records was never sent to the *Tribunale* and therefore never made its way to the provincial archives.

Provincial/State Archives (*Archivio di Stato*)

The provincial archives are in the *capoluogo* (capital city) of each province and called the Archivio di Stato di [insert name of province], comparable to US state archives in regards to their rich genealogical records and cultural artifacts. Records here include civil, census, military, court, notarial, family archives, and more. Some provincial archives have several annexes that contain the records of their *archivio di stato*.

These archives all have a s*ala di studio* or research room, which is open to the public. The rules of researching in a particular *archivio di stato* vary by province. Some only allow consultation of three to four registers a day, while others will allow more if they know you are coming a long way to research the documents. Some require you to write for permission or reserve common materials ahead of time. Therefore, requesting permission several weeks in advance of your visit is always a good practice, and you should always visit an archive's website to learn about its rules and procedures.

For an example of the rules governing record access in these archives, take a look at the website of the Archivio di Stato di Foggia **<www.archiviodistatofoggia.beniculturali.it/index.php?it/31/sala-di-studio>**. Click the link titled *Regolamento della Sala di studio (file PDF)* to bring up the regulations for accessing the records of this particular archive. The file even shows how much it costs to have the archive make a copy or provide a digitized image of a document.

Just like when researching at any US state archive or historical society library, you have to register and leave the majority of your belongings in a locker to enter the *sala di studio*. Some provincial archives allow you to have only blank paper, a pencil, and perhaps your laptop, as they want to make all photographs or digital copies for you and collect fees. Others will make you check large bags but allow computers, digital cameras, and notepads. You will be asked to put your phone in the locker if your Twitter feed or volume of phone calls become disruptive. For the provincial archive in Foggia, the form to request access to the *sala di studio* can be found at **<www.archiviodistatofoggia.beniculturali.it/ index.php?it/104/modulistica>**. Also, be sure to use cotton conservation gloves when researching to make sure the oils from your skin don't damage documents. You can purchase these gloves from archival and conservation companies, such as Gaylord **<www. gaylord.com/c/Conservation-Supplies>**.

Once admitted, you have to submit requests for archival materials (or copies of archival materials) using small forms designated for that purpose, then wait for them to bring the material to you for researching. This is a process US researchers are not unfamiliar with, as many US state archives and historical societies operate in a similar manner.

Most *archivi di stato* have pages on their websites dedicated to their research rooms. The hours are usually posted on this page. What is contained within the collection of a particular *archivio di stato* can often be found through a link on its website, typically titled *patrimonio archivistico* or *patrimonio*.

Parish Archive (*Archivio Parrocchiale/Archivi Ecclesiastici*)

A parish is an individual church serving a specific area within a town. Small towns may have a single parish while large towns or cities could have dozens. Parish archives contain baptismal records, ecclesiastical birth records, confirmation records, death or burial records, multiple kinds of marriage records, and ecclesiastical censuses. The actual parish archives may be in the parish building, in the priest's home, or in another building owned by the Church. This varies with no apparent pattern. Earlier records (often pre-1900) from all parishes within a town may be combined into one parochial archive in the *chiesa madre* (mother church), *duomo* (cathedral), *basilica* (basilica), or *cattedrale* (cathedral).

If you want to determine what parishes are in your ancestor's hometown and what diocese they belong to, the Chiesa Cattolica Italiana's (Italian Catholic Church's) website is a good start **<www.webdiocesi.chiesacattolica.it>**. You can use it to find current parishes and what diocese they belong to, and you can do the same on the Motore di Ricerca Par-

Online resources, like the Motore di Ricerca Parrocchie, can help you find your ancestor's parish.

rocchie's website **<www.parrocchie.it>** (image C). However, remember these are the current parishes and diocesan jurisdictions, so there may be some differences from when your ancestors resided in Italy. The *Annuario delle Diocesi d'Italia*, available on microfilm from the Family History Library, can be used to find when a parish was created and what parishes were in operation at the time your ancestors resided in Italy. Italia.Indettaglio.it **<italia.indettaglio.it>** also allows you to search for Italian parishes, as well as hamlets, towns, provinces, and regions. Diocesan archives may also have information about boundary or jurisdictional changes that have occurred over the years.

Diocesan Archive (*Archivio Diocesano/Archivio Storico Diocesano*)

A diocese is a group of parishes within an ecclesiastical district, and each diocese has its own archive. An archdiocese, likewise, is a group of dioceses within a particular region. Some records for larger cities may be found within an archive at the archdiocese (when the seats of the archdiocese and the diocese are in the same town), but they are usually found within the *archivio diocesano*. These archives are usually quite organized, but only open one or two days per week and have limited staff.

The diocesan archives are generally less useful to researchers than parish archives, though they may contain additional copies of post-1900 parish records, including marriage documents (and especially marriage dispensations, which gave couples specific permission to marry). They often contain the documents relating to the various priests/nuns who served within their diocese and the records of defunct parishes.

Local Library (*Biblioteca Comunale* or *Biblioteca Municipale*)

Local libraries often have town and provincial histories and manuscripts on the noble or more prominent members of a town. Local libraries contain a wealth of information about the town, and some have distinct sections and collections for genealogists. Understanding your ancestors' town history may be the key to answering one of the many questions you have, and historical resources can add "meat" to your family history book. The majority of these resources will obviously be in Italian but, depending on the area of Italy, there could be resources in other languages.

Many of the larger local libraries have websites with online catalogs you can research to determine useful resources. For example, the website of the Biblioteca Comunale di (Municipal Library of) Palermo has many resources, including an online catalog **<librarsi. comune.palermo.it/polo/home>**. Likewise, the website of the Biblioteca Comunale di (Municipal Library of) Trento **<www.bibcom.trento.it/info/archivio_storico>** notes you can access the archive without a reservation during certain days and hours. This library also has many genealogical resources, some of which can be accessed online **<www. bibcom.trento.it/patrimonio_e_risorse/archivi>**.

USING MAPS AND GAZETTEERS

There are many different types of maps useful for genealogical or historical research, and you should have several good maps in your collection for the time periods and area of the country your ancestors came from. These maps come in a handful of general categories, many of which are available online:

- Pre-Unification: Maps that show the various historical kingdoms and provinces that make up modern Italy

- Post-Unification: Maps that show how the various provinces came together to form a unified Italy

- Sectional: Excerpts covering specific regions (northern, central, southern) or former kingdoms (Kingdom of Naples, Kingdom of the Two Sicilies), often showing more detail than maps of the whole peninsula
- Topographical: Geographic features of an area, including elevation, geological landmarks, rivers, lakes, etc.
- Satellite: Detailed images captured by modern satellites
- Cadastral: Used to show property (real estate) boundaries for legal taxation purposes (but now can be used to determine town boundaries more than one hundred years ago), held by the provincial archives (image **D**)

Though Italian maps will most often be written in Italian, you can find them in nearly any language due to the country's changing historical boundaries. For example, you'll often find German-language maps in the border areas of northeast Italy once ruled by the Austrian-Hungarian Empire. Also keep an eye out for historical maps as you travel in other parts of Europe. While in Amsterdam, my husband found a Dutch-language map of Italy in 1300, printed in 1886. This is now the oldest map I have in my collection, and it provides an interesting look into the territory that is now modern-day Italy.

D

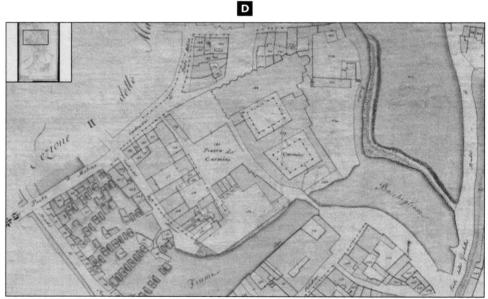

Cadastral maps, available online from some provincial archives, are among some of the useful geographic resources available to researchers.

While maps are graphical depictions of a specific area, gazetteers are geographical dictionaries (many times arranged alphabetically) that can help you find towns and smaller localities or determine town name changes. Gazetteers, combined with maps, reveal topography (what mountains or rivers are nearby, how easy would it be to travel between two towns in order for ancestors to meet, etc.). They help us place our ancestors within their specific geographical place.

One of my favorite resources is the "Italian Town Database in One Step" database **<www.rootsweb.ancestry.com/~itappcnc/pipcntown.htm>**, which allows you to search for places in several different ways, including a "sounds like" feature. This is a good place to start, especially if all you have is the name of the town as your remember your *nonno* (grandfather) saying it thirty years ago.

Where to Find Maps and Gazetteers

The Comuni-Italiani.it website **<www.comuni-italiani.it>** (an online gazetteer) has information on each town, such as what hamlets are under their jurisdiction, population statistics, and current maps for each town, province, and region. You can search by using topographical or satellite maps. The satellite maps are a unique way for you to get the feel for the topography of a certain town (mountains, streams, etc.). In the same way (as they are powered by the same database), you can use Google Earth **<www.google.com/earth>** to find a locality through satellite imagery, the parish your ancestors attended (if it survives), or an address listed on an Italian birth record. Geoplan **<www.geoplan.it>** and Mapquest **<www.mapquest.com>** are also useful resources for finding the street or address your ancestors resided on, as well as parishes close to their location. Be aware that some Italian towns have renumbered houses and/or changed street names at different points in time.

Take some time to explore the gazetteers from different kingdoms and time periods available on Google Books or Amazon Italy, such as the various printings of the *Dizionario del Comuni delle circoscrizini amministrative, delle frazioni e delle localita (Dictionary of the municipalities of administrative districts, districts and localities)*, a gazetteer published through Tribuna Dizionari. You can also find the *Dizionario del Comuni del Regno d'Italia (Dictionary of the Communities of the Kingdom of Italy)*, which is dated 1861 but has been reprinted, on Amazon Italy or (in 1871 form) for free on Google Books **<books.google.com>**. Another reprinted gazetteer useful for researchers is *Circoscrizioni Amministrativa, Giudiziaria, Elettorale e Diocesan e Dizionari dei Comuni del Regno D'Italia Compres Le Province Venete (Administrative, Judicial, Electoral and Diocesan Circumscriptions and Dictionaries of Municipalities of the Kingdom of Italy Comprising Provinces Venete)* by Pietro Castiglioni. Of particular interest is the inclusion of diocesan and judicial sections, including sections on the Kingdom of Italy as well as Veneto.

Many of the *archivi di stato* are creating databases containing old cadastral maps. These maps usually note large landowners and topographical features, allowing you to better understand the area your ancestors came from.

You can find historical maps of Italy (and of other parts of the world) online at the Perry-Castañeda Library Map Collection <www.lib.utexas.edu/maps/italy.html> and the David Rumsey Map Collection <www.davidrumsey.com>, which have many historical Italian maps (including several city maps). Edmaps.com has historical Italian maps <www.edmaps.com/html/italy.html>, including a digitized version of the map that my husband found in Amsterdam. Wikimedia Commons, part of the Wikipedia <www.wikipedia.org> organization, has a useful Atlas of Italy <commons.wikimedia.org/wiki/Atlas_of_Italy> that has many historical maps, along with more specific depictions showing Italian regions and provinces. Most images are in the public domain and free for use, but check the copyright information before downloading. Maproom.org <www.maproom.org/index.html> also has historical Italian maps available for a nominal fee.

The Family History Library in Salt Lake City is one of the best places to find physical maps and gazetteers of Italy. The library catalog has twenty-one entries for maps of this country and fourteen for gazetteers. The *Nuovo dizionario dei comuni e frazioni di comune con le circonscrizioni amminisrative (New dictionary of municipalities and hamlets of comune with administrative constraints)* is a gazetteer of localities, hamlets, and neighborhoods within Italy. It even includes other useful information like military districts, population information, postal jurisdictions, and court jurisdictions. This gazetteer is available at the Family History Library in book form. This reference is especially helpful when you have only a phonetic spelling of an Italian location and can also be used to narrow down the place of origin for your Italian ancestors.

The *Annuario generale: comuni e frazioni d'Italia (General directory: municipalities and districts of Italy)*, created by Touring Club Italiano, was printed regularly into the 1990s. You can find various editions through online booksellers like Amazon Italy <www.amazon.it> or AbeBooks.com <www.abebooks.com>. The Family History Library in Salt Lake City holds the 1961, 1980, and 1993 editions in its collection

If you're looking to buy print maps, you can purchase a detailed Pre-Unification map (as well as other historical Italian maps) titled "Italy 1815–1859" from Fun Stuff for Genealogists, Inc. <funstuffforgenealogists.com>, which specializes in genealogy merchandise and usually has a booth in the exhibit hall at state and national genealogy conferences. Maia's Books <www.maiasbooks.com> also has historical Italian maps and can be found in the exhibit hall of genealogy conferences.

CHANGING BOUNDARIES

Italian jurisdictional changes happen today, as well as hundreds of years ago. Natural disasters can also cause reorganization and jurisdictional changes, leaving a researchers searching for surviving records. (For example, earthquakes in central Italy in 2016 destroyed whole towns. Despite this, officials salvaged many of the civil and ecclesiastical records with the help of Italian and international archivists.) In some instances, authorities have chosen not to rebuild a particular town hall but instead to merge the town with a larger one. Surviving civil records for the destroyed town would then be transferred to the town hall of the town they were being merged into. Additionally, with political and governmental changes, Italy is constantly looking for ways to manage its national expenditures. Sometimes whole provinces are dissolved, merged, or renamed in an effort to gain economic stability.

There is no one place or archive in Italy that maintains a master list of all name and jurisdictional changes. However, each provincial archive has some form of internal reference materials concerning these changes that they use when processing document requests. These archives can be contacted by e-mail for guidance, if you are unable to find a locality (writing in Italian is suggested).

FamilySearch's online catalog **<www.familysearch.org>** can also be used to find information on town name and jurisdictional changes and has become the number-one resource for these changes. As the organization digitizes records in Italy, it continues to add these details to the descriptions in their online catalog.

For example, the town of Santa Flavia in the Palermo province of Italy was once called both Solunto and Sòlanto prior to 1880. Records between 1820 and 1879 can be found listed under these other names. Therefore, if you didn't know about this name change when researching this record (or that the family came from this town), you may not find the documents you are looking for.

KEYS TO SUCCESS

- Learn the administrative districts used by Italy during the time your ancestors lived there, as what town/comune your ancestor lived in will affect what records were kept, what archives they were recorded in, and where those records reside today.

- Determine what archives hold records of your ancestors. Understand what types of records are found in each archive.

- Consult geographical resources like maps and gazetteers to determine where your ancestor's town was in a province or region, plus what topographical features (rivers, mountains, etc.) and other towns were nearby.

6

Deciphering Italian: Language, Names, and Surnames

nless your ancestors came to the United States only a generation or two ago, you likely don't speak Italian fluently. And that's okay! Most records use only a limited vocabulary, and you don't have to be a linguistics expert to interpret Italian-language records and place names. Rather, you'll need to learn just a basic primer on the Italian language and a handful of vocabulary words common to Italian records. This chapter will provide Italian-language basics to help you interpret records, plus describe Italian naming traditions.

LEARNING THE BASICS

You may be thinking, "All the records will be in Italian, right?" Not necessarily, as what language is used in records depends on location, time period, and record type. From about 1806 onward (in most of modern-day Italy), the majority of the records were written in Italian (civil records) or Latin (parish records). You'll occasionally find a word from a local dialect, likely in a Latin-language parish record rather than an Italian-language civil record. (Priests were more apt to slip into dialect than were civil officials.) In areas ruled by France, Austria, or Spain, you could find records in French, German, or Spanish—but even still, the great majority of records will be in Italian and Latin.

RESEARCH TIP

Mind the Dialect

When you travel to Italy, don't be surprised to hear people speak in their dialect first. However, once the locals realize where you're from, they'll usually slip back into standard Italian (or some of the English they were taught in school) to communicate. Italians are an amazingly friendly people and often go our of their way to help a foreign visitor.

Since Italy did not become a unified country until about 1865, the use of a standardized Italian language was not common in most public settings until the end of the nineteenth century, sometimes later. As we've discussed in previous chapters, pre-unification Italy comprised various city-states, kingdoms, and duchies (ruled by foreign powers), and each locale spoke its own language or dialect. Most continued to speak this dialect long after unification, so the history of the location you are researching affects not only what records were created, but also what language they were written in.

In addition to minding dialects, you'll also need to brush up on your Italian history to find what language records of your ancestor's hometown might be kept in. As you learned in chapter 4, various parts of Italy were ruled by Spain, France, and Austria, so you can expect some records from occupied regions to have the languages of those countries. For example, records of the *Mezzogiorno*, which then included southern Italy and Sicilia (once called the Kingdom of the Two Sicilies), were kept by the ruling Spanish and so were sometimes written in that language. Likewise, northeastern Italy was once part of Austria, meaning some of the records there will be in German. (Note that ecclesiastical—or parish—records are nearly always in Latin, no matter the time period or region.)

In addition, some previously Italianate areas of the world belong to other countries. For example, the island of Corsica has been a part of France since 1768. Yet most of the island's records prior to the 1830s are in the Genoese dialect (very similar to modern Italian) or one of the Corsican dialects because the island was under Genoese rule for several hundred years. Corsicans were originally an Italianate people, yet the island has been a part of France for nearly 150 years.

While the Italian-Latin-French-German combo can be intimidating, you don't need to be fluent in any of these languages to extract information from genealogical documents. Rather, you'll just need some basic genealogical terms and language skills (as well as some easy-to-use language resources) to research Italian records. This section will provide you with some of these, plus important abbreviations.

Dual-Speaker System

Cultural legacies in some parts of Italy are particularly complex, and some of these areas have incorporated non-Italian languages into their day-to-day activities. Here are some bilingual (or even trilingual) regions in Italy, along with what other language(s) beside Italian are spoken there.

Region	Language(s)
Valle d'Aosta	French
Trentino-Alto Adige/Südtirol	German, Latin
Friuli-Venezia Giulia	Friulian, Slovene
Sardinia	Sardinian, Catalan
Sicilia	Sicilian (includes several dialects)

Key Genealogical Language Resources

As stated earlier, you'll only need to recognize a handful of Italian words while searching through records. Appendix D includes several useful word lists, but in this section we'll discuss what other resources are available for learning key Italians words and phrases. You can find similar resources online for the other languages you might encounter within Italian documents, and the worksheet at the end of this chapter contains examples of each Italian letter in script (taken from actual documents), which will help as you read and interpret Italian genealogical documents. You'll also find some key words and titles, plus examples of how double consonants are written in Italian.

The FamilySearch Wiki, a free database organized by the FamilySearch organization, has genealogical word lists for both Italian **<www.familysearch.org/learn/wiki/en/Italian_Genealogical_Word_List>** and Latin **<www.familysearch.org/learn/wiki/en/Latin_Genealogical_Word_List>**. Google Books **<books.google.com>**, which has an agreement with the Italian Ministry of Cultural Heritage, has digitized tons of Italian-language books, including Italian-English dictionaries and guides to various Italian dialects.

Another free resource, RootsWeb, has two lists of occupations in Italian: **<freepages.genealogy.rootsweb.ancestry.com/~mmange/itengocc.html>** and **<freepages.genealogy.rootsweb.ancestry.com/~calitri/Calitri/History/occupati.htm>**. The Coniglio Family website **<www.conigliofamily.com/SicilianAndItalianOccupations.htm>** and Ancestry.com **<c.ancestry.com/Affiliate/Knowledgebase/Guides/Ancestrylibrary/Italian_Occupations.pdf>** also offer free lists of occupations, as does Wikibooks **<en.wikibooks.org/wiki/Italian/Vocabulary/Professions>**.

Those who want to dig deeper into foreign languages also have online resources available to them. For example, the University of Notre Dame has an online guide to Latin **<archives.nd.edu/latgramm.htm>** (featuring both a dictionary and a grammar guide), and Brigham Young University has an online Italian script tutorial **<script.byu.edu/Pages/Italian/en/welcome.aspx>** (plus tutorials for other languages) that will help you decipher text.

Those seeking a more formalized or immerse experience can take advantage of other online resources for learning Italian. Language-learning software can help you learn Italian in your own time, or you could find a group of English-speakers and native Italians who chat over video-calling software like Skype **<www.skype.com>** to help each other learn Italian and English, respectively. Explore what is available, and choose the tool that best reflects how you learn.

Automated Translation Services

Automated translation services are programs that convert documents between languages, and they have both their benefits and drawbacks. The translations produced by these services can often give you the gist of a document, but they may misinterpret (or outright mistranslate) words or phrases, especially those that have different meanings depending on context. Therefore, use these services sparingly.

Let's look at an example of a translation done by Google Translate **<translate.google.com>**, one of the most popular tools. I typed in the following paragraph:

> Ed a richiesta di Francesco, Vitantonio, Rocco, Angelo, Arcangelo, Giuseppe fratelli Nuzzi, nonché da coniugi Teresa Nuzzi, e Francescantonio Elia, coniugi Porzia Nuzzi, e Giuseppe Saccente nella qualità essi fratelli e sorelle Nuzzi di eredi del fu lor genitore Francesco, e di detti Elia, e Saccente per la sola autorizzazione maritale delle di loro rispettive mogli, tutti proprietari domiciliati, e residenti in questo suddetto Comune di Palo del Colle, meno il primo che domicilia in Grumo Appula, e tutti elettivamente per la presente procedura in Bari in casa del di loro avvocato procuratore Sig. Vincenzo Cursoli [?] Strada Calefati n. 91.

Google Translate provided this translation:

> And at the request of Francesco, Vitantonio, Rocco, Angel, Archangel, Joseph's brothers Nuzzi, as well as spouses Teresa Nuzzi, and Francescantonio Elijah, spouses Portia Nuzzi, and Joseph Saccente in the quality they Nuzzi brothers and sisters as heirs of their father was Francis, and Elijah said, and Saccente for the single authorization husbandly of their respective wives, all owners are domiciled and resident in the aforesaid City of Palo del Colle, not the first one

that domicilia in Grumo Appula, and all electively for this procedure Bari in the house of their attorney lawyer Mr Vincenzo Cursoli [?] Calefati Road n. 91.

So how did Google do? Let's take a look at the same Italian-language paragraph as translated by an actual person:

> And at the request of Francesco, Vitantonio, Rocco, Angelo, Arcangelo, and Giuseppe Nuzzi, brothers, as well as the spouse of Teresa Nuzzi, Francescantonio Elia, and the spouse of Porzia Nuzzi, Giuseppe Saccente, it is declared that these brothers and sisters are heirs to their father Francesco [Nuzzi], the named Elia and Saccente, by authorization of their respective marriages, all landowners and residents in the above-named Town of Palo del Colle, except for the first [Francesco Nuzzi] who resides in Grumo Appula, and they all elect to record the present act in Bari before the prosecuting attorney Mister Vincenzo Cursoli [?], Calefati Street, number 91.

As you can see, Google Translate only got part of the translation correct, and it took certain phrases out of context (for example, translating names) while not filling in other kinds of information. These shortcomings can cause you to miss important parts of a document or misinterpret what a document is saying about your ancestor.

As a result, you should only use automated translation services when you need to understand individual words or phrases. A human translator (whether yourself, a professional, or a native speaker) is best for longer, more nuanced documents. Human translations have the added benefit of dynamic comments that can help explain unusual sections or how the document fits within its historical or social context.

CULTURAL NAMING TRADITIONS

Understanding Italian naming customs can help you differentiate your ancestor from other similarly named people, as well as provide some insight into your family's history. Since it was common practice to name children one of a small handful of family names, you could have many ancestors of the same name and approximate age, all born within the same town. The standard naming customs were as follows:

- First son is named for the paternal grandfather
- First daughter is named for the paternal grandmother
- Second son is named for the maternal grandfather
- Second daughter is named for the maternal grandmother

Subsequent children were often named for their parents, aunts, uncles, or a patron saint. If a child died, the next child of the same gender born within that family would be given the same name. As a result, the presence of a second child with the same name as a sibling likely indicates the first sibling's death, so that can be a clue to look for a death record if you don't already have one.

The majority of Italian families followed the naming customs, but (of course) there were exceptions. All the children's names in one family I researched came from Shakespearean plays, while another family named all its children Maria, with most having distinct middle names that they used throughout their lives. A third (very unfortunate) family named the first four sons Francesco, all of whom passed away before reaching a second birthday. It seems the family gave up trying to give a child this name, because the fifth boy was named Giovanni.

Furthermore, names were often abbreviated in certain distinct ways, and knowing these abbreviations can give your research a leg up. Here are some abbreviations for a few common Italian given names:

- *Ant^o* or *Ant^{no}*: Antonio or Antonino
- *Agost^o*: Agostino
- *Ang^a*: Angela or Angelina
- *Bart^{meo}* or *Barte^o*: Bartolomeo
- *Batta*: Battista
- *Cal^o* or *Cal^a*: Calogero or Calogera
- *Cat^a* or *Cat^{na}*: Caterina
- *Dom^{co}* or *Dom^{ca}*: Domenico or Domenica
- *Filom^a*: Filomena
- *Franc^o* or *Franc^a*: Francesco or Francesca
- *Giac^o* or *Giac^a*: Giacomo or Giacoma, Giacomina
- *Giusp^e* or *Gius^e*: Giuseppe
- *Giov^a* or *Giov^i*: Giovanna or Giovanni
- *Giov. Batta* or *Gio. Batta*: Giovan Battista, Giovanni Battista
- *M^a*: Maria

It's possible that home records list a slightly different first name for a person than do official records, as Italians often went by nicknames or middle names. Given names that end in *-ino* or *-ina* are diminutive forms of that given name, used by families and close friends to express affection. Be aware of these possible variations as you search for your ancestors in records, particularly when using search engines. For example, *Nino* is often Antonio or Antonino, *Nel* might be Carmela, and *Nina* standing for Antonina.

A list of Italian given names and their English equivalents can be found at **<www.oocities. org/irishkenj/givename.html>** and **<www.conigliofamily.com/SicilianAndItalianGivenNames. htm>**, useful when determining what an Americanized given name was in Italian or vice versa. D'Addezio.com also has a first-name translator **<www.daddezio.com/genealogy/ italian/names.html>**, and you can use the Reverso Dictionary **<dictionary.reverso.net/ italian-english>** to determine what the English equivalent of an Italian name (or any other Italian word) might be. Google Translate's mobile app (downloadable from the Google Play store or from the Apple Store) is another handy tool.

UNDERSTANDING ITALIAN SURNAMES

Our surnames are part of who we are. We write them every day on documents, receipts, and checks. We hear them everyday as others address us in formal situations. We pass them down to our children and our grandchildren, and we use them to identify individual lines of our family trees. But where did our surnames come from, and what do they mean?

In this section, I'll briefly cover the basics of Italian surname origins. So much could be said about this subject that it would be a separate book in itself. In fact, it already is: Joseph G. Fucilla published *Our Italian Surnames* (Genealogical Publishing Company) in 1949, with several subsequent reprintings. This book also contains a whole chapter discussing Italian given names, a subject we'll address briefly in this chapter. Use Mr. Fucilla's book to expand your knowledge in this area.

Initially, prior to the fourteenth or fifteenth century, most of our ancestors did not use surnames. Instead, individuals were known by a given name or nickname, sometimes with the name of the fiefdom or region they lived in attached to it (i.e., "Giovanni di Messina" for a man who lived in Messina with the given name Giovanni). With the onset of

---

RESEARCH TIP

Look for Letters

If a particular letter stumps you, look for additional examples of this letter in the rest of the document or the documents surrounding it in the register. The documents before and after were more than likely written by the same scribe. However, this may not hold true in large cities where there are several civil officials recording documents during any given day. In these cases, you may have to expand out a little further to find another example of a particular letter written by the same person.

written records and establishment of noble families in Italy, surnames began to be used as a means to identify a person, not only individually but also as a means of knowing where the person came from.

Surnames evolved in four main ways and were derivatives of geographic or ethnic origins, nicknames, occupations or titles, and personal (given) names. Were there other forms of surname origination? Sure. However, these four categories cover the majority of surnames one can find in Italy today:

- **Geographic or ethic**: These surnames derived from an ancestor's ethnicity or place origin in another country or region, such as Greco (Greek), Tedesco (German), and Albanese (Albanian). Giuseppa di Catania, a resident of Roma, might have an ancestor who originated in the town or province of Catania. You'll find several variations, such as the suffixes *–ni* or *–an*, but all denote the person came from a certain region or place (i.e., Trevisan—from Treviso). These names were more common in northern Italy than in southern Italy because (as we've discussed in previous chapters) poverty-stricken southern Italians were more likely to move between towns and regions to find work, while northern Italians usually didn't migrate until the early twentieth century.

- **Nicknames**: Nicknames often evolved from physical characteristics, mental capacity, or something our ancestors did in the past and could be used as given names and surnames. Rossi (red) could mean someone whose skin was rosy in appearance or had red hair, while Grasso (big) could refer to a large person.

- **Occupations or titles**: Some surnames derived from occupations or the vocation a person had at the time the family took a surname. Some examples would be, Barbieri (from *barbiere*, or "barber"), Ferrarri (from *ferro*, or "iron"), and Mastro-giovanni (a combination of Giovanni and the Italian word for "teacher" or "master," *maestro*). One of my family's surnames, Lo Schiavo (literally "the slave"), may indicate an ancestor's occupation and place within his society. Antonina de Duca may descend from someone with the title of a duke (*duca*), while Cesare di Marchese may descend from a marquis (*marchese*).

- **Personal (given) names**: These surnames were usually taken from the given name of the ancestor's parents. For example, Maria, the daughter of Domenico, became Maria di Domenico. Likewise, Giovanni (whose mother was named Maria), became Giovanni Di (or Dei or De) Maria. Naturally, the most common of these surnames where those derived from given names popular at that time, often Catholic saints. A person's appearance or stature may also determine the ending of a particular surname derived from a given name. For example, if Giovanni Battista, the son of Domenico, was quite short in stature, he might be called Giovanni Battista di Domenicini. *-Ini* and *-etti* endings denote smallness, while a surname ending in *-one*, *-oni*, *-otto*, and *-otti* may indicate a large person.

Abandoned children were often given surnames that were meant to provide luck or to wish them the best (e.g., Buonaventura, meaning "good fortune," or Benvenuto, meaning "welcome"). They were also given surnames that denoted their physical or social condition (e.g., Brutto, meaning "ugly" or Esposito, meaning "exposed").

A quick note: Di (alternate spellings: De, Del, and Dei, all meaning "of" or "from") or Lo (meaning "the") often preceded a surname, although the use and spelling of them varied by region, family, and across documents relating to an individual ancestor.

As you can see, there is much to learn about the origins of our surnames. Did surnames evolve over time or after immigration? Definitely. Due to the racism faced by Italians after immigration, many Italian surnames evolved into a more "American-sounding" name. This helped the everyday lives of Italian immigrants, as it made more jobs available to them and lessened daily conflict due to racism or xenophobia. Some ancestors took entirely different surnames than the one give at their birth, like my ancestor, Matteo Catanese, who used many different surnames throughout his life (see chapter 13 for more).

In a growing trend, many Italian-Americans, seeking to reconnect with their ancestral history, are retaking the original spellings of their surnames. This is a wonderful way to honor the ancestors whose sacrifices provided you with the lives and opportunities that you enjoy today.

The GENS website has an interesting Italian surname distribution tool **<www.gens.info/italia/it/turismo-viaggi-e-tradizioni-italia#.WJERK7YrLSc>**, and you can use the online Italian whitepages, *PagineBianche* **<www.paginebianche.it/index_en.html>** and Whitepages.it **<whitepages.it>** to determine the current distribution of a surname in a town or province (though you should note this doesn't necessarily reflect the historical distribution of surnames in an area).

UNDERSTANDING ITALIAN HANDWRITING

As you begin to research Italian records, you will notice distinct differences in how some letters are written, most especially the *ss*, which look like an English *js* or *sj*. You can find good handwriting references in most Italian genealogical research books, and be sure to consult the examples at the end of this chapter. Brigham Young University also has a script tutorial for Italian handwriting **<script.byu.edu/Pages/Italian/en/handwriting.aspx>**.

Let's look at a few handwriting examples. The first example (image **A**; excerpted Italian text below the image, and the translation in the caption) provides several words

A

In this document, the capital *S* appears in several words or names, but the letter's appearance varies. The translation reads: "...Civil Records Official of the Town of Sant'Anna there appeared Salvatore Sabella, age thirty-six, a barber, resident of S. Anna [Sant'Anna], who declared that on the first of the current month at 4:02 p.m., in the house at 16 Largo Vasca, [a child was born] from Concetta Taleo, [daughter of the living] Giuseppe Antonio [Taleo], age thirty-two, the legitimate wife [of the declarant], farmer, residing with her husband. A male child was born and presented to me [who goes] by the name of Giuseppe Sabella."

TRANSCRIPTION:

Uffiziale dello Stato Civile del Comune di Sant'Anna é comparso Salvatore Sabella, di anni trentasei, barbiere domiciliato in S. Anna, Il quale mi ha dichiarato che alle ore po meridiane [combines to form pomeridiane] Quattro e minuti due, del di primo del corrente mese, nella casa posta in largo Vasca al number Sedici, da Concetta Taleo di Giuseppe Antonio di anni trentatre sua legitima moglie Contadina domiciliata, e residente con esso marito é nato un bambino di sesso maschile che lui mi presenta, e a cui da il nome di Giuseppe Sabella

B

TRANSCRIPTION:

Numero d'Ordine 31
Celebrazione di Matrimonio tra

Vincenzo Gasparrino
E Caterina Federici

This record has several letters that might look like other letters. Notice the *G* in Gasparrino almost appears to be a *P*, and the lowercase *s* and *p* next to each other make them hard to distinguish. The translation reads: "Order Number 31: Celebration of Marriage between Vincenzo Gasparrino and Caterina Federici."

or names that begin with the capital *S*, but the writing varies slightly in format. In addition, the lowercase *a*, *e*, and *o* may look slightly different at the end of a word than they do within a word, and noting that subtlety can change a word's meaning. On the second to last line, we see the word *maschile* (meaning "male"), a good example of how the lowercase *s* extends below the line. If there were a double *s* in this word, then only one *s* would extend below the line.

The capital *G* in Italian often looks like a capital *P* in English. In this second example (image **B**), the surname *Gasparrino* places an *s* and a *p* next to each other. You'll need to carefully watch the pen strokes to be able to determine the correct spelling of this name. Similarly, the capital *F* in *Federici* looks like an English *S*.

In this example (image **C**), the word *Gennaio* ("January") on the first line shows how a lowercase *i* can extend below the line when not on the end of the word. You may also want to note how the double *n* in this word can very easily appear to be *un* to an English speaker/reader. Lastly, this civil official appeared to still be using the pen and quill, as evidence by the inkblots where the pen reversed direction.

This example (image **D**) shows several abbreviations, which you will get more comfortable with as you encounter them. This example is part of a *riveli* record, a disclosure (type of census) taken in Sicilia between the sixteenth and early nineteenth centuries for taxation. Note the ink bleed-through from the opposite side.

C

A lowercase *i* in a word in the middle of a sentence (in this case, *Gennaio*) can extend below the line, making it look like a *j*. The translation reads: "The year 1886, on the 28th of January, at 10:05 a.m., in the Town Hall. Before me Ferdinando Colotti[,] Municipal Agent Functioning as the Civil Records Official of the Town of Onore, there appeared Andrea Colotti, [son of the living] Giovanni [Colotti], age thirty-eight; Farmer, residing..."

TRANSCRIPTION:

L'anno milleottocentoottantasei, addi ventiotto di Gennaio, a ore ante meridian dieci e minuti cinque, nella Casa Comunale.
Avanti di me Colotti Ferdinando Assessore Municipale facente le funzioni di

Uffiziale dello Stato Civile del Comune di Onore, e comparso
Colotti Andrea di Giovanni, di anni trentaotto; Contadino, domiciliato..."

D

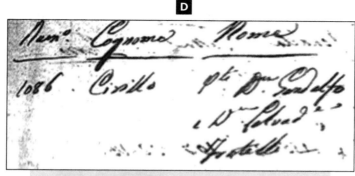

This record contains a number of abbreviations: *Num⁰* (numero/number), *Ptᵉ* (*prete*, or priest/father) and *Dⁿ* (Don). The translation reads: "Number: 1086, Surname: Cirillo, Given Name: Father [Priest] Don Gandolfo and Don Salvadore, Brothers."

TRANSCRIPTION:

		Num⁰ [Numero]	Cognome	Nome
	1086	Cirillo	Ptᵉ [Prete] Dⁿ [Don] Gandolfo	
			e Dⁿ [Don] Salvadᵉ [Salvadore]	
				Fratelli

In this record, two brothers owned the property being taxed, and the first listed was a priest. *Don* is a title of respect given to those of the upper class and/or priests. Occasionally you will see this title used for an ancestor not in the top layer of society who had done something particularly respected, but this is not the norm.

These examples show different aspects of handwriting that I found challenging when I first began researching Italian records. Each time you translate a record, the process will get easier, as you learn more about the language and the trickier parts of Italian handwriting.

KEYS TO SUCCESS

- Learn some Italian-language basics. Knowing a handful of useful vocabulary words in the language records were kept in will help you decode records without being fluent in Italian.

- Double-check translations provided by automated tools/websites.

- Bear in mind cultural naming traditions as you work back in time. While not all families followed these norms, names that repeat throughout your family tree can provide valuable research leads.

- Research how Italian surnames evolved and what your surname might mean.

- Be flexible when trying to decipher handwriting in records. Consider what other letters could appear in a word, as bad penmanship and years of record damage can make it easy to confuse letters for each other. Use the handwriting examples as guides.

HANDWRITING LETTERS GUIDE

	Uppercase	Lowercase			Uppercase	Lowercase
A			N		
B			O		
C			P		
D			Q		
E			R		
F			S		
G			T		
H			U		
I			V		
J	n/a	n/a	W	n/a	n/a
K	n/a	n/a	X	n/a	n/a
L			Y	n/a	n/a
M			Z		

*The letters J, K, W, X, and Y are not found in the standard Italian alphabet. You'll only find them in foreign-language words that have been incorporated into modern Italian.

HANDWRITING LETTERS GUIDE

Double consonants can be written different ways, depending on their place within the word. Here are some of the more difficult-to-discern pairs.

Double consonants	Sample text
bb	
gg	
ll	
nn	
pp	
ss	
tt	
zz	

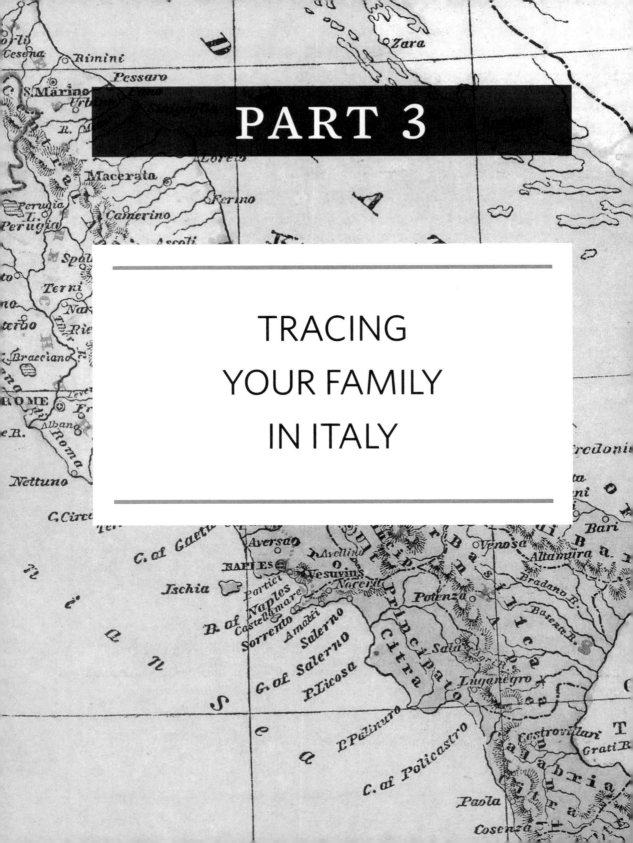

PART 3

TRACING
YOUR FAMILY
IN ITALY

7

Civil Records

C ivil registration is one of the largest and most important record sets in Italian genealogical research. Thanks to the efforts of FamilySearch International, which has microfilmed and/or digitized civil records held in the *archivio di stato* (provincial/state archives) of Italy, these records are also among the most widely available.

In this chapter, we will discuss in depth the various forms of civil registration documents you might encounter in your research, including (but not limited to):

- birth records (both regular and supplemental)
- marriage records (marriage banns, marriage promises, marriage records, and marriage supplements)
- death records (both regular and supplemental)

Each type of record presents different challenges and varies based on time period and/or location. In this chapter, we'll discuss various types of records created by the civil authorities, as well as modern-day extractions from the original documents that might be useful in your research. You can read about more kinds of civil records, including population registers, by visiting **<bit.ly/italian-guide>** and downloading our free bonus chapter.

UNDERSTANDING CIVIL REGISTRATION

Civil registration records the vital events in Italy and is governed by the Italian Civil Code (Il Codice Civile Italiano). The civil code has changed over the years, and you can find various versions of it in digital format on Google Books **<books.google.com>**. For example, couples being married were read specific articles directly from the Civil Code that stressed the importance of cohabitation, loyalty, and duty.

In addition to documenting the births and deaths of citizens, civil records are also used in court cases, for inheritance purposes, for military matters, in support of passport applications, and as documentation in citizenship cases.

For our purposes, Italian civil records are divided into three categories based on when they were created:

- *Stato civile napoleonico* (Napoleonic civil records or SCN), 1804–1815: Named for Napoleon Bonaparte, these were modeled after the *code civil des Français* (French civil code) and introduced by the King of Naples, Gioacchino Napoleone Murat, to the area under his control. He declared records should be kept from 19 October 1808, and these continued to be maintained until 1815. At this time, civil registration did not extend to every current-day province of Italy. (Sicily, for example, did not begin civil registration until 1820 because it was under Bourbon control.)

- *Stato civile restaurazione* (Restoration civil records), 1816–1865: Coverage for this time period varies by location, but in general civil records were kept in the southern part of the peninsula (mainland Italy) from 1816 to 1865 and in Sicily from 1820 to 1865. Because these lands were ruled by the Bourbon-controlled Kingdom of the Two Sicilies, these records are sometimes called *stato civile borbonico* (Bourbon civil records). In this time period, marriages were required to be performed in the Catholic Church, and civil birth registers included both birth and baptismal information. (Note: Northern Italian regions generally didn't keep records at this time, but a few provinces restarted civil registration in the 1840s and 1850s.)

- *Stato civile italiano* (Italian civil records), 1866–present: Italian Unification may have created a singular Italian state, but changes to the civil registration process varied considerably across the young kingdom. In this new era of records, baptismal information was no longer required on civil birth records. Parishes continued to keep baptismal records, and a few northern dioceses also maintained a separate parish birth record. In addition, at least two witnesses (often relatives, friends, or municipal employees) were required for each civil record, and marriage records required four witnesses.

Regardless of time period, civil records may be found in multiple volumes depending on how large the town was. Particularly large cities, like Palermo or Naples, kept separate registers by neighborhood. In these instances, you need to have the name of the neighborhood they lived in. Otherwise, you will have many volumes to search, each with hundreds or thousands of entries. Fortunately, officials often made annual and decennial (ten-year) indexes for these resources, and many of these have been microfilmed or digitized by FamilySearch.org **<www.familysearch.org>** and Ancestry.com **<www.ancestry.com>**. For example, indexes for Palermo can be found on Ancestry.com **<search.ancestry.com/search/db.aspx?dbid=5778>**, and genealogist Hugh Tornabene created and digitized extractions of these records **<freepages.genealogy.rootsweb.ancestry.com/~tornabene/index8.htm>** as he researched his ancestors from this city.

CIVIL BIRTH RECORDS

Civil birth records, commemorating the beginning of your ancestor's life, are useful because they set a start date for your research. These records verified the child's gender and declared his name. Typically the father or midwife presented the child for registration, and the bottom of a record will note if he was born while his father was out of town—important because the father had the right to change the child's name upon his return. Image **A** shows an 1896 civil birth record from the Pescara province. Note how

ATTI DI NASCITA

This 1896 birth record for a male child has two columns. The left column (not shown) provides the record number and name of the child whose birth is being recorded, while the right column (translated at left) gives many details.

the official merely filled in information on a pre-printed form, making it easier to read and translate. Preprinted forms like these began in the 1870s. Prior to that, the documents were totally handwritten, following directions laid out in the civil code.

Civil births did not need to be recorded until three days after the actual birth occurred, and records will give a reason when a child was presented more than three days after birth. The child may have been sickly, or the father/midwife may have had to travel long distances or through bad weather to reach the record office. If the child was too sickly for a trip to the town hall, a civil official may have come to the family home to record the

Know Who Did What

Despite their importance to genealogists, civil birth records were not a first priority for many Italian families. In fact, families didn't have to register a birth with the government for up to three days. Instead, the infant was taken to the nearest parish for baptism almost immediately (usually the same day). The child's father, if present and available, would then take the child to the town hall to have its birth recorded. The midwife who performed the child's birth could stand in either the father or godparent's place if necessary. Understanding this process may help you determine relationships and solve genealogical problems.

birth, particularly in small towns with fewer births to track. In one instance, I discovered a midwife who recorded six births at once, all of which occurred over a ten-day period in a hamlet about six kilometers outside the nearest town. The midwife was likely too busy with the six birthing mothers (and crossing six kilometers in the dead of winter was no easy task) so instead recorded them all at once, rather than making individual trips to record each birth.

As we discussed briefly in the previous section, the time period your ancestor lived in will affect what birth records you're able to find, how they'll be formatted, and what information they'll include. Prior to Italian Unification (a process which occurred between 1865 and 1871), most areas of current-day Italy required birth records to include baptismal information in addition to birth registers, and this can be found in the right-hand column of these documents. After 1865, you'll have to go to the parish archives for baptismal records.

In addition to civil birth records, researchers might also find supplemental birth records, transcriptions, or extracts of original documents created for various administrative or legal purposes. They are usually found in registers titled *allegati* or *processetti* but occasionally in *atti diversi* registers (see the bonus download at **<bit.ly/italian-guide>**), depending on town procedure. Occasionally, records weren't transcribed upon receipt, and you will find the original document that was received from the other town was simply placed within one of these civil registers. Note that, because supplemental birth records are transcriptions of the original documents, they're more likely to contain errors.

Supplemental birth records were created for a variety of reasons, including births that occurred outside of the parents' town of residence or in unusual places (on a train, at sea, etc.). Birth record abstracts may also have been created for marriage, military service, or passport/identification card applications. If the transcribed document was sent from outside the country, you may even find translations included with the documents, often routed through the *Tribunale* (court) and a local university for translation.

Supplemental birth records can be found for abandoned, stillborn, or miscarried children. Whether the town placed these births in the regular birth register of the supplemental varies by town. If you find a birth record within these registers that says the child was born *senza vita* (without life), then the child was either stillborn or the mother miscarried.

Occasionally, the birth of an abandoned child will be registered on a *notamento di nascita* (notice of birth) birth record form. This form allows more room to discuss the specifics of the child's abandonment than does a regular birth record and leaves space for the specifics of the child's abandonment and baptism. These records are more likely to be found prior to 1861. See the free bonus download at **<bit.ly/italian-guide>** for more on researching abandoned children.

CIVIL MARRIAGE RECORDS

As it is today, marriage for our Italian ancestors was a time of joy. Marriage ceremonies were often followed by a feast that lasted all day and far into the night. Marriages were also a time of fulfillment for parents; mothers in traditional Italian families were tasked with finding spouses for all of their children, as well as saving money so they could provide a dowry for each daughter and a bridal gift for each son. (The size of these gifts, of course, depended on the parents' financial stability.)

Your ancestors' "big day" also has use for your genealogy research, as marriage documents provide a snapshot of your ancestors' lives at the time and help establish

Civil Law Changes in the Kingdom of the Two Sicilies

As we discussed in chapter 1, many of the Italian immigrants to the United States came from modern southern Italy and Sicily, which was once the Kingdom of the Two Sicilies. King Ferdinand I, the ruler of that kingdom, made two important changes to the format of civil registration during in the early nineteenth century, and these changes can be important for researchers:

- In Royal Decree No. 15, dated 21 June 1815, it was decreed that all marriages must occur in the Church. As most Italians were Catholic, this translates to marriages in the Catholic Church for most ancestors. Civil marriage records prior to 1861–1865 are not the actual marriage record but rather a marriage promise, which stated the couple's intent to marry within the Church. These marriage promises were a form of civil engagement and were posted on the door of the town hall, like the marriage banns, so anyone who objected to the marriage could make their objection known.
- In Royal Decree No. 20, dated 5 July 1815, it required that baptismal information be included on civil birth records. This is when birth records began to have two columns, with the birth information on the left and the baptismal information on the right.

Marriage Impediments

During the marriage bann process, couples could encounter a number of impediments that would keep them from going through with the ceremony. *Finding Your Italian Ancestors: A Beginner's Guide* by Suzanne Russo Adams (Ancestry.com, 2009) describes several possible obstacles to marriage, organized into two major categories of varying severity:

- **Prohibitory impediments** make a marriage illegal but don't invalidate it should they be discovered after the ceremony. These include previous betrothals, unions between Catholics and non-Catholics baptized into other faith traditions, or marriage during certain high holy times.
- **Direct impediments** immediately make a marriage null and void. These include a lack of consent between the two parties, insufficient age (defined as the beginning of puberty), a lack of parental support, or marriage banns not being read. More scandalous direct impediments include the presence of other living spouses, relationship by "consanguinity" (related by blood up to the fourth degree/the great-great-grandparent level) or "affinity" (related by marriage, such as to in-laws), adultery, impotence, or crimes like homicide. Despite the severity of some of these conditions, bishops could dispense certain indiscretions to allow a couple to get married—often because the couple had a child on the way.

relationships. Marriage was a legal process, and civil law necessitated several types of marriage documents, each of which served a specific purpose. Like other kinds of Italian civil records, coverage and formatting varied by location, but the major kinds of marriage documents were:

- *Atto di pubblicazioni* or *atto di notificazioni*: Act of publications/notifications or marriage banns
- *Atto di solenne promessa di celebrare il matrimonio*: Act of solemn promise to celebrate marriage or marriage promise
- *Atto di matrimonio*: Act of marriage
- *Allegati di matrimonio* or *processetti di matrimonio*: Marriage supplements or attachments

In this section, we'll discuss each type of record in detail.

Atto di Pubblicazioni/Notificazioni (Marriage Banns)

As in other countries, Italian civil marriage banns were required to be posted on the door of the town hall and read aloud on two consecutive Sundays to alert the townspeople of the impending marriage and allow time for any objections or obstacles to be made known. The couple, armed with copies of their birth or baptismal records (usually created a few

Marriage by Proxy

When researching an Italian couple's marriage, you may find an anomaly: a marriage by proxy. Marriage by proxy occurred when a designated proxy (often a relative or close friend) stood in for the bride or groom during the marriage process. Marriage proxy documents are interesting because they often reveal the name of the relative or close family friend who served as a proxy, the names of the bride's and groom's parents, and why your ancestor needed one in the first place. While most proxies were for brides, grooms might be represented by proxies when called away for military service or some other legal obligation.

The proxy document, usually created by a notary, may be found in the marriage supplements and can be quite revealing about what was going on in that ancestor's life. A second copy of that document will be found in the notaries' files, provincial archives, or in the notarial district archives, depending on the year of creation. See chapter 10 more details on notarial records.

days ahead of time) would request that the banns be posted at the town hall and read aloud from their parish pulpits over the next two weeks. Should you find marriage banns for a marriage that never took place, the couple likely faced some impediment (perhaps a marriage contract with someone else) that prevented them from marrying; see the Marriage Impediments sidebar for more information.

If the bride and groom resided in different towns, banns would be posted in both towns, so be on the lookout for multiple sets of banns in these cases. Often you will find one set of banns differs from the other, as additional information may appear on only one set of banns. The town the couple did not marry in (usually the groom's hometown) would then send notification to the other town when the process of the banns was complete. The couple could not proceed with their marriage until the banns were completed in both towns of residence.

Marriage banns (see image **B** for 1907 marriage banns from the Palermo province) can be found in registers with several different titles, depending on the time period and place where they were created. These records were known as *pubblicazioni di matrimonio* (publications of marriage) or *notificazioni* (notifications). Between 1830 and 1865, marriage banns were included in *memorandum* registers, which contained a full set of banns in at least two parts, though they are not necessarily organized together or numerically. Occasionally, a third part of the banns indicates the banns process was complete. Unless both towns were particularly close together, you'll find a few days' difference between when the banns were posted in each town.

The year 1907, on the 16th of November, at 6:40 p.m., in the Town Hall.

Before me Salvatore Di Gesaro, Mayor [and] Civil Records Official of the Town of Isnello

and there appeared Calogero Albanese, a widower, age sixty-five, a farmer, resident in Isnello, son of the deceased Antonio [Albanese], age [blank], a farmer, and resident in life in Petralia Sottana, and of the deceased Maria Malla, a housewife and resident of Petralia Sottana in life, and [also appearing was] Domenica Gervasi, a widow, age fifty, a housewife, resident in Isnello, daughter of the deceased Nicolo [Gervasi], age [blank], a resident in life in this Town and of the deceased Felicia Sbriglia, housewife, resident in life in Isnello;

who states that Albanese and Gervasi requested the marriage banns in this office: and I declared that the groom was born in Petralia Sottana and the bride was born in Isnello. The spouses state that they have resided in Isnello from one year ago to today, that they have no adoptive parents to present impediments to the marriage, or no other parental or through affinity marriage impediments, nor any other impediment determined by the law.

PUBBLICAZIONI DI MATRIMONIO

These declarations were supported with oaths in legal formats from: Salvatore Giorgi, age thirty-five, a municipal guard, and from Andrea Sicli, age thirty-three, a sexton, both residents of this Town and witnesses of the present act. I have examined the documents presented, and with my own initiative, have placed them in the supplemental volume of this register. I declare that the banns were posted in Isnello and Petralia Sottana.

The documents are: copies of the birth records of the bride and groom; [a statement of] release from the civil records office in Petralia Sottana and certificate of free state for the same, dated 7 November of the current year, the [statement of] release issued by this civil records office, and copies of the acts of death for Calogera Ganci, first wife of Albanese, and the same for Salvatore Di Francesca, first husband of Gervasi, all dated the 19th of the current month.

The present act was read aloud to all those concerned and signed by me and the witnesses only, and the bride and groom stated they were not literate.

Signature of Salvatore Giorgi witness

Signature of Andrea Sideli witness

Signature of S. Di Gesaro

This 1907 marriage banns (called *pubblicazioni di matrimonio*) for Calogero Albanese and Domenica Gervasi contains a lot of valuable information about the couple and their families, including that the Albanese family originated in a different town, Petralia Sottana.

Marriage banns often contain more information than marriage records, especially after 1865. They provide the couple's names, ages, birthplaces, residences, occupations, parents' names, amongst other information like the names of witnesses, whether parental consent was required, and notations about unusual circumstances surrounding the marriage (legitimization of children born out of wedlock, or a marriage permission received from a commanding officer if the groom was in military service).

Unlike most civil records, marriage banns were not kept in duplicate. The original register was transferred to the *Tribunale* at the end of each year, then to the *archivio di stato* after seventy years. FamilySearch.org has microfilmed or digitized the majority of these registers being held in the *archivio di stato*, and it's seeking to digitize records that never transferred from the *Tribunale*. In addition, all digitized Italian records conserved in the provincial archives, will eventually be available for free on the Italian archival website, Portale Antenati <www.antenati.san.beniculturali.it>.

Atto di Solenne Promessa di Celebrare il Matrimonio (Marriage Promise)

In some areas of Italy (notably in the areas of the Kingdom of Two Sicilies), a civil marriage document before the Unification of Italy is actually an *atto di solenne promessa di celebrare il matrimonio* (marriage promise), rather than a technical marriage record. They are a form of civil engagement, providing information on a couple and their proposed marriage, as well as containing derivative information on the couple's actual marriage within the Catholic Church.

Once the marriage banns were complete, a couple had to record a marriage promise in the town hall with four witnesses present before proceeding to the church to get married. And like marriage banns, marriage promises had to be posted on the door of the town hall, though only once for an unspecified amount of time. (In fact, the couple was free to marry as soon as the promise was posted; I have seen many 10 p.m. marriage promises followed by a parish wedding ceremony the next morning.)

Once the civil official recorded the marriage promise and posted it on the door of the town hall, he gave the couple two copies of the document to present to the parish priest, plus a certificate authorizing him to perform the marriage. The priest would then fill in the specifics of the marriage on one copy of the marriage promise and return it to the town hall. The wedding details were transcribed onto the two original marriage promises. The priest then used the second copy to create the parish marriage record. (As you can see, a couple's marriage generated a lot of work for the civil records office and parish!)

Marriage promises contain more information than later marriage records because they also recorded the parish marriage. The documents are two or four pages long and also list what documents were presented, especially useful when you research marriage supplements that don't have a cover page. Marriage supplements not having cover pages makes it difficult to separate the documents pertaining to the marriage you are interested in from the previous and subsequent marriages. The two-page marriage promises often have more handwritten portions, and the closeness of the lines makes the translation process more challenging.

Marriage promises contain the following types of information, each of which is valuable to your research:

- The date the couple and their witnesses appeared to record the marriage promise (note this is likely separate from the day of the actual wedding ceremony)
- The couple's names, ages, birthplaces, place(s) of residence, and occupations
- Whether the bride and groom were single or widowed, sometimes with a deceased spouse's name and date of death
- The names of their parents, usually with their ages, professions, and places of residence
- The names, ages, occupations, and places of residence for all four witnesses
- Other documents that varied based on province
- The date of the marriage, the date it was recorded in parish records, the record number, and what sheet/page (*foglio*) the document can be found on

Atto di Matrimonio (Act of Marriage)

The act of marriage can be found in nearly all areas of Italy from 1865 onward. This document is easier to understand than the marriage promise and was nearly always recorded on a pre-printed form.

After Unification, everyone was required to marry civilly. A couple may also choose to marry in the Church, but legally they had to also have a civil marriage. The church and state had serious disagreements over who had the power to administer marriages

RESEARCH TIP

Keep in Mind the Age of Majority

Parents could make decisions about who their children married well into the twentieth century, and keeping this in mind can be useful as you research and analyze marriage records. In the nineteenth century, the age of majority (the point at which individuals could choose partners for themselves) was twenty-five for a male and twenty-three for a female.

between 1865 and 1875. Children born during this time period whose parents had not married civilly were noted to be illegitimate on their civil birth record. Couples may have eventually had a separate civil wedding ceremony, but the government did not go back and correct these notations when the parents married.

Marriage records usually contain all of the same information as marriage banns, except the couple's towns of birth. You may also find that the witnesses on a couple's marriage record were relatives or close friends. Don't gloss over those witness names because they could potentially reveal relationships.

Processetti/Allegati (Marriage Supplements)

Called *processetti di matrimonio* or *allegati di matrimonio* depending on the location of their creation, marriage supplements (also called marriage attachments) are records required (by Italian civil law) to be filed with the civil record office so a couple could marry. They're among the most useful and detailed records available in Italian records, and a single record set can contain two to four generations of a couple's ancestry. Most supplements include:

- Cover page: If included, this document will state the name of the couple, the year, often a record set number, and how many documents are included within the supplements. You can use the number of documents given to make sure you find all of the documents pertaining to the couple you are researching. Cover pages also make marriage supplements much easier to find, as they will help you more easily identify relevant records. The record set number does not necessarily correspond to the record number of the marriage record or marriage promise.

- Extracted birth or baptismal records of the bride and groom: These records determined whether the bride and groom could consent to their own marriages. Extracted birth records could be civil or ecclesiastical records, depending on the location of their creation and whether that particular diocese kept separate birth registers in addition to baptismal registers. You are more apt to see ecclesiastical birth records in northern or central Italy, and these records often pre-date civil registration, allowing one to extend an ancestry beyond what is normally possible by using other civil records.

- Extracted death records for any parents deceased at the time the marriage banns and/or marriage promise was recorded: These documents explained (without saying it outright) why the parent wasn't present and/or why their permission was not indicated.

- Extracted death records for the paternal or maternal grandfather, if either father was deceased: If the father was deceased, the bride's/groom's grandfather was next in line to give permission for the marriage. After that, you often see the mother (or possibly another male relative) give permission. These records could come from the local hospital, another town, or possibly from a foreign country where the person died.

- Extracted death records for any previous spouses of the bride and groom: These documents served as additional proof that a widowed person was free to marry. Notations about the death of previous spouses were placed on the marriage banns, the information taken from the extracted death records presented by the couple.

- Extracted copies of the first and second marriage banns: As discussed earlier, couples needed proof that their banns had been published in the appropriate fashion.

- A certificate of no opposition: This document stated that the banns process was complete and the couple faced no civil or ecclesiastical opposition to the marriage.

- Extract of the marriage promise: This was required for most parts of Italy prior to 1865; see the previous section for more.

Accessing Civil Records

So where do you find these records? All civil records except for marriage banns and *allegati* (birth, death, and marriage) were kept in duplicate. One copy of each register remained in the town hall and the other copy was sent to the *Tribunale* (district court) at the end of each year, where it remained for seventy years. After seventy years, the documents were transferred to the *archivio di stato* (provincial archives) for conservation.

You can access original civil records at the town hall and provincial archives, either by visiting the archive or by submitting a letter requesting individual records (see appendix C). We've noted any exception to this blanket rule.

FamilySearch has microfilmed or digitized many Italian civil records, and how you can access the records through FamilySearch depends on its agreement with the main Italian archive in 2014. Civil records digitized in this second initiative will also be placed on the Portale Antenati website and freely available for anyone to research. You can also access these documents at the Family History Library or at a FamilySearch Center. Ancestry.com has a moderate amount of Italian civil records available to its subscribers, though you'll need the World subscription to access them.

Supplemental birth, death, and marriage records (as well as marriage banns) were not kept in duplicate. The original register was transferred to the *Tribunale* at the end of each year and then to the *archivio di stato* after seventy years. FamilySearch has microfilmed or digitized most of these registers, and is seeking permission to digitize even those that haven't been transferred to the provincial archives.

All digitized Italian records conserved in the provincial archives will eventually be available for free on the Italian archival website, Portale Antenati **<www.antenati.san.beniculturali. it>**. They will also be available to access at the Family History Library in Salt Lake City.

- A certificate of poverty: This document (common amongst the impoverished Italians who later came to the United States) was included if a couple had insufficient funds to pay the fees normally associated with the marriage paperwork, confirming the couple's economic state to exempt them from the fee.

- Notarial documents: These documents created by notaries gave permission from an absent parent or explained why a birth or baptismal record was not included for the bride or groom. Notaries could have created other documents pertaining to a marriage contract or land transaction for a dowry, but these documents are not usually attached. They would be found amongst the notarial records within the *archivio di stato* or provincial/state archives.

- Extracted death records of the paternal and maternal grandmothers: These were normally included when the bride or groom was underage and their parents and grandparents were all deceased. In this way, they showed the civil authorities why an uncle or other relative was giving permission for the young person to marry.

- Miscellaneous documents needed to understand a particular part of the couple's marriage: This could include permission from the military command office (if the groom was still in the service), *atti di notarietà* (which was an act that detailed why the bride or groom's birth and baptismal records couldn't be found and wasn't being presented), etc.

- Documents or notations regarding the abandonment or reclamation of the bride or groom: If the bride or groom was reclaimed as a child (i.e., abandoned but then taken back by the birth parents), birth parents often did so informally, with no legal paperwork filed. This may be the only document you find that tells you more about the bride's or groom's familial situation.

CIVIL DEATH RECORDS

While Italian death records are generally considered the least reliable source of civil genealogical information, they are still valuable sources of information. Civil death records are particularly important near the beginning of civil registration, as these are some of the few documents allowing us to extend a family line beyond the beginning of the nineteenth century.

Death records usually contain the following valuable information about the deceased:

- Name
- Age
- Marital status and spouse name, if applicable

- Place of residence, may include a street address
- Parents' names
- Date and place of death
- Names of witnesses and their ages, occupations, and places of residence

The deceased's town of birth is not usually found, nor is a cause of death unless it was something unusual. I once found a death record in the town of Isnello, Palermo province, that stated the deceased was "shot dead in the piazza," perhaps indicative of a story yet to be discovered. This particular ancestor was a soldier born on the mainland and so may have been assigned to Sicily to squash the rebellions happening there at that time, unrest caused by the changes in the aftermath of Unification.

Image **C** shows an 1879 death record from Palermo province in the standard format. Death records varied little in format, except for those from the early nineteenth century, which contain different wording to describe the recordkeeping process.

Tread lightly when reviewing information in death records, as recordkeeping procedures invited great potential for errors. Depending on the time period, some civil officials had to go to the deceased's home and physically see the body to verify his death, but other information in death records may be questionable. In many towns, neighbors (not necessarily close ones) would report a person's death to the civil records office, and it's difficult to determine how well they knew the deceased and how accurate the information they provided was. Typically, the date/time/place of death and the deceased's spouse's name are likely to be correct, but age and name of parents could be incorrect depending on how well the declarants knew the family.

Note that you may find many death records for your ancestors' young siblings or children, as infant mortality was high in nineteenth-century Italy. Epidemics, lack of medical care, and insufficient food for a breast-feeding or pregnant mother are just three reasons for the high mortality rate, and abandoned children (foundlings) had an even more difficult time.

As with birth records, death records could have transcriptions or extracts made when an ancestor passed away in unusual circumstances, such as outside of the Italian town where he was a citizen, in a hospital, or while he was working overseas. These supplemental death records were created after an Italian town hall that held the deceased's original birth record received a notice of a person's death (called *annotazione di morte* or *annotazione di decesso*, "annotations of death" if it occurred in country) or transcriptions of the person's death record (if it occurred outside the country). Officials in the town hall (*ufficio dello stato civile*) and district court (*Tribunale*) were supposed to annotate the person's birth record with this information (the date and place of death, act number,

TRANSLATION:

The year 1879, on the 22nd of May, at 10:00 a.m., in the Town Hall.

Before me Giovan Battista Palma...Civil Records Official of the Town of Termini [Imerese], there appeared Andrea Mercurio, age sixty, a porter [perhaps carrier], resident in Termini, and Vincenzo Mercurio, age fifty, a porter [perhaps carrier], resident in Termini, who declares to me that yesterday [21 May 1879] at 2:00 p.m. in the home at 11 Vico Cannitello, Salvatore Arrigo passed away.

Salvatore was thirty years old, a farmer, resident in Termini, born in Termini, and of [meaning born to] the deceased Carlo [Arrigo], a resident of Termini in life, and from [the living] Francesca Azzarella, a farmer, resident in Termini; widower [meaning the deceased] of Giuseppa Lo Bianco.

For this act the witnesses present were: Vincenzo Di Lissi, age sixty, a bricklayer, and Vittorio Alberti, age forty, a bricklayer, both residents of this Town. The present act was read aloud to all and signed by me, the others stating they did not know how to write [were illiterate].

Italian death records are generally less reliable than other kinds of civil records, but you can still learn a lot from resources like this 1879 act of death for Giovan Battista Palma from Termini Imerese, Italy.

register and/or part number, location, and date of transcription), but this didn't always occur. Records from outside the town were transcribed into the Italian registers, just like was done for supplemental birth records. These records can be found in the *allegati* or *processetti* registers, but occasionally are found in the *atti diversi* registers.

An 1812 supplemental death record for Vincenzo Matarese (digitized on FamilySearch.org) is below. As you can see, these records can provide rich detail:

Order [record] number One

On 14 May 1812...was recorded the death record of Vincenzo Matarese.

The copy [meaning the original notice being transcribed] was number 592 and dated 12 May 1812. Before me Giuseppe Monaco, civil official for the town of Vicaria in the province of Napoli there appeared Giuseppe della Gatta, age thirty, a clerk at the Hospital of S. Francesco di Paola, and a resident of Vicaria, as well as Pietrantonio Ginetti, age forty-six, a guard at the Hospital, and resident of this same town...They declared that Vincenzo Matarese passed away on 12 May 1812 at 7:00 a.m. in the Hospital of S. Francesco di Paola. Vincenzo was eighteen years old, a farm laborer, the son of the living Giuseppe [Matarese], and a resident of Fontana in Ischia, Province of Napoli...

As with other kinds of record transcriptions, supplemental death records are more likely to contain transcription errors, though you may be able to find the original extract in the register. If transcriptions were sent from outside the country, you might also find a translation of the document.

However, unlike birth, death, and most marriage records, the supplemental death records were not kept in duplicate. The original register was transferred to the *Tribunale* at the end of each year and then to the *archivio di stato* after seventy years. FamilySearch.org has microfilmed or digitized all of these registers in the *archivio di stato*. If the records haven't been transferred from the *Tribunale*, they are seeking permission to digitize them at the district court archive. All digitized Italian civil records conserved in the provincial archives will eventually be available for free on the Italian archival website, Portale Antenati.

KEYS TO SUCCESS

Determine when civil registration was taken in your ancestor's part of Italy, as civil registration laws varied throughout history and from place to place.

Define the different types of records that might be useful to your research. Find out where the records are now and how to access them.

Continue digging if you find a supplemental birth or death record for your ancestor, as the presence of these records points to unusual circumstances surrounding these events. Look at the pages before and after the record to find other documents that might have been attached.

Be on the lookout for marriage supplements, which often contain records concerning other vital events or special situations surrounding the marriage (e.g., birth or baptismal records). This one resource could provide two to four generations of your ancestry!

8

Church Records

C
hurch records are the second largest record set in Italian research, and also among the most useful. Many Italians (most of them Roman Catholic) centered their lives on family and the Church, and their major life events are recorded in records held by parishes and dioceses. Church records began as early as 1563, when priests and bishops were instructed to maintain records of their parishioners' baptisms, marriages, and burials. (Many also kept records of confirmations.) Towards the end of the seventeenth century, Roman Catholic parishes also began keeping a type of family book called the *status animarum/stato delle anime* (state of the souls), a type of parish census used to track parishioners for taxation and sacraments recordkeeping.

There are two main types of archives where church records can be found; check out image **A** to see a map of current dioceses and archdioceses.

- **Parish archives (*archivio parrocchiale*):** Baptismal, marriage, confirmation, and death/burial records are usually found in the parish. (The *status animarum*, which we'll discuss further in this chapter, can be found in either the parish or diocese.) The physical parish archive may be in the church, in an attached building, in the priest's residence, or in another building across town. If the town is large, then

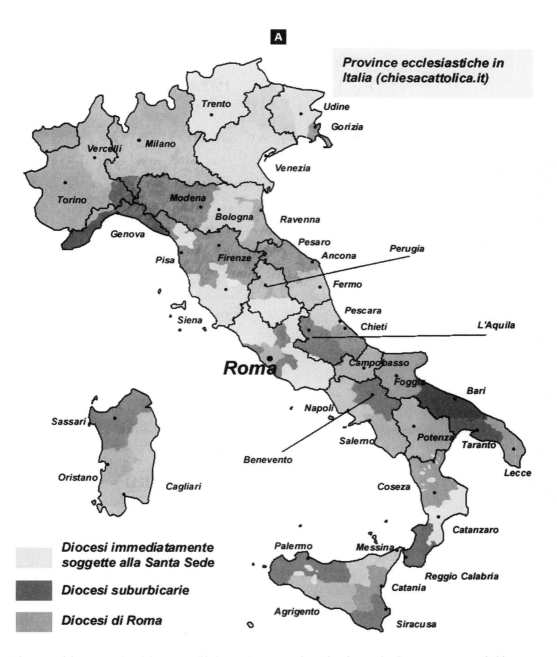

A

Province ecclesiastiche in Italia (chiesacattolica.it)

Trento

Udine

Gorizia

Vercelli • Milano

Venezia

Torino

Modena

Bologna

Ravenna

Genova

Pesaro

Perugia

Pisa

Firenze

Ancona

Fermo

Siena

Pescara

Chieti

L'Aquila

Roma

Campobasso

Foggia

Bari

Napoli

Sassari

Salerno

Potenza

Taranto

Benevento

Lecce

Oristano

Cagliari

Coseza

Catanzaro

Palermo

Messina

Reggio Calabria

Catania

Agrigento

Siracusa

Diocesi immediatamente soggette alla Santa Sede

Diocesi suburbicarie

Diocesi di Roma

This map of dioceses and archdioceses will help you determine where church records of your ancestors are held. Specifically, this map denotes what areas are under the dominion of the diocese in Rome but don't border it.

the pre-1900 parish records have likely been combined into a single archive in the mother church, *duomo*, or *cattedrale*. Few parish records have been microfilmed or digitized, but FamilySearch.org <www.familysearch.org> has a modest collection.

- **Diocesan archives (*archivio diocesano*):** Marriage dispensations and ecclesiastical marriage supplements are almost always found within diocesan archives, as are confirmation records and records from defunct or closed parishes. In the northern areas of Italy (pre-1900) and all throughout Italy (1900–present), you may also find duplicate copies of baptism, marriage, and death records at the diocesan level. Diocesan archives also hold records of a priest or nun's service, and these records can

Finding Your Ancestor's Parish

A parish (or *parrocchia*) is an individual church within the town your ancestors resided in. Small towns will often have a single parish, while large towns or cities could have many. People often attended the parish that was closest to their place of residence and families attended the same parish for generations. This is helpful when researching our ancestors, as we can often find records for several generations of a family within a single parish's records. Likewise, a diocese is a group of parishes within a particular ecclesiastical district, and a collection of dioceses in a region is called an archdiocese. Each diocese has a diocesan archives, usually named *archivio diocesano* or *archivio storico diocesano*.

To start searching for parishes in your ancestor's hometown (and what diocese they belong to), visit the Chiesa Cattolica Italiana's (Italian Catholic Church) website **<www. chiesacattolica.it>**, which has a database of all currently active parishes and dioceses in Italy. (Though, of course, parish boundaries may have changed since your ancestor's time.) To view historical parish and diocese boundaries, check out Italia.Indettaglio.it **<italia.indettaglio. it/ita/parrocchie/parrocchie.html>** and the digitized three-volume *Guida degli Archivi diocesani d'Italia* (*Guide to the Diocesan Archives of Italy*) by Vincenzo Monachino, available on the Direzione Generale Archivi (General Directorate Archives) website:

- Volume I **<www.archivi.beniculturali.it/dga/uploads/documents/Quaderni/ Quaderno_61.pdf>**
- Volume II **<www.archivi.beniculturali.it/dga/uploads/documents/Quaderni/ Quaderno_74_II.pdf>**
- Volume III **<www.archivi.beniculturali.it/dga/uploads/documents/Quaderni/ Quaderno_85.pdf>**

The Family History Library also holds on microfilm the *Annuario delle Diocesi d'Italia* (*Annals of the Dioceses of Italy*), published by the Catholic Church in 1951. See chapter 5 for more on using geographic resources to locate your ancestor's hometown.

be very descriptive and provide information on the person as well as their family. They also contain the records of any charitable organizations or orphanages run by the Catholic Church in that diocese. (Some records for larger cities may be found within the archdiocese building, but the archive is still usually called the *archivio diocesano*.) These archives are often well organized, accessible only by appointment, and open only a few days a week for limited hours. Many dioceses have their own websites that contain information and hours of operation, and you will likely need to set up an appointment to research there. Some dioceses are partaking in La Memoria dei Sacramenti **<registriparrocchiali.weebly.com>**, a project that details the holdings of parochial archives and how to access them.

In this chapter, we'll discuss the major kinds of records kept by parishes (and other religious organizations), plus where you can find them and how to use them in your research.

ITALIAN ECCLESIASTICAL RECORD TYPES

There are only a few types of records created by the Catholic Church (often based around the sacraments), and they're held in ecclesiastical registers (image **B**). We will describe each one in the sections that follow, along with any challenges or quirks you might encounter within them. Note that, as with Catholic Church records in other countries, Italian church records are generally kept in Latin (though you may find some priests who record in Italian).

B

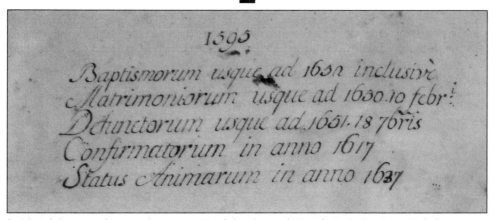

Parish and diocese archives can house a variety of church records in ecclesiastical registers, including baptismal, marriage, death/burial, and *status animarum* (state of the souls) records. This example shows a register where five different types of records were included in one register for a range of years.

RESEARCH TIP

Go to the Street Where They Lived

Some Italian civil records will provide a street address your ancestors resided on. This information may be helpful in narrowing the choices of what parish your ancestors might have attended in order to research in the ecclesiastical records. However, this tactic doesn't always work because some parishes have been closed and/or rebuilt in different locations over the years. Use your ancestor's street address in conjunction with contemporary atlases or city directories to help pinpoint where parish records containing your ancestors were kept.

Battesimo (Baptismal)

Baptismal or *battesimo* (sometimes called *battezato*) records are usually quite basic in terms of the details they provide. You'll find the date of baptism, sometimes the date of birth, the name of the father, the name of the child's godparents, and the priest who baptized the child. About 40 percent of the time, a mother's name is included, often without her maiden name. The baptismal record of Maria Maddalena Novella (image **C**) is in the typical paragraph format for church records. A symbol in the top-left indicates that she was deceased. This symbol did not indicate that she passed away in childhood, as further research revealed that she married and had children; rather, her baptismal record was updated upon her death, as per custom.

Baptizing children was a high priority for Italian families. As discussed in chapter 7, a child was usually baptized within three days of birth, and his parents had to physically present him before the priest in order to be baptized. If the record indicates a longer period of time between birth and baptism, the child may have been sickly at birth, or the family may have lived in a hamlet far from the nearest parish. The father, the midwife, or the godparents usually presented the child for baptism (though the latter two would only serve in

Role of Midwives

Midwives were extremely important to the Italian family. While they were obviously charged with safely birthing children, they also were granted special liturgical privileges, including the ability to baptize children only in certain dire situations. These privileges were closely monitored by the local priests. As a result, local priests were in charge of choosing who could be a midwife, and they often preferred women who had finished raising their own children.

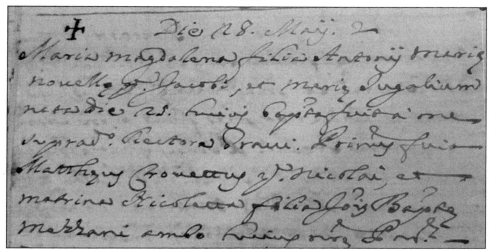

This baptismal record for Maria Maddalena Novella contains an interesting detail: The cross symbol on the top left indicates Maria is deceased. Further research revealed that Maria died after having children, and her baptismal record was updated with the symbol after her death, as per custom.

this role if the father was out of town or otherwise unavailable). Midwives or the woman in charge of the town's foundlings would bring an abandoned child to the parish for baptism. If a child appeared to be in danger of dying during childbirth, the midwife may have already baptized the child. Occasionally, you will find a child who was baptized twice, once in the womb (presumably as insurance in case the child died during birth) and once after birth.

Ecclesiastical birth records, often kept by parishes before the start of civil registration, contain the same information as baptismal records, but also include the actual birth date. Civil registration largely made ecclesiastical birth records redundant, but each diocese had some leeway in what they instructed the priests under their guidance to do when it came to recordkeeping. As a result, some parishes (such as those in the Bergamo province) continued to keep both birth and baptismal records long after civil registration began.

Confirmazione/Cresima (Confirmation)

Called *cresima* or *confirmazione*, this type of record documented a person's confirmation, a coming-of-age rite that usually was performed once a year when the bishop visited the parish. During the ceremony, a child (usually from eight to twelve years old) would reaffirm his or her Catholic faith. Even now, a child's confirmation is celebrated with pageantry, often with a parade of children, family, and priests across town, with those being confirmed dressed in white. The ceremony is often followed with a day of feasting with family and friends.

Confirmation records include the date of confirmation, the name and age of the child, and occasionally his father's name. Because the age of confirmation extended across a five-year time span, you will often see several children within one family receiving the sacrament of confirmation at the same time. When baptismal and birth records have been destroyed, these records can be especially helpful in determining when an ancestor might have been born. These records can often only be found at the diocesan archives.

Matrimonio (Marriage)

Ecclesiastical marriage records are proof of a couple's marriage within the Church and can usually be found within the parish or diocesan archives. These records come in multiple formats, depending on where and when you are researching. For example, you are more apt to see a marriage record that is totally handwritten before the year 1900.

As we discussed in chapter 7, marriage rites required several different kinds of documents. Among the first are marriage banns that announced an upcoming marriage, and these would be read from the pulpit on three consecutive Sundays and also posted on the door of the parish. (This would happen in both parishes if the bride and groom were not members of the same one.) Another kind of records, *dispensazioni* (marriage dispensations), can sometimes be found in the diocesan archives or attached to the parish marriage record. A dispensation allowed a marriage that otherwise would have been forbidden to take place, such as if there were less than four degrees of familial relationship separating the bride and groom, or if marriage banns needed to be waived because the bride was already pregnant and didn't have time to wait. Dispensation requests may include hand-drawn family trees depicting the relationship to the bride and groom—a valuable resource for genealogists. (See chapter 7 for more information on the various reasons that a dispensation may have been necessary.)

If no objections were found (and any necessary dispensations granted), the couple would be married in front of their parents and four witnesses with a large celebration to follow. Parents with limited finances and several children of marriageable age would often marry off two children at once, saving themselves the cost of a second marriage celebration. As a result, always look at the record before and after to see if it might be for a sibling of the ancestor you are researching. Depending on the time period and region, there may or may not have been a subsequent civil marriage required.

> RESEARCH TIP
>
> **Remember—Here Comes the *Bride***
>
> It was customary for a couple to marry in the bride's parish. Therefore, if you don't find an ecclesiastical marriage record in the town an ancestor lived in, look in surrounding towns, as the bride may have come from a different town.

Sepoltura (Death/Burial)

Parish death/burial records are usually very brief, and often indicate any sacraments that were given to an individual immediately preceding his death—in fact, only some parish death records provide both the death date and burial information, and you will sometimes see only the death information or only the burial information. All of these records are *sepoltures* and found within the same parish registers. Older parish death records (mainly pre-1700) often read more like a burial record than a death record, and they may or may not indicate the date of an ancestor's death.

The size of a city will help determine where a person was buried and how it was indicated in records. Death records from small towns, for example, will often not indicate the name of the cemetery where the ancestor was buried, as there was only one cemetery in town. Records from large cities with multiple cemeteries, however, usually listed a cemetery.

A burial record should also note if an individual was buried within the church building—an honor usually reserved for the rich or religious person who lived and worked in the Church—or on the church grounds. However, you will sometimes find that other people of prominence were also buried within the Church. For example, the death and burial record of Cattarina Ferrari, translated below from the parish records of Bogliasco, shows a woman (likely a nun) being buried within the Church of San Giacomo in Parma, Italy. While she is not given the title of "Sister" in this document, the record suggests she may have been a nun because she served for so many years at the hospital.

> On the 28th day of October 1741.
>
> Cattarina Ferrari, daughter of the deceased Francesco, age sixty-six "more or less," who has lent her hand in servitude at the Venerable San Giacomo hospital for the incurably ill in the town of Parma for forty-nine years continuously and in the past at our best city hospital. This was where she received the Eucharist sacrament and had her last confession with the chaplain. Her body was buried on the 29th of the current month in the church associated with the hospital.

A woman's surname is often omitted on parish death records. You may be able to get it from her father's surname (which is sometimes listed) or glean at least her married name from her husband's information. In image **D**, a seventeenth-century death record for Clara [no surname given], taken from Family History Library microfilm, lists her as the wife of Michele Novella. In cases like this one, you'll need to find more sources to determine if this truly is the ancestor you're looking for.

D

TRANSLATION:

13 February [1673]

Clara [no surname given], wife of Michele Novella, passed away at the age of thirty [born about 1643] and was buried in this church after receiving the sacraments from Reverend Paolo Gordesco, Curate.

Unfortunately for researchers, Clara's surname was not listed on her burial record. The record does, however, give her husband's name, her age at death, and the name of the priest who give her the final sacrament.

Status Animarium/Stato Delle Anime (State of the Souls)

Status animarum (also called *stato dello anime* or *stato d'anime*) or "state of the souls" records can be wonderful sources of genealogical information because they recorded whole family groups and their vital statistics, along with what sacraments each family member had received. Since you often find several generations of an Italian family residing in one household, this particular record type can expand the research on your Italian ancestors very quickly.

Catholic priests were required to keep baptismal, marriage, and death/burial records since the Council of Trent in 1563, but just fifty years later Pope Paul V prescribed the keeping of confirmation records and parish family books called *status animarum* in Roman Catholic parishes worldwide. The intent of these family books was to record the vital events and sacraments (baptism, communion, confirmation) of parishioners, but they were also used for taxation in most time periods and localities of Italy. They were continually updated, created, and revised by a potentially revolving door of priests during annual visits (allowing for more transcription errors and inconsistencies).

Despite potential inaccuracies and inconsistencies with other kinds of records, state of the souls records can be tremendously helpful in extending a family's ancestry in those areas of Italy that did not keep civil registration before its peninsula-wide adoption in 1865. They're also useful for tracking mobile ancestors as well as remote/rural localities or places with changing names, and social historians often use them to gage a community's population size throughout time.

What information they recorded varied depending on the time period, the priest's education level or age, and the location in which it was recorded. Having said that, they often include birth, marriage, and death places and dates for each member of a household, plus women's maiden names. Names of godparents were sometimes provided, as were double surnames (e.g., "Martini Ardenghi Alessandra" for Alessandra Martini Ardenghi) and individual or family nicknames (e.g., "Maria Francesca, daughter of the deceased Francesco Petrogalli, also known as Zampeder").

Records can also contain more obscure information. For example, you may find information about occupation and financial status. Depending on the year and diocese, confirmation (*cresima*) records may or may not be listed separately, and married children were noted on the parental families' record with information about transfer to the entry for their marital household. The sheet or page number of the new entry is often referenced. Note that parishioners with cognitive and developmental disabilities were generally not recorded, as they did not receive sacraments and were not eligible for taxation. If they were recorded, the reason for the lack of sacraments is indicated.

The records may be written in Latin, Italian, French, or any one of dozens of dialects, though Italian and Latin were the most common. Some records contained two or more languages/dialects within the same register or even in the same record, and the documents' frequent use of abbreviations can sometimes make translation difficult. Some abbreviations include *C* or *Con* for Confirmation, *C* or *Con* for Confession, *C* or *Com* for (First) Communion, and (for children over ten years old) an *X* for "soon to be confirmed."

Most *status animarum* records are held in the parish archive, but you can sometimes find duplicate copies in the *archivio diocesano* (diocesan archives). Some ecclesiastical

More Records Resources

What other resources would be helpful as you research Italian church records? Understanding the language and therefore the records is the biggest concern for most genealogists, as they begin this type of research. We've provided several language resources in chapter 6, but you may find the following additional resources useful as well:

- The UK National Archives' online tutorial for beginning Latin users **<www.nationalarchives.gov.uk/latin/beginners>**
- *An Introduction to Greek and Latin Paleography* by Sir Edward Maunde Thompson (Clarendon Press, 1912), available digitally at **<archive.org/details/greeklatin00thomuoft>**
- The Latin Library **<www.thelatinlibrary.com>**

records have been digitized or microfilmed by FamilySearch and are found on microfilm or its online database, and they often contain *status animarum* records and are labeled *stato delle anime*. Check the FamilySearch.org catalog **<www.familysearch.org/catalog/search>** for what records are available for your ancestral town. Documents are sometimes simply an entry on a single page, while later *status animarum* records typically contain more information and are on two facing pages.

In the state of the souls record in image **E**, two brothers—one a priest and the other married with children—live together. In this instance, the priest was keeping separate counts of the adults and children right on each family's *status animarum* record. The entries on this particular record likely extended through 1788, when the last child listed on this record was born, despite the fact that the register cover stated the years included to be 1780 to 1785.

Below is a translation of a seventeenth-century, single-page *status animarum* record, found in the town of Bogliasco in the Genova province. If the person was old enough for communion or confirmation, the priest began an individual's entry with what sacraments had been given. This record did not extend over a series of years, but instead was solely for the year 1699:

[Family Number] 11

Confirmation, Communion, Michele Novella, [in household] in 1699.

Confirmation, Communion, Angela Novella [married surname given], "from [the parish of San] Michele," [in household] in 1699.

Communion, Tecla [Novella], "in Genova" [likely meaning physically].

Communion, Barbara [Novella], age [blank], [in household] in 1699.

Communion, Giovanni Antonio [Novella], "99" [likely meaning in household in 1699], age 13 [born about 1686].

Angelo Maria [Novella], "99" [likely meaning in household in 1699], age 11 [born about 1688].

Lorenzo [Novella], "99" [likely meaning in household in 1699], age 8 [born about 1691].

Another type of parish census record (often called a disclosure), the *riveli dei beni e anime*, was created solely within the region of Sicily. However, because its main purpose was taxation, we'll discuss that type of record in more detail in chapter 9.

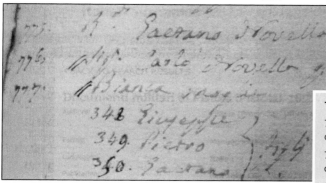

E

TRANSLATION:

773. Reverend Gaetano Novella, son of the deceased Giuseppe [Novella]

776. Mister Carlo Novella, son of the deceased Giuseppe [Novella]

777. Bianca [no surname given], wife

348. Giuseppe [Novella], son

349. Pietro [Novella], son

350. Gaetano [Novella], son

This *status animarum* record for the Novella family shows Reverend Gaetano Novella living with his brother (Carlo) and sister-in-law (Bianca), along with three nephews.

RECORDS OF OTHER RELIGIONS

Italian communities were overwhelmingly Roman Catholic, but you'll occasionally find ancestors who adhered to other religious traditions. Some of these records will be very similar to the ones you'll find for Roman Catholic ancestors—records of the Eastern Orthodox Catholic Church, for example, are identical to those found within the Roman Catholic Church and can be found in the individual parishes or diocesan archives. In addition, their civil registration, military, and notarial records were recorded just like those who attended a Roman Catholic parish. The Venetian archives have a useful English-language guide about Eastern Orthodoxy in Italy <benedett.provincia.venezia.it/comenius/multicult/benedetti/en/enortodossia.html>, and the Orthodox Archdiocese of Italy and Malta has a similar history on its website <win.ortodossia.it/The%20Holy%20Orthodox%20Archdiocese%20of%20Italy%20ed%20Malta.htm>.

Other faith traditions had more divergent recordkeeping systems. We'll discuss two of them (Judaism and Waldensianism) in this section.

Jewish (*Ebrei*)

The arrival of Jewish immigrants in what is now Italy began long before the Roman Catholic parish records. The book *Finding Italian Roots* by John Philip Colletta (Genealogical Publishing Co., 2008) has a great section on researching Italian Jewish ancestors, a must-have if your Italian ancestors were Jewish. He includes multiple reference materials that will help as you pursue your ancestry.

Records of circumcisions, births, deaths, and marriages are the main forms of genealogical resources. Your ancestral homeland may have local Jewish history museums or libraries, and the rabbi there can inform you of what resources exist for that particular town. Ecclesiastical records of Italian Jews are often only available to practicing Jews whose rabbi asks for access on their behalf, but you should research the community your ancestors lived in and write a letter to the local synagogue anyway. You can also find great information about Italian-Jewish genealogy on the JewishGen website **<www.jewishgen. org/infofiles/italy/italian.htm>**.

Waldensian (*Valdese*)

Waldensian churches were found mainly in northern Italy, and their records follow the same standard format seen within the records of other Protestant religions. The majority of Waldensians lived in three communities in the Piemonte region, which was under Italian and French rule during different periods of time and so naturally has records written in both languages. Learn more about the Waldensian community on the Chiesa Eveangelica Valdese (Union of Methodist and Waldensian Churches)'s website **<www. chiesavaldese.org/eng/indexen.php>**.

FamilySearch International has the "Piedmont Project" (a collection of Waldensian family group sheets created from the parish records) on microfilm, and the Archivio di Stato di Torino (State Archives of Turin) has notarial records dating back to the early seventeenth century. The FamilySearch Wiki has a useful guide to Methodist and Waldensian churches in Italy **<www.familysearch.org/learn/wiki/en/Italy,_Waldensian_ Evangelical_Church_Records_(FamilySearch_Historical_Records)>**, and the Waldensian Families Research website **<www.waldensian.info>** has extensive information on parish, notarial, tax, and census records, as well as compiled genealogies.

KEYS TO SUCCESS

- Look for clues about your ancestor's life in records left behind by their religious observances—notably the sacraments of baptism, marriage, and burial. The vast majority of Italians were Roman Catholic, but you may occasionally find adherents to the Eastern Orthodox, Jewish, and Waldensian faiths. Understand what resources are available to help you translate these mostly Latin-language records; see chapter 6 and appendix D.

- Trace your ancestor and his family through the *status animarum* (state of the souls) records, also kept by parishes. This is a great place to find whole family groups.

- Understand the history of your ancestor's parish, as whether or not a parish is still operating and what diocese it is part of today will affect where you can find its historical records.

9

Census and Taxation Records

Researchers who have spent time on US ancestors know that census records created by the government are among the most useful records available to genealogists. The same is not true for all types of Italian census records, which are diverse and can extend as far back as the fourteenth century. It can take some time to understand them within their historical and social contexts. Normally called *catasti, estimi catastali, censimento, riveli,* or *censo*, these records were primarily used for taxation. As a result, these census records can also be considered a type of tax record.

Census and tax records' format vary by location, time period, and who was in power at the time (i.e., what laws governed their creation). What's available for Bologna, for example, differs from what is available for Reggio Calabria, not only in the years they were taken but also in the information included, determined by the laws of the time and place of creation. What title each state archives gives census records in their collection also differs, although the archives have been working toward a more uniform way of labeling the historical collections across the country.

In this chapter, we'll discuss the census records created in each major historical time period, plus where to locate online resources and what you can expect to find in them.

EARLY CENSUSES (PRE-1700s)

The earliest records in this era have little information, sometimes only the name of the head of household (or all working males), with no females mentioned. As the censuses became more frequent, the government needed more-specific tax calculations and so began to include all family members, their ages, and often their relationships to the head of household. The censuses vary dramatically because Italy's regions were under the rule of different governments, monarchies, and duchies at different points in time. We'll discuss the specifics of each type of census (and reasons for their creation) in the following sections.

The Papal States/Central Italy

The first relatively modern census was taken in the fourteenth century within the Papal States, which included the current regions of Emilia-Romagna, Lazio (then called Latium), Marche, and Umbria. In the early seventeenth century (around 1614), these records evolved into the *status animarum* (state of the souls) records, discussed in chapter 8. The first census in the Papal States is stored within the Archivio Segreto Vaticano (Vatican Secret Archives). Once accessible only to researchers who were clergy or scholars, much of the collection of the Vatican Archives is now being digitized and will be available for consultation from the comfort of your home (though, as of this book's publication, census records have not yet made it to the forefront of the archives' digitization efforts) **<asv.vatican.va/content/archiviosegretovaticano/en.html>.**

Venice and Lombardy

The Serenissima Repubblica di Venezia (Republic of Venice) also began taking random *catasti* in the late fourteenth century. Therefore, if your ancestors came from this area of the country (which included parts of modern Albania, Croatia, Cyprus, Greece, Italy, Montenegro, and Slovenia), records prior to 1700 were created under the laws of this Republic. Few of these records have been microfilmed or digitized, but archivists may have created indexes or other guides to the census records that could prove valuable to your research (such as one from the state archives in Venice **<www.archiviodistatovenezia. it/siasve/cgi-bin/pagina.pl?Tipo=inventari&Lettera=5>**, seen in image **A**).

These records usually contain only the name of the property owner or tenant and information about his taxable property. Since other family members were not taxable, the records don't include information about them. Therefore, these records hold limited genealogical value. If you still wish to research these records, search the state archives in Venezia, where you can find these records labeled *catasto austriaco* or *catasto austro-italiano*. The archives also have more modern types of census records under different titles, including *censo provvisorio* and *censo stabile*, though these also have limited genealogical value.

Archivio di Stato di Venezia

La guida al patrimonio documentario

| Home | Patrimonio documentario | Navigazione | Ricerca | Credits |

Fondi

- Contesto politico istituzionale e tipologia
- Elenco in sequenza istituzionale
- Elenco alfabetico
- Repertorio dei fondi e degli strumenti di corredo
- Elenco alfabetico degli strumenti per la ricerca

Soggetti produttori

- Enti
- Persone
- Famiglie

Ricerca

- Fondi

Elenco alfabetico degli strumenti per la ricerca

5 |A |B |C |D |E |F |G |I |J |L |M |N |O |P |Q |R |S |T |U |V |Z |Tutte

« precedente | pag. 2 di 6 (142 risultati) [ ] vai | successiva »

26   Cataloghi degli studenti, Inventario - 166/b

27   Censo provvisorio. Notifiche di Treviso, elenco, 2012 - 539/b

28   Censo provvisorio. Notifiche. Padova, Indice, sec. XX - 425/I-II

29   Censo provvisorio. Notifiche. Venezia, Indice, sec. XX - 424

30   Censo stabile attivato, elenco, sec. XX - 438

31   Censo stabile e censo stabile attivato [Catasti], Indice, 2005 - 22/RIS

The Archivio di Stato di Venezia's website contains information about the census records it holds, including the time period each type of record covers and whether an index to the records has been created.

Florence

In the fourteenth and fifteenth centuries, Florence taxed its residents using the *catasto fiorentino*, mainly because of a financial crisis stemming from past skirmishes with Milano and the projection of more. Because Florence then controlled some semi-independent areas, taxation was met with resistance. The citizens of San Gimignano and Volterra, for example, rebelled against the taxes and had to be put down by Florence's army, and the government issued fines to those who didn't pay.

Historians interested in the region have extensively studied these censuses, and their work can help you learn more about these documents and your ancestors recorded in them. Take a look at the Brown University project on the 1427 *catasto fiorentino* **<www.dellai-aedis.com/INCORSO/fimon-jpj/FIMON.html>**, and you can search the catasto at **<cds.library.brown.edu/projects/catasto/newsearch>**. The French website L'Atelier du Centre de recherches historiques **<acrh.revues.org/7458>** has more information on the census, including what the various codes in the census mean. David Herligy and Christiane Klapisch-Zuber's book *Tuscans and their Families: A Study of the Florentine Catasto of 1427* also lends great insight into migrations, occupations, family structure, gender roles, and the processes around major life events (birth, death, marriage).

REGIONAL CENSUSES (1700s–1860)

Some censuses were taken by region or city-state, and the specifics depend on the taxation laws in place at that time. More and more of these records are becoming available through various initiatives and digitization projects, as well as individual historians' efforts to record the history of these regions.

Catasto Generale Toscano (Tuscany)

The website of the Archivio di Stato di Firenze contains information about the *catasto generale toscano* (general census of Tuscany) and a digitization project it has under way <www.archiviodistato.firenze.it/catastotoscano/index.html>. The project is aimed at researchers who need to perform historical and real property research in this region between 1832 and the 1960s. The collection contains three thousand registers and more than five thousand maps.

After more than thirty years of conservation and collaboration, archivists have made these records available to search on the Castore catasti storici regionali website <www502.regione.toscana.it/castoreapp>. Select your town of interest and the year you're searching from the dropdown menus (in my case, Bagni di Lucca in 1863), then click Esegui to search the databases. Select a search result by clicking the button at left, then click Visualizza to view a map.

Catasto Onciario (Kingdom of Naples)

The *catasto onciario* was taken in the Kingdom of Naples between 1747 and 1755 after a mandate from King Charles III of Spain. At the time, the Kingdom of Naples consisted of the areas of southern Italy remaining after the island of Sicily seceded from the Kingdom of Sicily in the thirteenth century. The Kingdom of Naples was ruled by both Spanish and French dynasties over the centuries, with their systems of governance and taxation designed to enhance the ruling country's coffers. The *catasto onciario* was not popular amongst the common people, who were already struggling to survive under an excessively high tax burden, little food, non-existent medical care, and rampant disease. The *catasto onciario* continued when this area of Italy became the Kingdom of the Two Sicilies, but only for those provinces on the mainland. (Sicily had its own system, called *riveli dei beni e anime*, that we'll discuss later in this chapter.)

The *catasto onciario* was designed to bring uniformity to land registration and taxation. Prior to its formation, Italian municipalities (then called *universities*) could tax in two different ways, although most used only one system for clarity. The *gabelle* system allowed them to charge tax only on property in use, while the *battaglione* system required calculation of all real property (whether in use or not), so that an appropriate tax amount could be calculated. Farmers who let fields go fallow for a season or two would conceivably not have to pay taxes on those fields under the *gabelle* system for the years they were not in use. With nearly 90 percent of the population working in agricultural jobs, this was a significant consideration.

These census records (like the one in image **B**) can be an invaluable source of information on your ancestor, as they were taken prior to civil registration in most areas of Italy and record information on all members of a household, not just the heads of household (*capo di famiglia*). You can commonly find the names of all family members living in the household (which could include several generations of ancestors), relationships to the head of household, occupations, and ages. If the record was for a non-resident landowner or foreign landowner, you may also find their town of residence or origination. If your ancestor was a servant in the home of a wealthy person, you may find her listed within her employer's household.

The *catasto onciario* separated landowners into six different categories:

- Citizens of the kingdom (regardless of whether or not they were residing on the land)
- Widows and unmarried women
- Churches and other ecclesiastical organizations
- Secular clergy
- Foreigners residing on the land
- Non-residing foreigners owning land (often having tenant farmers work their properties)

Property and Taxes in Sicily

What exactly was taxed? Land, buildings, and large animals were often taxed, with taxable animals including mules (*muli*), donkeys (*asini*), horses (*cavalli* or *giumente*), cows (*bovi* or *vacche*), goats (*capre*), and sheep (*precore*). If an animal could pull a cart, it was taxed at a higher rate. Buildings were taxed by the number of rooms the taxpayer owned. It was not unusual to see multiple family members owning and paying taxes on different rooms in the same dwelling. Taxable property in relation to a building included homes as well as things like sheds, farm tools, household furnishings, and water wells, and topography sometimes affected how a plot of land was taxed (e.g., a sloped hillside would be taxed differently than a wooded plot depending on its usability for farming).

TRANSLATION:

Angiolo Masucci Chianchiero, unable, age 55

Agnese Feonla, wife, age 69

Marco, son [of head of household], married, age 32

Brigida Pecce, wife of Marco, age 25

Ciriaco, son of Marco, age 1

[Taxable] industry for Marco, 12 onze.

He owns a house in which he resides with household members...with a courtyard and a small kitchen garden [continues with taxation specifics]...

Animals

Three old mules, aged fruit ...[continues with taxation specifics]

This *catasto onciario* documents Marco Masucci Chianchiero, who lived with this father at the time. Marco was the only taxable household member because his father was no longer working and his son was too young. (Unless widowed or orphaned, women did not work outside the home.)

The *archivio di stato* in Napoli holds the original records, and the other provinces that were part of the Kingdom of Naples maintain second copies of these documents. Many of them have been microfilmed or digitized, with some available on the websites of these *archivi di stato*. An online PDF details the *catasto* for many towns in the Kingdom of Napoli <media.regesta.com/dm_0/ASNA/xdamsProgettareFuturo/allegati%20/IT/ASNA/ CATA/LOGO/0002367/IT.ASNA.CATA.LOGO.0002367.0001.pdf>. You can also search the

The Sistema Informativo degli Archivi di Stato contains an online catalog for what records each *archivio di stato* has.

online catalog for each *archivio di stato* on the Sistema Informativo degli Archivi di Stato's website **<www.archivi-sias.it>** (image **C**).

Sometimes individual researchers or groups may have transcribed or digitized the *catasto onciario* for their region or town of interest. Use search engines like Google **<www.google.com>** to see what is available for your town of interest. Books detailing the *catasto* of a certain town or province have been published by historians, and you can find these on Amazon Italy **<www.amazon.it>**, Ebay **<www.ebay.com>**, or AbeBooks **<www.abebooks.com>**. They can also be found through the websites of a variety of Italian booksellers.

Additionally, FamilySearch.org **<www.familysearch.org>** has thirty different microfilmed or digitized *censimento* collections within its holdings, and more are in the process of being digitized. These records are separated by town and province, and online catalog entries will tell you where the original records are conserved.

Catasto Teresiano (Duchy of Milan)

The *catasto teresiano* was a census of all properties in the Duchy of Milan, taken between 1718 and 1760. The purpose was taxation, to see who owned what land, and who the government could tax. As did the citizens of the Kingdom of Naples, residents of the Duchy of Milan, especially noble families who owned a lot of land, opposed this effort to create a taxable land registry. Officials worked on this *catasto* on and off for more than forty years, and what can be found for one town will not necessarily be found for another. Because many individuals were too poor to own land during this time, these records hold limited value for most genealogical research—unless you are researching a wealthy or noble family from areas formerly in the Duchy of Milan.

Note that, at the time, the Duchy (which existed between the late fourteenth century and the beginning of the eighteenth century) consisted of the city of Milano and twenty-five surrounding towns. In 1714, it became a possession of the Austrian Empire until 1796, when Napoleon Bonaparte arrived and took possession for France. In 1815, it was merged with other territories and became a part of the Kingdom of Lombardo-Veneto.

Catasto Napoleonico Particellare (Northern Italy)

The *catasto napoleonico particellare* was created between 1807 and 1817 in those areas of northern Italy then ruled by Napoleon Bonaparte. Because it includes only part of northern Italy (and because it does not contain a full census of the population, but rather a collection of cadastral land maps showing property boundaries and maybe landowners' names), these records aren't especially useful for genealogists. You'll see some variation in when these records are created; for example, the province of Bergamo has records only from 1808 and 1813. However, the records are historically valuable because they represent the first uniform mapping of certain parts of Italy, and this system of land recordation and mapping served as the basis of the land registration system Italy employs today.

You can usually find the originals of these records in the state archives. Some individual Italian towns conserve their old *catasto napoleonico*. Take a look at the website of the town of Chiavari in the Genova province for an example **<www.comune.chiavari.ge.it/pubblicazione.aspx?Id=208&IdCat=180>**. This town's website shows two examples of the separate sections of *catasto napoleonico particellare*. Take some time to explore this webpage, then dig into what is available for your towns and provinces of interest.

Catasto Gregoriano (Papal States)

The *catasto gregoriano* was created in the Papal States beginning in 1816 and ending in 1835 during the reign of Pope Gregory XVI, after whom it's named. It was modeled after the *catasto napoleonico particellare* and therefore is more of a tax record and set of maps than a census of the population. The government created two copies of this *catasto*, one to be kept for use by the local Chancellor and one to be sent to the central office in Roma. The maps were used in these areas until 1870.

These records can be found in the Vatican Archives. Information useful to genealogists and historians includes the names of property owners, the location and size of the property, and taxes owed.

Search for Adopted Ancestors

A key use of censuses that listed all family members is to track orphaned or abandoned children. Since civil and ecclesiastical records rarely recorded what household such a child might have grown up in (either through adoption or fostering), the census is a valuable way to find out more about who raised these ancestors and perhaps where the child was born. Formal adoptions were rare due to the costly paperwork such a thing involved. Instead, these children were often given to a foster family to raise, a situation which left little paper trail.

Catasto Lombardo Veneto (Lombardy and Venice)

After the regions of Lombardia and Veneto were no longer under Austrian rule, they had to decide what to do about the *catasto napoleonico particellare*, which was never completed in these regions. The process of decision-making and discussion of the errors made in the *catasto napoleonico* took many years (1814–1853). The main difficulty was determining how to value taxable assets. Finally, in 1854 the government began creating the *catasto lombardo veneto*.

This *catasto* was similar to the *catasto napoleonico particellare* in that it was a collection of cadastral land maps that showed the boundaries of property and that its purpose was to administer taxes, not to document the population. Some examples of this *catasto* can be found on the websites of the state archives in Milano **<www.asmilano.it/Divenire/collezione.htm?idColl=10665301>** and Bergamo **<www00.unibg.it/dati/corsi/24132/45202-Geografia%20Regionale_Fonti_3.pdf>**.

While of limited value to genealogists, these records provide historical information for those researching land-owning ancestors in this area and time-period.

POST-UNIFICATION CENSUSES (1871–PRESENT)

Not all areas of current-day Italy became a part of the country of Italy in 1861. Some areas weren't fully absorbed into the country until after one of the World Wars. Studying the history of the time and place your ancestors lived can be an important step in your research journey (see chapter 4). In this way, you can understand these census/tax records within their historical context and shed some light on the lives of your ancestors.

Because of the diversity of censuses taken in different areas of Italy, no one set of guidelines applies to this type of record. As a reminder: Most taxation records mention only those individuals who were eligible for taxation—I've noted any exceptions in this chapter. This was especially true in southern Italy and Sicily, where wealthy individuals

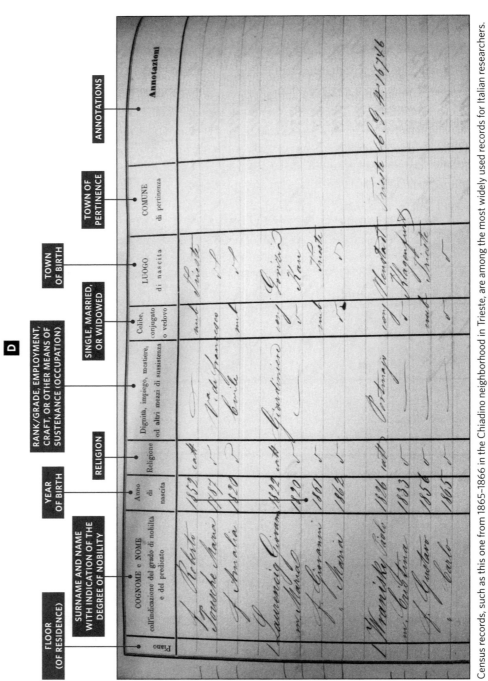

FLOOR (OF RESIDENCE)

SURNAME AND NAME WITH INDICATION OF THE DEGREE OF NOBILITY

YEAR OF BIRTH

RELIGION

RANK/GRADE, EMPLOYMENT, CRAFT, OR OTHER MEANS OF SUSTENANCE (OCCUPATION)

SINGLE, MARRIED, OR WIDOWED

TOWN OF BIRTH

TOWN OF PERTINENCE

ANNOTATIONS

D

Census records, such as this one from 1865–1866 in the Chiadino neighborhood in Trieste, are among the most widely used records for Italian researchers.

owned large pieces of land called *latifundi* (see more about this under in the *riveli dei beni e anime* section). Most of the common people either rented the land for their use or were tenant farmers.

Therefore, if you don't find your ancestors in these records, that doesn't mean they weren't there. They simply may not have had any taxable holdings at that time. Those who rented someone else's land or were sharecroppers may be found within the tax record of the landowner, if they were required by their rental or sharecropping contract to pay a portion of the taxes for the land they used. These individuals usually aren't indexed, making them more difficult to find than the primary landowner(s).

However, one kind of census record does apply to most of Italy: federal censuses. Italy began taking federal censuses in 1871 and has continued them every ten years. The 1871 to 1941 censuses are usually held in the state archives of each province. What information was included was not consistent, as each area of the country faced unique challenges in the post-Unification period—but, unlike the other kinds of records we've talked about, these were used primarily for census-taking and so contain little genealogically useful information. Between 1871 and 1901, not all members of each household were included, and women were only named if they were the head of household. The civil statuses (married, single, widowed) of the heads of households, whether they owned any property, and how many people were in the household may also be found.

It wasn't until 1911 that the federal census became more uniform and included all members of a household. These censuses were taken every ten years and continue today. Between 1911 and 2011, a federal census record contained the following types of information:

- Names of all household members
- Ages
- Places of birth
- Occupation for head of household

Theses censuses are held in the *ufficio dello anagrafe* in each town and are not open for research. These records (and any surviving form of municipal census; image **D**) are what they use to compile the *stato di famiglia storico* (historical state of the family certificate), *certificato di residenza* (residency certificate), or *certificato di cittadinanza* (certificate of citizenship). While these certificates can be very valuable to the researcher, not all towns are willing to spend the time necessary to compile one for you.

RIVELI DI BENI E ANIME (SICILY)

The *riveli di beni e anime* (*riveli* meaning "to reveal" or "disclose"; *beni e anime* meaning "taxable possessions and souls/inhabitants") were census-type records created for taxation, and (unlike some other taxation records from modern Italy) can be valuable sources of genealogical information. These records contain every Sicilian living within a locality, as well as their taxable property and animals.

In addition to knowing how to tax each individual, the landowner would have a better idea of how many males were able to be conscripted (for military service or infrastructure improvements) and what resources could be taxed and/or used for the good of all those within the *feudo* (feudal estate). Many people owned small plots of land but had limited powers or ways they could use the land and its resources. The local lord had to grant permission to do many things. Not only the wealthy owned land and property in Sicilia, and not all *contadini* (farmers, peasant class) that you see paying taxes on land were tenant farmers. However, tenant farming was a common way of life for many people.

These records are found exclusively in the region of Sicilia prior to 1817, often back to the sixteenth century. Other areas of present-day Italy had comparable records, often called *catasti onciari* (singular, *catasto onciario*). The *riveli* are separated by the three valleys of Sicilia, then arranged alphabetically by community:

- Val di Mazara: The western half of Sicily, with the border starting between Termini Imerese and Cefalù (north) and Licata (south)

- Val di Demona: The northeastern part of Sicily starting at Enna and extending south to Catania

- Val di Noto: The southeastern part of Sicily starting at Enna and extending south to Licata

Many of these communities now go by different names than they did in the old feudal system, either because of changes in land ownership or language used from the time when the records were created. For example, you will find Agrigento's records under *Girgenti*, the Sicilian name for this city.

Originally created by the Tribunale del Real Patrimonio and later by the Deputazione del Regno, the *riveli* for all communities are being conserved in the Archivio di Stato di Palermo. Second copies of these records can sometimes be found in the other *archivi di stato* in Sicily. Years of availability vary depending on community/location of feudal land and when records were created for each area, with some of the earliest dating to 1548.

The *riveli* for Luca Setti Pani (image **E**) provides a good example of the type of information that can be found within these records. This record is a listing of "souls" and real property. The head of household is seventy years old and appears to have a wife, two sons, a grandson, and a young granddaughter. His wife's age was not given, and she is listed with her husband's surname (as was custom; unlike normal Italian practive, nearly all 1793 *riveli* in this town listed the wife under the husband's surname). Luca doesn't have a

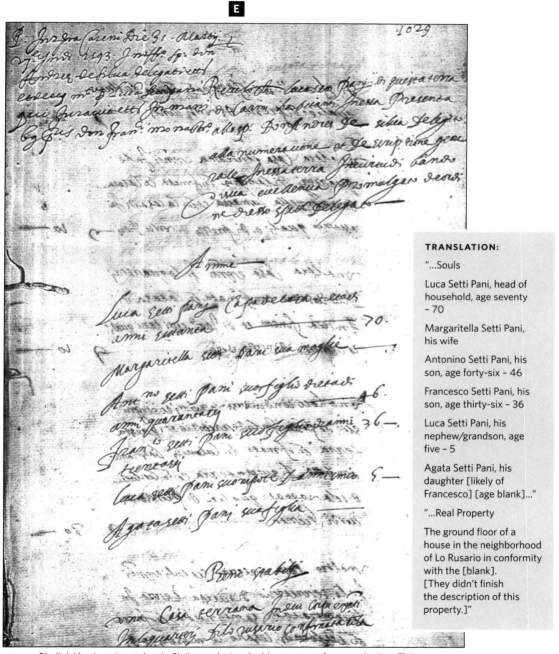

TRANSLATION:

"…Souls

Luca Setti Pani, head of household, age seventy – 70

Margaritella Setti Pani, his wife

Antonino Setti Pani, his son, age forty-six – 46

Francesco Setti Pani, his son, age thirty-six – 36

Luca Setti Pani, his nephew/grandson, age five – 5

Agata Setti Pani, his daughter [likely of Francesco] [age blank]…"

"…Real Property

The ground floor of a house in the neighborhood of Lo Rusario in conformity with the [blank]. [They didn't finish the description of this property.]"

Riveli dei beni e anime, taken in Sicily, can be invaluable resources for genealogists. This one provides a snapshot of Luca Setti Pani and his household.

daughter-in-law in his household, suggesting she died after giving birth to her daughter (Luca's granddaughter). The description of real property is incomplete, and no numbers were included to indicate taxes due. This is likely because of the taxpayer's age, as he may have been exempted.

As a result, *riveli* are extremely valuable when performing a variety of genealogy tasks, such as attempting to find replacements for destroyed ecclesiastical record or tracking rural properties using notarial records (see chapter 10). You can also use *riveli* when studying whole families or communities, as well as to find abandoned or orphaned children.

However, like any record set, *riveli* can present problems for researchers. Many of them were handwritten, meaning the script can sometimes be hard to read (either due to bad handwriting or to the record's condition). Records could also be in a combination of languages (Latin, Italian, Sicilian), making them hard to translate even if you do manage to interpret the letters. As mentioned earlier, town names may have changed, making them more difficult to translate. Sometimes only the heads of household were listed, and the information taken on any individuals (usually men) can be inaccurate—especially ages, which census-takers often rounded to the nearest ten years. Additional mistakes may have been made when indexes were created.

FamilySearch has more than four hundred microfilmed *riveli* collections within its holdings. Several collections are labeled *Riveli di beni e anime di Sicilia (comuni vari)*, but they don't include records from unknown towns/localities. However, the collections are usually organized by town; read the Notes section of each collection's record for more on its coverage. Because of FamilySearch's efforts, this particular census/tax record is the one that it is easiest to access.

KEYS TO SUCCESS

Study the history of your ancestor's region to know what censuses were taken during his lifetime. As with other recordtaking procedures, censustaking practices varied throughout time and across the Italian peninsula.

Track families across census years, as this will open your eyes to changes in family structure (e.g., new marriages or the births/deaths of siblings, parents, and other relatives) or location.

Use census records as a springboard for finding other resources, as census records are one of only a few records available prior to the start of parish records in 1583. Notations in census registers can lead you to parish or notarial records, as well as provide information about your ancestor's financial status.

10

Notarial Records

A s in other parts of the world, Italy's notarial system kept records of a wide variety of important legal documents, and these documents can provide valuable information for genealogists. While sometimes difficult to find and interpret, these legal records (called notarial records because of how they were recorded) are a must-see for researchers. This chapter will show you how.

WHAT ARE NOTARIAL RECORDS?

In Italy, all legal transactions by private parties are handled through notarial documents prepared by a *notaio*, or civil law notary. A civil law notary (also known as a "Latin notary") is usually a professional with specific training in notarial law who can prepare, record, and certify legal documents that are requested by private parties. Since they're only allowed to prepare non-contentious legal documents, notaries practice civil and family law. Like lawyers, they give legal advice and hold law degrees, though (depending on time and place) they don't need to be attorneys and their examination (while rigorous) is not the equivalent of the bar exam. Laws regarding this have changed in current-day Italy, where one cannot practice law and notarial law at the same time; you can't be an *avvocato* (lawyer) and a *notaio* (notary) simultaneously.

Between the sixteenth and eighteenth centuries, becoming a notary required at least two years of a university education, which meant that only the wealthy had the means to prepare for such an office. However, when notaries first appeared in the Roman Republic, they were public secretaries who took a type of shorthand (called *notae tironinae*) and would set their stands in public markets to draw up contracts and other types of documents. Over time (and by the Middle Ages), being a notary developed into a lucrative and respected profession. Notaries were treated with great respect, and the office was often hereditary (i.e., you often find many generations of a family holding notarial office).

In general, a civil law notary could prepare any form of legal document to which the nation-state (i.e., the republic, duchy, or Italian government) had no legal stake in. These can include, but are not limited to:

- wills
- marital documents (dowries, marital contracts, and marital permissions)
- legalizations
- adoptions
- indentures
- property deeds (both real property and personal property)
- inventories
- mortgages
- loans
- building contracts
- personal declarations (including declarations of death and documents certifying a person's birth when no birth record was recorded)
- partnership papers
- acknowledgements of receipt
- power of attorney documents

Notarial records often pre-date ecclesiastical records, beginning in the century prior to the Council of Trent in 1583. Italians from all social statuses can be found within notarial records, as even the poorest individuals might need a marriage contract or have a small plot of land they want to deed to their daughter.

Prior to Italian Unification, what we now know as modern-day Italy was ruled by multiple city-states, each of which had different laws that influenced the format and even language of the civil law notaries working within its jurisdictions. In addition, notarial documents are often rife with abbreviations and in a form of notarial Latin, not the standard Latin that one might find in ecclesiastical records of the same time period. Trafford R. Cole, Pys.D., writes in *Italian Genealogical Records: How to Use Civil, Ecclesiastical, & Other Records in Family History Research* (Ancestry.com, 2013):

> There was no established format for these [notary] records; each notary created the record according to his style and the desire of the parties involved...
> Until about 1865, the official language used by notaries was Latin; and they used abbreviations and codes to make documents as obscure as possible so that only notaries could read them.

However, Latin was not the only language the records can be found in. Depending on where and when they were created, they may be written in Italian, French, or even German. The document in images **A** and **B** provides an example of a notarial document (a consent to a mortgage so that an annual mass could be said for the departed) that was written in French. This document displays the wide variety and complexity of the documents one might find within the notarial records.

Despite the great variance in these kinds of records, notarial registers are usually separated into three basic formats.

Minuto

This is the short form or rough draft of the document, of which only one copy was made. This document was for the individual notary's use as he prepared the full document, and was not sent in duplicate to the notarial district archives. *Minuti* (plural) that are over

---

Notarial Translation Help

The following books, which you can find online at websites such as Amazon Italy **<www.amazon.it>** can help you translate Latin in notarial documents:

- Berhard Bischoff, *Paleografia Latina Antichita e Mediovo* (Padova, Italy: Editrice Antenore, Italian edition, 1986) originally printed in German, Italian translation of second edition
- Giulio Battelli, *Lezioni di Paleografia* (Città del Vaticano: Libreria Editrice Vaticana, 2007, seconda ristampa della quarta edizione)
- Luca Sarzi Amadè, *L'Antenato Nel Cassetto: Manuale di Scienza Genealogica* (Sesto San Giovanni, Milano, Italy: Mimesis Edizioni, 2015)

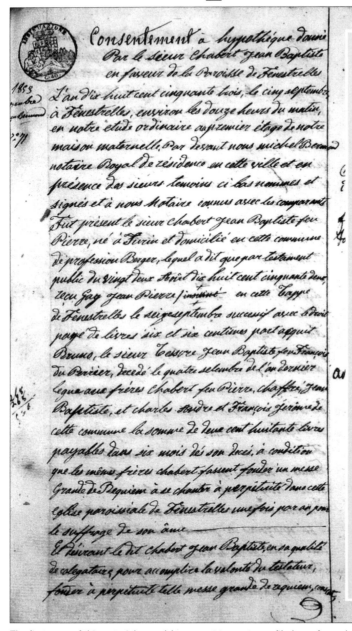

TRANSLATION:

No 79

...Consent to a mortgage given by Monsieur Chabert Jean Baptise Consentement in favor of the parish of Fenestrelles.

In 1853, the 5th of September at Fenestrelles, about twelve o'clock in the morning, in our usual study on the first floor of our maternal home, in front of us Michel Bermond royal notary, residing in this town and in the presence of the sirs, witnesses, below named and signed with us and our notary known to those appearing. Present was Monsieur Jean Baptiste Chabert, of the late Pierre, born in Turin and living in this town, profession of shepherd, stated by public will of 22 August 1852, received [by] Jean Pierre / insessinéin this Cappe of Fenestrelles the following 16th of September, with the right of payment of six livres and six centimes part acquit Bruno, Monsieur Cessore Jean Baptiste of the late François from Perrier, died the 4th of September of last year bequeathed with brothers Chabert of the late Pierre, Jean Baptiste Chaffeé, and Charles Andre and François Jerôme of this town the sum of 280 livres payable in six months from his death, on the condition that the same brothers shall hold a Grand Requiem Mass to be sung in perpetuity in the Fenestrelles Parish church once a year for the suffrage of his soul.

And desiring the said Jean Baptiste Chabert, in his role as co-legator to accomplish the will of the testator, to found in perpetuity for such grand requiem mass, consecrated [hard to read]

The first page of this notarial record (a consent to mortgage filed so a funeral mass could be held, written in French and translated by Corey Oiesen) gives a death date for Jean Baptiste Chabert (4 September 1853).

TRANSLATION:

is obliged and summons oneself for the payment and the insurance of such a perpetual foundation to this guaranteed by this mortgage specially in favor of the Parish of this town and for it [marked out letter] in favor of the Priest, guaranteed by the same, here presently represented by Monsieur the Priest Jean Baptiste Giugas of the late Jean Baptiste born at Granges de Pragelas, and living in this town, and at present and accepting by means of _____ the superior, ecclesiastic authorization, so much that its portion of the body of the building not yet individually divided by the brothers named below, situated in the center of this town Rue de porte France, holding at the levant Jean Jerôme Bompard['s land], north of Felix Ducka and couchant at the road , declaring that such a mortgage is sufficient for guaranteeing its obligation

_____

As this act requires, our notary hereby received and we have read, pronounced, and published and all its contents in plain language, in clear and intelligible voice to the appearing persons in the presence of sirs Joseph Chabert of the late Barthélemy, born at Pignérol and Jean Louis Ravial, son of Jean François, born in this town, living here, the required and competent witnesses who signed with the parties or were appearants and our notary....

The second page of Jean Baptiste Chabert's notarial record further specifies the conditions of this "mortgage" agreement, which arranged for Chabert's surviving family to have a mass celebrated in his memory each year in exchange for a donation to the parish.

one hundred years old can often be found amongst the notarial records in most provincial archives.

Below is a translated abstract of the most important details found in a *minuto* document from Renno, Corsica, France (included here because it concerns an Italian family, was written in Italian, and was created on an island that was once under Italian rule):

> Record number 69, 21 September 1777...Reverend Francesco Antonio De Luca
> and his brother, Domenico Michel [sic, Michele] De Luca hereby loan 1,800 lire
> of Genoese currency to Giuseppe Antonio Mattei, son of Giovanni Battista [Mat-
> tei], and his wife, Donna Barbara Maria De Luca, sister of the lendees...

In this record, the De Luca brothers (one of whom was a priest) were lending money to their sister and her husband, showing how even a *minuto* can reveal familial relationships and provide insight into the ancestors' lives and financial matters. The De Luca brothers are also mentioned in the marriage record of Giuseppe Antonio Mattei and Donna Barbara Maria De Luca. However, their relationship to the bride was not stated in that record. When combining the information from the marriage record with the information from this *minuto*, we can learn about the sibling relationship of the three De Luca's. In this particular case, only the *minuto* record survives, and the full notarial act could not be found.

Atto Notarili or *Atto di Notai*

Atto notarili or *atto di notai* are the full versions of notarial documents, kept in whatever form was applicable for the type of document it was. Two copies of this document were required to be prepared, one to be kept by the individual notary and another to be conserved and reviewed at the notarial district office. All original copies are then sent to the notarial district office after one hundred years, with many then being sent on to the *archivio di stato* (provincial archive) for historical preservation.

Bastardelli

The *bastardelli* (referring to illegitimate acts) are an index of documents maintained by each notary, usually arranged chronologically for personal reference. Each individual notary retained the *bastardelli* even after the rest of the records were sent for conservation. They may be labeled *Inventario* or *Indice dei Atti Notarili* in modern archives. These indexes were especially helpful to the notary when he needed to research the past transactions concerning a piece of real property, in order to create a new notarial document with all of the details of property transfer over the years. Many families used the name notary or notarial family for many generations. Image **C** provides an example of

This *bastardelli*, a notary's personal index, can provide you with an at-a-glance summary of what notarial records were performed by a notary—including those that might have involved your ancestors.

a notarial register index (a *bastardelli*) that was written in a combination of Italian and Latin. The records referenced were also written in both languages.

USING NOTARIAL RECORDS IN RESEARCH

Notarial records can provide unique information about your ancestors that can really breathe life into your research. I once found an amazingly helpful property transfer that detailed three generations of a family, complete with death dates and places for the initial couple on the deed. Since access to parish records was not permitted in this area of Italy, the pre-civil registration information included was especially valuable.

Below is a portion of a four-page mortgage transfer that revealed a lot of genealogical information about the family being researched:

> Number 16131, 12 August 1868 in Palo del Colle. By enforceable copy of a judgment issued by a Judge in the District Court on 7 March 1868...And at the request of Francesco, Vitantonio, Rocco, Angelo, Arcangelo, and Giuseppe

Nuzzi, brothers, as well as the spouse of Teresa Nuzzi, Francesantonio Elia, and the spouse of Porzia Nuzzi, Giuseppe Saccente, it is declared that these brothers and sisters are heirs to their father, Francesco Nuzzi, the named Elia and Saccente by authorization of their respective marriages, all landowners and residents in the above-named town of Palo del Colle, except for the first who resides in Grumo Appula...

This document revealed several siblings of Francesco Nuzzi that we did not know about previously, as well as who each of his sisters married. It also provided a link between the Nuzzi family of the town of Palo del Colle, and the Nuzzi family from the town of Grumo Appula (both in the Bari province) by noting the residence of one of the siblings in Grumo Appula. The document also reveals that all siblings were landowners, which can be a good indication of social status and should point you to other notarial records for this family that concern real property or financial transactions. Landowning Italian ancestors often did not own just one property. They often held at least partial titles to several different properties.

Here are some other notarial records worth researching:

- **Property deeds or transfers** often list all of the changes that occurred on a particular property over many years. They may concern personal property or other possessions like ownership or use of trees or water wells, or how such resources can be accessed.

- **Wills** can name living and deceased family members, vital statistics, place of residence, an account of assets upon death, and detail financial transactions (mortgages, rental contracts) that need to be resolved. These documents often show the marital surname of a female ancestor (even though Italian women went by their maiden name), details of transfer and ownership of any real property under the deceased's name, and provide details of dowries previously bestowed upon female children.

- **Dowries** and **marital contracts** can name family members, vital statistics, place of residence, details of property (real or personal) being bestowed, and the conditions surrounding the acquisition of the property, meaning how it would be paid or transferred. Dowries were given to daughters and bridal gifts to sons (usually in the form of money for male ancestors).

- **Adoptions** often list the names of the adoptive parents, the child being adopted, details regarding the birth of the child and abandonment (if appropriate). If the child was orphaned, you could find details of its birth parent's death and the subsequent housing and support of the child until adoption.

- **Recognitions** can provide the name of birth parents for abandoned children, plus details about their dates and places of birth, abandonment, and recognition or legitimization. When birth parents reclaimed an abandoned child and legitimized him upon their marriage, this was often done informally, without a notarial act and with the inclusion of a note within the couple's marriage documents. Recognitions, on the other hand, were formal legal documents created by a notary and enabled the child to inherit from its parents, not just use their surname.

- **Marriage permissions** can provide names and vital statistics for family members. They may also help you track an ancestor around the world. I've seen several instances of Italian immigrants sending marriage permissions back to Italy through their local Italian consulate, in order for a daughter to marry. I've seen several marital permissions that indicate a parent was in military service or too ill to travel to the town hall to give permission.

The details notarial documents can provide are endless. Individuals could have notarial documents created for nearly any event they felt needed to be addressed legally. Therefore, these records have the ability to provide the intricate details of your ancestors' lives—details found in no other Italian genealogical resource.

ACCESSING NOTARIAL RECORDS

Most notarial record collections are located in the collections of the *archivi di stato* (provincial/state archives), normally arranged by the town the notary operated in, the name of the notary, the time period, and the type of notarial register. Often they will also have a schedule of the years, towns, and notaries whose records are within their collection. A few provincial archives (such as the archives in Genova) have the notarial records in an unorganized bunch, though even they are working on reorganizing and indexing their notarial collection. This will help those researching in this province in the future. Until that is complete, notarial research in this province will be especially challenging.

The Family History Library (FHL) has a book on microfilm and in its international book collection that is a guide to notarial archives and might be helpful: *Gli Archivi notarili: ordinamento e funzioni guida practica per I concorsi negli archivi notarili*. The FHL also has a limited amount of these records on microfilm or digitized but their collection is increasing. A search for notarili in the FamilySearch online catalog <**www.familysearch.org**> brings up more than forty results or collections of notarial records.

For example, notarial records for the town of Luserna San Giovanni in the Torino province for the years 1610 to 1854 are available by microfilm from the Family History Library (image **D**). This record set's catalog entry notes some of the different types of

Atti notarili di Luserna San Giovanni (Torino), 1610-1854

Authors:	Luserna San Giovanni (Torino). Archivio notarile (Main Author)
Format:	Manuscript/Manuscript on Film
Language:	Italian
Publication:	Salt Lake City, Utah : Filmati dalla Genealogical Society of Utah, 1994
Physical:	in 317 bobine di microfilm ; 35 mm.

Notes

Microfilm dei registri originali nell'Archivio di Stato, Torino.

Wills, powers of attorney, inventories, marriage contracts, deeds, transactions, transfers and sales, etc.

Testamenti, inventari, contratti matrimoniali, atti di donazione, procure, transazioni, cessioni e vendite, ecc.

I registri non sono sempre in ordine cronologico.

Per gli anni 1709-1854, gli atti notarili per i frazioni e comuni d'intorno Luserna San Giovanni sono registrati insieme.

FamilySearch.org contains several collections of notarial records, such as this collection of *atti notarili* from Luserna San Giovanni in Torino.

records that are included; that the records are arranged chronologically and indexed; and that some records from a hamlet under the jurisdiction of this town are also included. These can be valuable details when researching for ancestors from this town.

The majority of Italy's pre-1900 notarial records can be researched onsite in the provincial/state archives or notarial archives. The location of notarial records varies by province and time period. In some provinces, one must visit the *conservatoria del registri immobiliari* (property registry office) first in order to find the original notarial document in the office's database, note its reference specifics, and order a copy from the provincial archives. Moving back and forth between archives can be time consuming, but most provinces make the process easier by allowing you to access surviving pre-1900 notarial records directly at the provincial archives.

If you are looking for notarial records after 1900, you need to start at the *conservatoria dei registri immobilari* or the notarial district in which you are researching. However, asking the provincial archives whether it has notarial records for the town and years you are seeking is always a good first step. Most provincial archives provide e-mail addresses on their websites for such inquiries. Allow plenty of time for a response, as archives can receive hundreds of inquiries from around the world each week.

If you know a notarial document exists and you have its location, date, and the notary's name, then you could request a search for it via Conservatoria.it **<www.conservatoria.it/ richieste/c47-archivio-notarile>** or other online providers. This is especially useful for notarial documents you find mentioned in the margins of birth records. You might also find reference to a notarial document in a couple's marriage supplements if one of them did not have a birth or baptismal record. In that instance, they had to file an *atto di notorietà* with a notary to be included within their marriage papers. This document provides the testimony of seven witnesses who personally knew the circumstances of the individual's birth.

REAL PROPERTY RECORDS

Deeds to Italian real property (land and buildings) are transferred or amended by notarial act, and these notarial records are worth discussing in detail. These are some of the most accessible notarial records, as the Italian government in 1977 began a project to extract the major details of all real property transactions that had occurred since 1910 (though this year varies somewhat by province). This information was placed in a database and was updated each time a change was made to real property. The property database is split into two sections: Catasto dei Terreni (land) and Catasto dei Fabbricati (buildings).

Until recently, a researcher could only access this database onsite in Italy's Conservatoria del Registri Immobiliari offices or through an Italian lawyer specializing in property and inheritance matters. However, changes to the laws have laid the groundwork for multiple service providers offering these services over the Internet. While other providers can be found by using Internet search engines, a few of the most commonly used providers are:

- Tuttovisure.it **<www.tuttovisure.it>**
- Catasto.it **<www.catasto.it>**
- Catastoinrete.it **<www.catastoinrete.it>**
- Televisure.it **<www.televisure.it>**

A national directory for Italy's Conservatoria's can be found on the website Conservatoria.it **<www.conservatoria.it/elenco-nazionale.html>** (image **E**), with each entry linked to a Google map to make these offices easier to find. Large cities may have more than one of these offices. Be aware that most of these offices work by appointment only.

Could your ancestors have left property in Italy? Maybe or maybe not. Even the poorest ancestors might have owned a small track of land or portion of a building. Many Italians intended their immigration to be temporary but later decided to settle permanently in the United States. As new generations were born, the details of property ownership

Conservatoria.it hosts a national directory of the Conservatoria's offices, allowing you to more quickly locate property records.

were often not conveyed to the descendants, and many of these properties can still be found in the names of the original owners.

For example, a home in Isnello, Italy, is still in the name of my great-aunt. She had no children to inherit the property, and no one likely knew about the land when she passed away in 1955. The property is not mentioned in the accounting of her possessions (found in her US probate file), nor did she mention it in her last will and testament.

Image **F** is a cadastral map that shows the location of this property in the town of Isnello; the nearby building with the cross on it is the church. The property consists of 5.5 rooms on Via Carmelo Virga, on the fourth floor (meaning the third floor in American terms). The property is parcel 526 on cadastral map 4, and is a home (not a vineyard, farm, or other sort of property). In addition to naming the property owner, the document says she was the daughter of the deceased Matteo Catanese, had married a man with the surname Gentile, and owned 100-percent interest in the property—all valuable genealogical information. The original notarial document(s) concerning this property may have additional information about my great aunt and the history of the property, including

This cadastral map shows the property owned by Carmela Catanese, marked here as lot number 526.

information on prior owners and transfers. Only the most important information about the property was extracted and included in the electronic database, so be aware that modern title reports record only part of the story.

You can perform or order several different types of searches depending on how much information you already have and what information you are looking for. No matter how you search, you should have the legal name of the immigrant, his birth date and birthplace, and his father's given name. These three items will help you narrow the choices of records that might pertain to your ancestor. Without these key pieces of information, you'll struggle to determine whether a particular property pertains to your ancestor, without going onsite in the Conservatoria and researching for the original notarial document at its base.

I have listed below several types of searches that might be useful. The titles for these searches vary slightly between providers, but the list will give you a good idea of what type of information can be found through each search. Of course, these searches cost money, though (when considering the time you would spend going to the Conservatoria yourself and searching in person) the price is worth it.

- ***Visura catastale su nominative***: You can specifically search by town or province, or search the whole country using name and birth date.

- **Visura catastale su immobile/visura storica per immobile**: Search using property description and the town, parcel, and map numbers. This usually shows any major changes made to property ownership in the last thirty years. Image  shows an example of this search.

- **Visura catatale con atti conservatoria**: Search for the actual notarial act concerning a property you have already defined is in the database. You will need the information from the above searches.

- **Mappa catastale**: Cadastral maps depict the outlines of a property and the land and buildings surrounding it.

- **Planimetria Catastale**: This drawing shows the divisions of a building's internal parts. These are specially useful when your ancestor owned one floor or one room of a home, a common occurrence in Italy. Image **H** shows the divisions of the building my great-aunt's property is a part of.

- **Elaborato Planimetrico**: These plans show a drawing of the building with entrances and common areas.

G

Search the Conservatoria to discover changes to property ownership over the last thirty years. This can help you track down property owned by your ancestors.

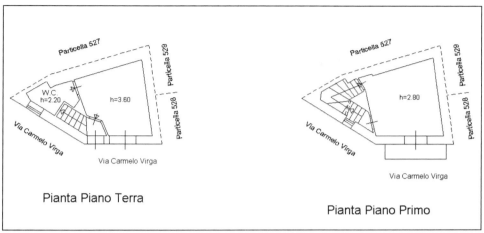

Planimetria catastale (cadastral plans) can show incredible architectural detail, such as this one that shows the first and third floors of a home.

If you find property in your ancestor's name and you want to find out more or if you are eligible to inherit the property, contact an Italian attorney that specializes in property and inheritance matters. The laws behind reclaiming such a property are tricky, and you'll need legal assistance in order to move forward.

KEYS TO SUCCESS

🌿 Seek out the notarial records your ancestors may have left behind, such as wills, marriage documentation, and deeds.

🌿 Learn what types of clues could be contained within notarial records and how to enhance your family history with these details.

🌿 Mine other genealogical records for clues leading to notarial records.

🌿 Explore the resources available to search in real property records in Italy. Find out whether Italian property is still in your ancestor's name!

Military Records

L ike young men and women today, our Italian male ancestors served their countries in the armed forces, and the records left behind by your ancestor's service can be useful to modern research. You can often find military records dating back to the late eighteenth century, though (as with other kinds of records) coverage and availability will vary by region. For example, the Italian draft officially began about 1860, while other areas of modern Italy required periods of conscription earlier depending on who governed your ancestor's area and what wars or conflicts the region was involved in.

Unlike other kinds of records (which are typically arranged by town or parish), military records were arranged by military district, and each province had several military districts. These military districts have been centralized into fewer military archives whose names usually begin with the words *"Centrale Documentale di"* followed by the name of the location. Use Google to find information on the documentation center for the area in which you are researching. You can find a list of other Italian military terms on the Portale Antenati website **<www.antenati.san.beniculturali.it/glossario>** (in Italian and English), which also discusses some forms of military documents **<www.antenati.san. beniculturali.it/Le-fonti-degli-Archivi-di-Stato>**.

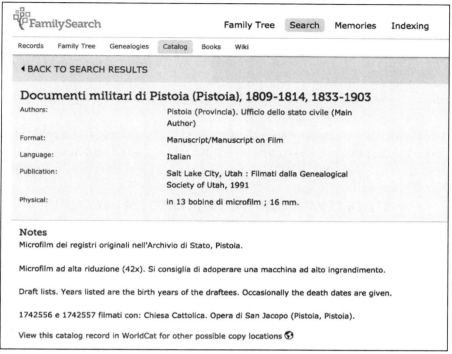

FamilySearch

Family Tree · Search · Memories · Indexing

Records · Family Tree · Genealogies · Catalog · Books · Wiki

◀ BACK TO SEARCH RESULTS

Documenti militari di Pistoia (Pistoia), 1809-1814, 1833-1903

Authors:	Pistoia (Provincia). Ufficio dello stato civile (Main Author)
Format:	Manuscript/Manuscript on Film
Language:	Italian
Publication:	Salt Lake City, Utah : Filmati dalla Genealogical Society of Utah, 1991
Physical:	in 13 bobine di microfilm ; 16 mm.

Notes

Microfilm dei registri originali nell'Archivio di Stato, Pistoia.

Microfilm ad alta riduzione (42x). Si consiglia di adoperare una macchina ad alto ingrandimento.

Draft lists. Years listed are the birth years of the draftees. Occasionally the death dates are given.

1742556 e 1742557 filmati con: Chiesa Cattolica. Opera di San Jacopo (Pistoia, Pistoia).

View this catalog record in WorldCat for other possible copy locations ⊕

Many Italian military records (held by *archivi di stato*, or state archives) have been microfilmed and/ or digitized by the FamilySearch organization. Look for the Family History Library's holdings online at FamilySearch.org.

Italian military records are increasingly being made available online. The Family History Library **<www.familysearch.org/locations/saltlakecity-library>** has many of the military records from the *archivi di stato* on microfilm or available digitally (image **A**). Italian military records are listed under various names within the FamilySearch online catalog. The Archivio Centrale dello Stato in Roma **<acs.beniculturali.it>** has military service records for those who served in both world wars. It also has information on Italian soldiers who were prisoners of war. If your ancestor passed away during his war-time military service, you may find information on him on the website of the Italian Ministry of Defense **<www.difesa.it/Ministro/Commissariato_Generale_per_le_Onoranze_ai_Caduti_ in_Guerra/Pagine/Ricerca_sepolture.aspx>**.

Most older military records are held at the *archivi di stato* (state archives), though archivists are often only willing to research the draft lists (and not other forms of military records) unless you give them a good reason why you need to consult other military records. However, be careful to fully evaluate any records that others research for you. I once had a client who thought he had been sent his grandfather's *lista di leva* (draft list) from the provincial/state archives in Bergamo. However, after evaluating the record, I saw that is was really his *ruoli matricolari* (muster list). Sometimes the archives have students who are studying conservation in their attached school perform the research asked for through postal inquiries, and they may not always have a full grasp of the different types of military records.

In this chapter, we'll examine the different kinds of military records that could include information about your ancestor's service, plus where to find and how to use these resources.

LISTE DI LEVA (DRAFT/CONSCRIPTION RECORDS)

In general, Italian conscription was mandatory from 1860 to 1923, though conscription laws varied based on location and time period. (See The History of Italian Conscription sidebar for more.) During these times, the *ufficio di leva* (draft office) in each town was required to send a list of males between the ages of seventeen and twenty to the *consiglio di leva* (draft board) at the *mandamento* (military district office, a part of the *tribunale di militare*) each year. Called *liste di leva* (image **B**), these records can be found for all male ancestors born after 1855 (and earlier in some areas of the north). Italian military draft or extraction lists are especially useful when you know only the province or general area of your ancestor's birth, as these records can then be used as a resource to narrow down an ancestor's town of birth.

These records (such as the one in image **C**) can provide a large amount of information, including details about an ancestor's appearance that you won't find in any other resource:

- Draftee's name
- Date and place of birth
- Place of residence

RESEARCH TIP

Watch for Draft Dodgers

When a male was born in Italy but emigrated with his parents as a child, he was sometimes put on draft lists. This had consequences, most especially in times of war. The military offices would work with the Italian consulate closest to where the family settled to track down the draftee and provide him with his notice to appear.

B

MANDAMENTO   CIRCONDARIO

di *Donnas*   di *Aosta*

Comune di *Pont Saint-Martin*

LEVA SUI GIOVANI NATI NELL'ANNO 1885

LISTA DI LEVA

Chiusa dal Sindaco il *l'ultimo* del mese di *Gennaio 1905* — Verificata dalla Giunta
municipale il *primo* del mese di *Marzo 1905* — Spedita al Prefetto o Sottoprefetto
del Circondario di *Aosta* il *primo* del mese di *Marzo 1905*

Ordine di Estrazione	COMUNI	Iscritti	Capilista	TOTALE	ESTRAZIONE	Innanza definitiva	Doletà soppletiva	Chiusura della Leva	Chiamata alle armi

Draft lists (*liste di leva*) are among the most useful military records.

C

NUMERI	COGNOME E NOME DEGLI ISCRITTI E INDICAZIONI PER I PROVENIENTI DA LEVE ANTERIORI	NASCITA E RESIDENZA E VARIAZIONI ALLA LISTA DI LEVA	CONTRASSEGNI PERSONALI PROFESSIONE - ISTRUZIONE	DECISIONI DEL CONSIGLIO DI Annotazioni circa le decisioni di rivedibili
1	2	3	4	
N. d'ordine **91** (all' invio della lista all' ufficio di leva)	*Romano Salvatore* Classi di provenienza	Figlio di *Giuseppe* e della *Cosopola Giuseppina* nato addì *8 novembre 1917* nel Comune di *Pompliano* Provincia di *Napoli* dimorante in *Pompliano Via Firenze 50*	Statura m. 1, Torace m. 0, Capelli { colore / forma Viso Naso Mento Occhi Sopracciglia Fronte Colorito Bocca	Addì *17.5.* *1937* *abile arruolato*
N. d'ordine **86** (dopo la verificazione definitiva)	Motivo del primo rimando Motivo del secondo rimando N. del ruolo matricolare comunale	Motivo dell'aggiunzione e della cancellazione	Dentatura Segni particolari Arte o professione Sa leggere? Sa scrivere? Titoli di studio	L' Uff. deleg. Addì 19

Liste di leva can provide you with your military ancestor's name, date and place of birth, place of residence, and more.

- Parents' names (included through 1955)

- Occupation

- Whether or not he was literate

- Physical description: hair, eye, and skin coloration; height and weight in metric measurements; any scars or identifying marks.

- Notations of eligibility or if he never appeared for conscription (for example, because of emigration)

The *ufficio di leva* in each municipality continually update draft records, and this can provide valuable insight into these years of your ancestor's life. For example, if an ancestor had been listed as available for the draft but passed away before appearing for his physical, the office informed the *consiglio di leva* of this change in draft status and noted it on the deceased's record. It was also the office's responsibility to state any initial issues that would make a man ineligible for service, such as a mental or physical handicap. Normally, these potential draftees were excluded completely before the list was sent to the military district office, though you may see potential draftees not making it through the examination process for things that should have likely excluded them from the beginning.

Seventy years after each draft year, the set of the *liste di leva* and *liste di estrazione* (see the next section) at the military district office was sent to the provincial/state archive (*archivio di stato*) of the province in which it was created for preservation, and this is where you can access these records today. The various *archivi di stato* hold different degrees of draft lists, as authorities did not always transfer records to the state archives as they were supposed to. Each *archivio di stato*'s website will list what records it contains and where you can find them, usually under the Patrimonio heading. For example, the website of the provincial/state archives in Palermo shows that military records reside at the Gancia branch **<www. archiviodistatodipalermo.it/pagina.php?id=44>**. Consulting the online catalog provides the information you need for consultation or to ask the archivists to look for you. You can also use the database of the main Italian archive, the Sistema Informativo degli Archivi di Stato, to search for what types of records each *archivio di stato* has in its collection **<www.archivi-sias.it>**.

Conscription/draft lists are one of the most used resources at the *archivi di stato*, so archives began microfilming and digitization projects that included these records to make their jobs easier when asked to research for records by mail. The Portale Antenati website provides a list of links to the various military digitization projects at the provincial/state archives **<www.antenati.san.beniculturali.it/link>**, and the Archivio di Stato in Venezia provides a good example of a digitization project that has evolved into a searchable database of the draft lists **<www.archiviodistatovenezia.it/leva/navigation. php?group=12&L=it&subgroup=13>**. In addition, the Family History Library has preserved

The History of Italian Conscription

In some ways, Italy's conscription laws have mirrored its history: decentralized, and shaped by certain key events.

The earliest draft lists were modeled after the French draft, as many areas of Italy were once under French rule. At this time, soldiers were subject to be called to serve for a time period of twelve years in more of a militia-type army. If they did serve, they had to serve in four-month increments, after which they had twelve months off before they were called to serve again. By 1831, this form of the draft had ended. A more established military began about 1848–1849, with reforms in 1854 calling for soldiers to serve eight-year stints. However, regardless of when an ancestor served, his length of service depended on several factors, in particular whether he served in the army, the navy, or smaller militia-type regiments. The Italian military came under federal jurisdiction during the Unification process, at which time military service was reduced to four years and then three years by 1875.

After this time period, the process became more uniform. Each year, the Ministero della Guerra (Ministry of War) would determine how many servicemen would be called from each locality, usually based on the historical number of potential soldiers placed on the draft lists in each military district. The lottery (or draw) of draft numbers was done publicly in each municipality and in front of the city officials. A potential draftee could attend or be represented by a parent (usually his father). The order of the lottery draw was then sent to the local military district and the Ministry of War.

You will usually see a male ancestor's draft process start at the age of eighteen, though some localities began the draft at seventeen. Therefore, if your ancestor was born in 1858, he would have been conscripted in 1876 and required to appear for a physical and determination of eligibility in 1878. If he didn't show up for these appointments, he could be considered a deserter and lawfully prosecuted.

many Italian state archives on microfilm and has even digitized some of them on the free FamilySearch.org <www.familysearch.org>.

The *liste di leva* kept by the *comune* often included extracted birth or baptismal records, providing even more information. Individual *comuni* will sometimes have information on the local draft on their websites, such as the town of Ravenna <www.comune.ra.it/Aree-Tematiche/Anagrafe-e-immigrazione/Elettorale-e-Leva/Ufficio-Leva/Liste-di-leva>.

One particular quirk to be aware of when researching these records is that sometimes an ancestor did not appear for his physical and determination of eligibility when he was supposed to. He may appear three to four years later, likely when the authorities caught up with him. Therefore, if you are unable to find an ancestor in these records, research in the years following his estimated year of conscription.

LISTE DI ESTRAZIONE (EXTRACTION LISTS)

At the age of twenty, each Italian male was required to have a physical examination, and a final determination of his eligibility for service was made at that time. At this time, the information from his *lista di leva* was placed on another list, called the *lista de estrazione* (extraction list; images **D** and **E**). Extraction lists (*liste di estrazione*) were created through 1911, at which time the military laws were changed and it was no longer necessary to create this type of military record.

These lists were prepared numerically. If a draftee was determined to be eligible for service, he would then be placed in either the first, second, or third category, with those in the first category having the highest likelihood of serving.

D

The first page of this *lista di estrazione* (extraction list) reveals the draftee's name (Andrea Gaetano Barletta, nicknamed "Perasso"), parents (Rosa Barletta and an unknown father), birth date and place (February 1, 1859, in Genova), civil and military district (Genova), and occupation (mason). See image E for the second page of the record.

E

The second page of this person's extraction list (continued from image D) reveals his height (2.62 meters) and a decision about his ability to serve (able to serve), the date of the decision (September 22, 1879), and what category he was assigned to (second).

Extraction lists were often notated to include other information, useful to genealogists. Here, the recordkeeper noted the draftee had a *debole constituzione* (weak constitution).

Some of the most common notations regarding eligibility are listed below. However, you will see many other notations (image **F**), depending on the particular circumstances of the draftee.

- ***Abile arruolato***: Able to serve/be enrolled
- ***Renitente***: Most commonly used to state that a draftee was temporarily unfit, though it could also denote a deserter, conscientious objector, or emigrant
- ***Rivedibile***: Failed, usually meaning he failed his physical testing
- ***Riformato***: Exempted, usually contains a military law number relating to the exemption or a notation describing the reason for exemption.

RUOLI MATRICOLARI (MATRICULATION ROLLS/MUSTER ROLLS)

Ruoli matricolari (muster rolls) are other useful records for documenting your ancestor's military service and learning more about him. Like the *liste di leva*, these provide a physical description of the ancestor, his date and place of birth, and parents' names. The records also include a summary of the ancestor's military service, noting each major action taken. For example, it might list regiments served in, dates transferred, injuries sustained, desertions or disciplinary actions, medals received, and date of discharge. These records are usually organized by an assigned matriculation number and contain the original conscription number assigned to him at the time the *lista di leva* record was created.

These rolls may also contain a *congedo illimitato* (unlimited certificate of discharge; image **G**) if an individual who had completed his military service. Two copies of this document were made, one kept in his *ruoli matricolari* and the other given to the soldier for his personal reference. The soldier's copy of this document is often found within the personal files of an Italian-American family, as Italian men tended to bring this document with them so they could prove their military service and not be called into service again. These records were also supposed to be sent to the provincial/state archives after seventy years for conservation. However, whether this actually occurred varies widely by province.

FOGLI MATRICOLARI/FASCICOLO MATRICOLARE
(SERVICE RECORDS/PERSONNEL FILES)

These documents, which can be found using an ancestor's matriculation number, are detailed records of a soldier's service and contain more information than the *ruoli matricolari*, as they include regimental or brigade numbers, military campaigns served in, wounds or medals received, and if he served or is noted to be a deserter. You may also find extracted copies of the ancestor's birth record or death record within this file, plus requests for permission to marry and the subsequent marriage document. (If an ancestor wanted to marry but was serving in the military, he was required to get permission from his superiors to proceed with the marriage. You will also sometimes find a notification of this permission being granted on a civil marriage document.)

If a soldier passed away during his military service, details leading up to the event can often be found, as well as his death date and an extracted death record. I once saw a record for a soldier who had lost a leg during a well-known battle in World War I, including the date of his injury, the name of the battle, information about his transfers between three hospitals, and finally the date and place of his death. The document also included a

This intricately drawn *congedo illimitato* (unlimited certificate of discharge) can provide information about your ancestor's service—and the conditions surrounding his departure from the armed forces.

Saving Private Giuseppe: Family-Based Military Exemptions

If a draft-age male was the only son and his father was deceased, he was usually exempted from military service, as he was considered to be the family's sole support or breadwinner. In 1896, my great-grandfather was placed in the third category for this reason, and he never had to serve. If two or three of a draftee's brothers were already serving, he might also be exempted so as to not place an unnecessary burden on any one family. A draftee may also be designated for future service depending on his circumstances. For example, some draftees who had a temporary physical ailment were deferred for a period of twelve months, at which time their eligibility for service was reevaluated. In these cases, the draftee was usually noted to be *renitente*, or temporarily unfit for service. In times of war, it was harder to get an exemption from military service.

copy of the *annotazioni di morte* (annotation of death) form that would have been sent to the *Tribunale* and *comune* where the soldier was from so the office could annotate both copies of his birth record with a date and place of death.

KEYS TO SUCCESS

Search carefully for your ancestors' military records. Many are kept at the state-archives level and are being digitized, but some archives will only let you access draft lists if you appear in person to do research.

Understand how various military records relate to one another. Extraction lists, for example, contain excerpts from draft lists, and personnel files are more detailed than matriculation rolls.

Learn what conscription laws governed your ancestor's region during his lifetime. This will clue you in to what records you should be looking for. This knowledge may also reveal key details about your ancestor's life. For example, if a couple had no children during a twelve-year time period, you might guess the father may have been serving in the military, depending on the time and place.

Remember that some military records (such as matriculation rolls) were kept in duplicate, meaning copies of these documents may still exist even if a particular archive's copy was lost or destroyed.

12

Other Records

W e've already discussed the major types of records that are available to Italian genealogists: civil registrations, church vital records, censuses, and more. But what about the plethora of other resources containing information about your Italian ancestors? This chapter will discuss other documents, such as newspapers, directories, and university records, that can harbor details about your ancestors from the Italian peninsula. While these records may not be your first port of call, you should seek them out as your research progresses—especially if you're working on a detailed family history project and want as many sources as possible.

ITALIAN NEWSPAPER ARCHIVES

Italian newspapers can help you understand the history and cultural mores that governed your Italian ancestors. They can be used to add "meat" (that is, historical and social context) to your family history story, as firsthand accounts of historical events can bring you great understanding about what your ancestors' lives were like and why they made the choices they did. For example, entrenched feudal society—as well as the changes brought about by Italian Unification—created an impossible situation for southern Italians and Sicilians in the later half of the nineteenth century, and these historical events (which

you can glean from newspapers) caused poverty and famine that led people to emigrate. Families had to find a way to feed their children, and the possibilities offered by emigration were tempting. Some countries, such as Argentina, were even offering free land to settlers, an attractive option for Italian emigrants in particular.

Italian newspapers contain several differences from their American counterparts. First, they don't normally include obituaries (except for very prominent individuals), nor do they contain the "hometown happenings" sections that are commonly seen in twentieth-century US newspapers. In addition, you won't find the same volume of newspaper collections in Italy as you would in the United States, as newspapers were mainly published in the larger cities. And since the majority of the Italian population was not literate until after 1900 (when laws mandated schooling through the third grade), newspapers were less common and had lower readership. Because of the overall illiteracy, only wealthier ancestors (those who had the opportunity for more than a third-grade education) were able to read what few newspapers there were.

Digitized Italian Newspaper Collections

Despite their relative scarcity, more and more Italian newspapers are being digitized and made available to the general public. No longer do you have to be on site in Italian archives to access these resources. Some Italian newspaper archives charge a small fee for access, a growing trend as more newspapers complete their digitization projects.

Some of the major newspapers have digitized their own collections. For example, *La Stampa* has digitized newspapers between 1867 and 2005 <www.lastampa.it/archivio-storico/index.jpp>, while *La Repubblica* has an online archive that extends back to 1984 as of the writing of this book <ricerca.repubblica.it>. *Corriere della Sera* has digitized its newspaper as far back as 1874 <archivio.corriere.it/Archivio/interface/landing.html>, and *La Gazzetta del Mezzogiorno* also has an extensive digital archives <archivio.lagazzettadelmezzogiorno.it/gazzettadelmezzogiorno/archive/archive.jsp?testata=bari>. Biblioteca Comunale Dell'Archiginnasio (a municipal library in Bologna) has digitized the seventeenth-century newspaper, *Le Gazzette bolognesi* <badigit.comune.bologna.it/Gazzette/gazzettedefault.asp>, and you can find more than 960 collections of digitized newspaper links at L'Eeroteca Digitale <emeroteca.braidense.it>. Euro Docs also has a list of links to many digital Italian collections, including both newspapers and other resources <eudocs.lib.byu.edu/index.php/Italy:_Historical_Collections>.

Many Italian libraries have also begun to digitize their newspaper collections, not all of which have been placed online. For an example, see the website of the *biblioteca civico* in Trieste, Italy <www.bibliotecacivicahortis.it/periodici-digitali>. Likewise, Google Books <books.google.com> and the Italian Ministry of Cultural Heritage and Activities and

Tourism reached an agreement several years ago that allows Google Books to digitize thousands of books currently in Italian libraries. All of these books could be used as historical resources to understand the history surrounding your ancestors.

Italian-American Newspapers

Unlike Italian newspapers, Italian-American newspapers contain an amazing amount of information useful to your research. You may find obituaries for Italian immigrants, notices telling recent arrivals where to meet their families, what ships are due to arrive at what ports, and a wide variety of other types of articles and notices. These newspapers can be found in the collections of local historical societies, state archives, and local libraries, as well as in specific Italian-American collections held by various organizations such as GenealogyBank <www.genealogybank.com>. The Newspaper Archive <newspaperarchive.com/it> is also beginning to digitize Italian and Italian-American newspapers.

University archives, such as the one at the University of Minnesota <www.lib.umn.edu/ihrca/periodicals/italian-newspapers>, may also contain newspaper collections that are available via interlibrary loan. (The University of Minnesota also has a variety of resources for Italian researchers, including documents about the Order Sons of Italy in America <www.lib.umn.edu/ihrca/periodicals/italian-serials>.

Local historical societies in areas of the country with significant Italian-American populations will have Italian-American newspapers you can research, either by microfilm

A

HIS PASSPORT NO GOOD.

Italy Holds That "Once an Italian Always an Italian."

When on my first visit to Italy after an absence of twenty-five years, furnished though I was with a passport from Washington with the great red seal of state and with my naturalization papers, I was amazed when I was arrested and put in a den of a prison reeking with filth and vermin because I had paid no attention to the Italian laws regarding the matter of military obligation. I was under the impression, as I am sure many Americans are, that when once I had sworn off my allegiance to the king of Italy and had become an American citizen I would be recognized as such and not be required to fulfill the obligations of an Italian citizen.

The experience was not amusing, and yet as I look back upon it there was a ridiculous side to it. When with great dignity and pride I pulled from my pocket my passport I expected to see the little Italian official gasp for breath and humbly beg my pardon. Imagine my feelings when, glancing at the American eagle on my papers and the signature of the secretary of state, I at the same time exclaiming, "Sono citadino Americano" ("I am an American citizen"), he turned his back upon me and said most indifferently, "Fa niente; fa niente" ("That's nothing; that's nothing"). I was led away by two carabinieri and turned into a large room, where I found seven prisoners who were to be my companions for that day and night. The next day I was taken before the prefect of the province, and then it was learned that I was not obliged to serve the regular three years in the Italian army, not because I was an American citizen—that was not recognized—but because I was the only male in my family. The Italian theory is "once an Italian always an Italian." The government does not recognize the change of allegiance on the part of any of its subjects.—Antonio Mangano in "Charities and the Commons."

Even though the publication didn't focus on Italian immigration, the *Irish American Weekly* contained this insightful article about what Italian-Americans faced returning to Italy.

or digitally. Archives across the country have significant Italian-American collections, including newspapers. For example, the Detre Library & Archives, located at the Heinz History Center in Pittsburgh, has an amazing Italian American collection archive. Another example is the Western Reserve Historical Society in Cleveland. Take the time to explore what's available for where your Italian ancestors settled.

Accessing newspapers through a database, like GenealogyBank or Newspaper Archive, has its advantages. I even found one article (image **A**) in the *Irish American Weekly*, not where you'd expect to find information on Italian-Americans. However, this article discusses a little-known fact: When our ancestors returned to the old country to visit family, they ran the risk of being conscripted if they had not served their mandatory time in the Italian military. This happened even when our ancestors immigrated as children and when they had become naturalized American citizens.

ITALIAN DIRECTORIES

Do you want to find contact information for living relatives? Or determine what parishes still survive in your ancestral town so you can search for records? Italian church and telephone directories can help for these (and for a variety of other research objectives).

Church Directories

Church directories, generally created for ecclesiastical use, have many genealogical applications and can be used to determine:

- What parishes survive in a particular town or diocese and their contact information
- Contact information for diocesan archives
- Historical information about particular parishes or dioceses (including dates of operation, information about merged parishes, name changes, destruction of parishes due to natural disasters, etc.)

You can find some directories, such as this annual publication about organizations affiliated with the Catholic Church on FamilySearch.org, in various online databases.

Since parishes in Italy often contain valuable, historically significant artwork, you will also find other types of websites detailing what can be found in individual parishes or diocesan museums. For example, the website of the Italian archeological group, Gruppo Archeologico Torinese, provides a short history and discussion of the archeological significance of the parish of San Giacomo Maggiore in Gavi, Alessandria province, Italy **<archeocarta.org/gavi-al-chiesa-parrocchiale-di-san-giacomo>**.

Online church directories can be found at Motore di Ricerca Parrocchie **<www.parrocchie.it>**, as well as the website of the Catholic Church in Italy **<www.chiesacattolica.it>**. The collection of the Family History Library in Salt Lake City contains the *Annuario delle Diocesi d'Italia, 1951* (image **B**), a book including information about organizations affiliated with the church, such as orphanages, convents, monasteries, and hospitals.

You can also purchase copies of various church directories through Amazon Italy **<www.amazon.it>**, including some specific to a certain diocese, town, or region. Some church directories can also be accessed through Google Books. Be especially on the look-out for directories from your ancestor's home region.

PagineBianche is one of the most widely used telephone directories, and you can search it online.

Telephone Directories

While relatively recent records, telephone directories can provide you with contact information for organizations and individuals useful to your research. Directories can be used to determine surname distribution in a particular town or province, locate contact information for living relatives, or find information on active parishes. Some of the most widely used online Italian telephone directories are:

- *PagineBianche* <www.paginebianche.it> (image **C**)
- *PagineGialle* <www.paginegialle.it>
- *Pronto* <www.pronto.it>

You can access physical or microfilmed telephone directories at the Family History Library in Salt Lake City, and many of these have been made available online at FamilySearch.org <www.familysearch.org> by searching *Italy, Province – Directories* in the online catalog. The Family History Library also has a CD in its collection entitled *Indirizzi e numeri di telefono di tutta Italia* (addresses and telephone numbers for all Italy).

UNIVERSITY RECORDS

Italian universities began in the twelfth through thirteenth centuries, as small groups of wealthy male ancestors were sent to private tutors for study. At that time, the teachers

were not employed by a university entity (by modern definitions) but often operated out of their homes, which served as dormitories for non-local students. By the middle of the thirteenth century, universities as we know them today had begun in the northern areas of the country (specifically Bologna and Padua), and the first medical university was founded in Salerno. The university a man attended depended not only on location, but also by the language he spoke and what he wanted to study.

Despite the fact that many Italians couldn't afford university, the university records for those who did attend can provide valuable information. University records often contain enrollment information, the name of a student's father, names of siblings also in attendance, town of origination, records of payment, report cards, biographical information, disciplinary actions taken, and other information specific to the student's education. Higher education was required for your ancestors who became doctors, notaries, or lawyers, so you should be on the lookout for these records if your ancestor worked in one of those fields.

You can find records from universities that have closed at the *archivi di stato* (provincial/state archives). How extensive the collections are can vary by province, how carefully the records were conserved, and when the university was in operation. Note that most university records can be researched by appointment only. Universities that are still in operation usually have not transferred their records to the *archivi di stato*, but instead maintain their own archives. For example, the Università di Bologna's historical archive can be found at **<www.archiviostorico.unibo.it/it/?LN=IT#>** (image **D**). You can

The Skinny on *Scuola*

As we discuss in this chapter, university records apply only to the wealthiest of ancestors. Prior to the twentieth century, you needed a significant amount of money to attend a university, which made a university education out of the average person's reach.

Rather, many Italian ancestors only attended school (*scuola*) through the third grade before being asked to work to support the family. Other ancestors, particularly women, never had the option to attend school and were taught what they needed to know in the home. It wasn't until after 1900 that Italian law mandated school attendance.

Initially, enforcement of the law was sporadic, especially in the southern regions of the country and Sicilia, which viewed edicts from Rome with a fair amount of suspicion. Additionally, a child couldn't attend school unless he had shoes, putting poor families at a disadvantage because they couldn't afford to buy shoes for all of their children. Their financial realities were such that children had to begin work at an early age and to contribute to the support of their families. This happened less often in the more industrialized northern areas of the country, but there were still people in the peasant class in those regions.

University archives, like this one from the Università di Bologna, may have websites that describe their holdings. E-mails to these archives are often answered quickly, especially if you are simply verifying resources or making an appointment.

view a document detailing its collection (which extends back to the fourteenth century) at <www.archiviostorico.unibo.it/storico/PDF/inventario.pdf>.

MUNICIPAL AND POLICE RECORDS

You can find many other types of records while researching your Italian ancestors, and it's important to consider looking beyond some of the standard genealogy resources. Italian archives hold troves of hidden genealogical treasure, as do the private collections of Italian-American families. As we discussed in chapter 2, our ancestors brought documents with them for a variety of reasons: to prove they'd already served their mandatory military service, to apply for a passport using a birth record or penal certificate, to document their work experience, and more.

Because the territory now known as Italy once consisted of multiple city-states that had different laws, you might encounter many different types of records. Some of these records are specific to certain provinces or regions of Italy, while others deal with certain time periods and historical events. Others concern citizenship, military service and/or political affiliation (e.g., the Fascist era), population movement, occupational guilds or identification, infrastructure, and a host of other topics.

Below are a few examples of the various documents you might find when researching your ancestors. If you have something unusual within your family papers, do some online research to determine exactly what the document is and why it was created. This may require digging deep into the history of the time and place your ancestor lived, but this research can reveal hidden facets to your ancestor and why he felt the need to keep that particular document. In the process, you will not only learn more about your ancestors, but also the historical and social policies that affected their lives in Italy.

In the municipal archives (*archivi municipale*) of Italian towns and cities, you can often find various types of municipal administration records. Where these records are stored and their accessibility depends on the town. The records may have been combined with other historical records in the town library (*biblioteca comunale*). For example, the website of the Archivio Storico di Trieste (Historical Archive of Trieste) **<archiviogenerale.comune.trieste.it>** contains a summary of the archive's holdings, plus contact information and details about the center's hours of operation. This city also has a *biblioteca civico* (civic/city library), which contains a large collection of antique books **<www.bibliotecacivicahortis.it>**.

Municipal administration records can even be found within the papers your Italian ancestors brought with them from Italy, providing a unique glimpse into the lives of the ancestors you are researching and information that is hard to find in any other genealogical source.

Occupational/Guild

Municipalities would sometimes issue documents confirming an ancestor's occupation or work history. Image **E** shows part of a document issued by the town of Borgo Franco in the Torino province concerning Lazzarino Pitti's occupation. It contains occupational information, a physical description of Lazzarino, his father's given name, an estimated year of birth, and his town of residence in 1905. It also contains a handwritten recommendation that he could show to future employers, the civil laws allowing for the creation

RESEARCH TIP

Ask the Living
If you have family members living in Italy, don't hesitate to ask them about mystery documents. They can often provide great insight into why these records were created.

Some government-issued documents can clue you in to your ancestor's occupation and physical description. This booklet gives a lot of details about Lazzarino Pitti's physical appearance: grey eyes, curly hair, large mouth, no beard, etc.

of the record, and multiple blank pages (presumably for additional recommendations). What a wealth of information this document has!

Political Affiliation

You may find documents that show your ancestor was part of a political party. The booklet (seen in image **F**) shows this ancestor's participation in the National Fascist Party under Benito Mussolini in 1931. It provides his picture, his name, the given name of his father, the address where he lived, his town of residence, and where he was registered to serve military. Even if a document doesn't coincide with your political or religious beliefs (or even if it offends you, as this political affiliation might), it could have great value genealogically.

Decreti (Decrees)

City governments may also issue *decreti* (decrees) for various purposes. When researching in the city of Trieste, I found a notation on a population register page that stated there was some form of *decretto* for the individual, Giuseppe Fedele Covi.

This document, found in family papers, confirms Luigi Mattioli's membership in the National Fascist Party. It also gives his address (14 Via Galliera, Bologna) and father's name (also Luigi Mattioli).

I found the record (image **G**) in a collection of several hundred decrees that (unfortunately) lacked an index. The file was time-consuming to research, as the decree's number was faded on many of the documents, and the documents (which appeared to have come apart at some point) were not in order numerically. However, the extra work was well worth it, since the document contained information about this ancestor that is hard to find in other resources: his town of birth (new information to me), his father's name, when he moved to the town of Trieste, his marital status, how many children he had, and details about his character and current and former jobs.

Travel Papers and Border Passes

When immigrants returned from abroad and had no passport, they were often required by their Italian town of citizenship to have travel papers or border passes prepared at the town hall or *questura* (police headquarters) in order to travel between territories/provinces/regions. Travel papers were often fully hand-written (unless issued at the *questura*), spanned between two and four pages, were loose papers, and provided an

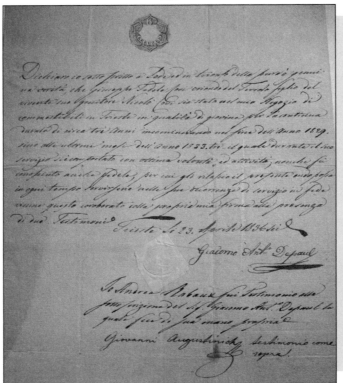

TRANSLATION:

I hereby declare, to the praise and triumph of the genuine truth, that Giuseppe Fedele Covi, a native of Tirolo and son of the living Nicoló Covi, was employed in my shop in his youth, from the end of 1829 until the last months of 1833. During his service to me, he behaved with great willingness and activity and was well known for his honesty. I hereby place my signature and seal in the presence of two witnesses.

Trieste, 23 April 1836

Signature of Giacomo Antonio Depaul

I, Andrea Rabaux, hereby witness the signature of Mister Giacomo Antonio Depaul, which was made by his own hand [written in the hand of Andrea Rabaux, likely in lieu of a signature].

Signature of Giacomo Augustinish, also a witness to the above [signature of Giacomo Antonio Depaul]

Government decrees issued for various reasons can reveal information about your ancestors. This one, which took me a long time to find, was the first to list my ancestor's town name.

ancestor's name, birth date, birthplace, parent's names, where he was traveling to, and who was traveling with him (especially for minor children). They may provide occupational information and contain a finite period of time that the travel papers or border passes were good for. These documents may only be found an Italian-American family's personal papers because, unless the documents were issued at the *questura*, Italian archives usually did not retain a copy of these records. They were considered temporary and did not have perceived historical value, an unfortunate reality that comes with Italian research.

The travel papers in image **H** concern Antonino Schiavo, when he returned to visit his family in 1906, with his four-year-old daughter, Maria. It provides the following information, useful for genealogical research:

- Names of Antonino and his daughter, Maria
- Birth date and places of birth for both (expressed as an approximate age for Maria)
- Parents' names, indicated to still be living on 31 December 1906
- A physical description of Antonino
- Return date and name of ship they returned to America on, written on the back in red pencil (perhaps by the office where they booked their return passage)

In some areas of Italy, you can find what is called a *tessera di frontiera* (border pass), which enabled an ancestor to travel across a border or between kingdoms. The *tessera di frontiera* pass in image 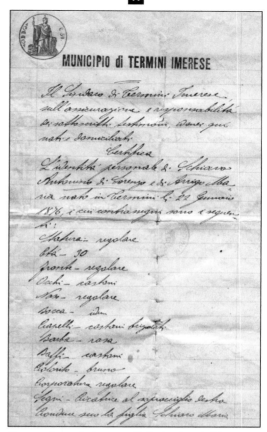 allowed passage between Italy and Serbia/Croatia/Slovenia. If an ancestor had a mobile occupation, being able to move across borders/kingdoms more easily would be a valuable asset. These papers were usually good for only one year or a designated travel period, after which time they had to reapply for further approval.

Border passes were usually issued at the *questura*, which may conserve some paperwork. While the records at the *questura* are not usually open for research, you may find the original passes within your family papers. The documents often contain valuable genealogical information, including:

- name of the ancestor
- father's given name
- physical description
- place of birth
- town of residence and address

Documents created upon an Italian's return to his hometown (such as this one for Antonino Schiavo) can provide a snapshot of his life at the time of his return: his name and birth date/place, the names of his relatives, a physical description, and more.

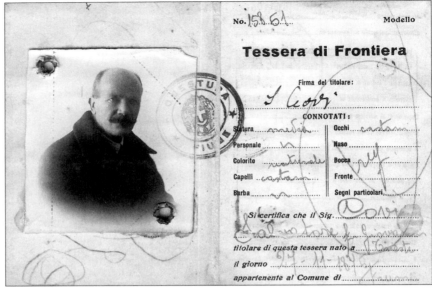

Border passes allowed individuals to cross the Italian border, and they can provide rich detail about your traveling ancestors.

- town of citizenship
- photograph of the ancestor
- occupational information

These are just a few examples of the various types of documents you might encounter when researching your ancestors. If you want to do quality genealogical research you should leave "no stone unturned," meaning no document unevaluated for genealogical clues.

KEYS TO SUCCESS

Be on the lookout for less-used records that can contain valuable details about your ancestors, particularly those created while he was still in the old country: newspapers, church or telephone directories, university records, and more.

Use modern resources, like currently published telephone directories, to give your research in Italy a leg up. These can help you get in contact with archives, genealogical or historical societies, and even distant family members.

Evaluate what municipal, police, occupational, or political records might exist for your ancestor and where to find them.

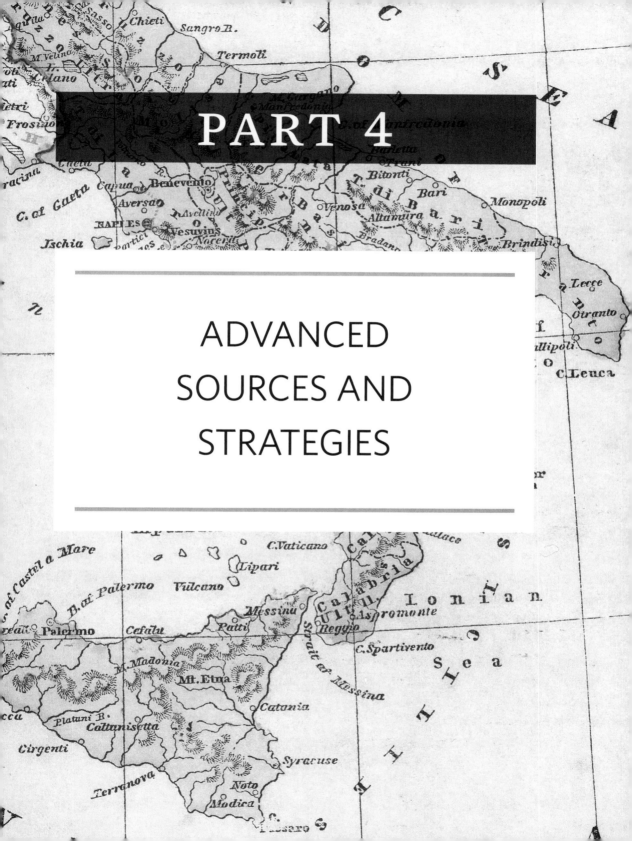

PART 4

ADVANCED SOURCES AND STRATEGIES

13

Putting It All Together

Throughout this book, we've discussed how to find and interpret records of your Italian ancestors. But how do all those pieces fit together, and how can you use all this data to piece together a family narrative? In this chapter, we'll take a look at a case study that will put this book's strategies into practice, helping us learn about an Italian-American man who used multiple names throughout his life.

MATTEO CATANESE: THE MAN WITH A THOUSAND NAMES

Matteo Catanese was a man of mystery. Like most Italian immigrants, he spoke little about the family he left behind, so his descendants knew little about the generations who came before him.

I had the following information when I began research:

- Family lore stated that Matteo Catanese married Maria Di Domenico in an unknown town in Italy. They immigrated to Pittsburgh and had two daughters, Carmela and Giuseppa Catanese. After a few years, they moved to Milltown, Pennsylvania, and eventually opened a small grocery store (image A).

- Matteo's immigration manifest shows he immigrated to the United States in 1893, with the intent of settling in Pittsburgh. His last town of residence was given as Isnello, Italy

Matteo Catanese and Maria (Di Domenico) Catanese stand in front of their store in Milltown, Pennsylvania, about 1919. My grandmother, Josephine Schiavo, is the young girl between them. The child to Matteo's left is Josephine's sister, Emily Schiavo.

(mistranscribed on Ancestry.com **<www.ancestry.com>** as *Isuello*). His ship left out of the port of Napoli, suggesting a southern Italian/Sicilian town of origination. Isnello, located in the Palermo province and the region of Sicilia, fits the bill.

- (Angela) Maria Di Domenico's immigration manifest showed that she immigrated with her two daughters—named Carmela Catanese and "Gpa" (Giuseppa) Catanese—in November 1898. They were going to her husband, Matteo Catanese, who lived at an Italian boarding house on Webster Avenue in Pittsburgh. Notably, the daughters' ages were flipped: Giuseppa was actually fourteen years old and Carmela was sixteen, but the manifest listed the reverse.

- Giuseppina "Catanisso" (likely a misspelling of Catanese) married Antonio Scava (again, likely a misspelling of Lo Schiavo) on December 24, 1899, at St. Peter's Church in Pittsburgh. The original record didn't contain the parents' names, but the marriage return includes the bride's father's consent for a minor to marry—plus his name, Matteo "Catanisso."

- Decades later, Matteo's granddaughter, Josephine Lo Schiavo, then in her eighties, told me Matteo "went by Martin." Was Martin an Americanization of *Matteo*, or the surname he went by? I didn't know at this point, but I dutifully recorded this clue in my family files.

With all that in mind, where should I begin my research? As we discussed in chapter 2, start with US records, as these are generally easier to access and can prevent unnecessary work later on. US draft records would be of little help (Matteo was born in 1856 and so was too old for WWI draft registration, and he passed away before World War II), and I couldn't find a naturalization record for him. I searched through US federal census records, but couldn't find any between 1900 and 1920 in Pennsylvania for Matteo Catanese, Maria Catanese, Carmela Catanese, or Giuseppa Catanese/Giuseppina Catanisso (though the latter was listed in the 1900 and 1910 census records in her husband's house). Broadening my search, I found one possible family in the 1930 US census who lived on Hilton Road in Allegheny County, Pennsylvania, and matched the Catanese family:

- Joe Martino, age 74 (born about 1856), born in Italy, alien, immigrated 1893, head, proprietor of fruit store
- Mary Martino, age 79 (born about 1851), born in Italy, wife
- Camilla [sic] Martino, age 47 (born about 1883), born in Italy, daughter

Could this be the Catanese family under a different name? I already knew that a descendant believed he went by "Martin," which could have been an adopted surname. Indeed, Joe Martino's age, occupation, place of birth, place of residence, and even immigration and naturalization information (per the 1930 census) match what I already knew about Matteo. The information in the census record for Joe/Matteo's wife and daughter is also consistent. (Again, the eldest daughter, Giuseppa, had already left the household; she married and moved out by the 1900 census, then passed away in the 1918 influenza epidemic.) This theory is worth exploring, but let's set it aside for now.

Matteo Catanese passed away on March 16, 1934, in Haffey, Allegheny County, Pennsylvania. His death certificate shows the Department of Vital Records made multiple amendments to the document after family members filed two affidavits that were used to correct information: one from his wife and daughter on November 17, 1934, and a second from only his wife dated February 1, 1935. Ancestry.com, where I found the death certificate, also digitized the amendments:

- Age changed from 67 years, 1 month, 14 days (born about 1867) to 78 years, 0 months, 20 days (born about 1856)
- Date of birth changed from February 2, 1867, to February 24, 1856
- Birthplace changed from Isnello, Province of Palermo, Sicily, Italy, to Polizzi Generosa, Province of Palermo, Italy
- Mother's name changed from Maria Liberti to Maria Alberti (father's name not changed)

Matteo Catanese is buried in Pittsburgh, and his tombstone includes a damaged picture of him.

- Matteo's obituary from the *Allegheny Valley Advance* in Oakmont, Pennsylvania was dated March 22, 1934, and stated the following:

  Mattio Catanefe [sic], 77 years old, resident of Milltown for 33 years, and proprietor of a small store there, died last Friday Morning. He is survived by his wife and daughter. Funeral mass was read in St. Joseph's church, Unity, Monday morning with burial in St. Joseph's cemetery.

Actually, Matteo was buried in St. John the Baptist Cemetery in Pittsburgh, not in St. Joseph's. Maria is buried next to him, and the date of birth on the tombstone (image **B**) doesn't match the one in his death certificate. The picture on his tombstone, typical for an Italian, could have provided additional proof this was the correct man—but it's faded and the majority of his head is damaged. However, the picture used is a recognizable copy of a picture in the families' collection. Maria's picture is clear enough to provide indirect evidence that the stone next to her is for her husband, Matteo Catanese.

Interestingly, I also found a death notice for a "John Martin" that is similar to the one for Matteo Catanese. On March 23, 1934, the "Milltown Musings" section of the Verona Leader read:

  "Milltown Musings…John Martin, grocery man for 40 years, died Friday, March 16th at the age of 77. He was buried in Unity on Monday and is survived by his widow, one daughter, and seven grandchildren."

The details in this notice (occupation, age at death, and surviving relatives) are consistent with what I knew about Matteo and his family.

Could Matteo Catanese, Joe Martino, and John Martin all be the same man? Legal records involving Matteo Catanese make a strong case that they are. Though Matteo died without a will, a 1935 bond within his Allegheny County probate file says, in part, that it is for the "Estate of Joe Martini alias Matteo Catanese, late of Haffy, Allegheny County, Pennsylvania..." Further, his wife is listed as Maria (Di Domenico) Catanese and his daughter as Carmela Catanese. Based on that, I can add Joe Martini to the list of names this ancestor was found to be using.

Fortunately, Maria (Di Domenico) Catanese did leave a will, having signed one shortly after the death of her husband in front of the Vice Consul at the Italian consulate in Pittsburgh. Her will contained several key details that provide information on this family:

> ...Before me, is Maria Di Domenico, daughter of the late Salvatore, widow of Matteo Catanese, born in Isnello, Prov. [Province] Palermo, Italy, domiciled in Millton [sic, Milltown], Allegheny County, Pa...

> ...I desire and demand that the sum of $100.00 be paid to the Holy Catholic Church of Isnello, Prov. [Province] Palermo.

> ...I desire and demand that the sum of $100.00 be paid to the Catholic Church of Isnello for Holy masses for the soul of my dear husband, Matteo Catanese.

> ...I desire and demand that the sum of $25.00 be paid to the Italian Orphans' Asylum of Oakmont, PA...

One key takeaway: Maria (Di Domenico) Catanese was born in Isnello, the town listed as the last place of residence for her and her husband on their immigration manifests. Note the request that money be given to help Italian orphans; this detail will later help understand Matteo Catanese's past as an abandoned child. (In her 1955 will, the couple's daughter Carmela also left the sum of one hundred dollars to an orphans' asylum, this time the St. Anthony Orphan's Asylum.)

In addition, I found two deeds concerning Matteo Catanese and this supposed Joe/John Martin. The first, from 1901, is between William Kidd and a "Joe Martin," arranging the purchase of Martin's store in Milltown (which I already knew Matteo Catanese owned). With this, I can estimate when Matteo moved out of Pittsburgh and establish that he went as Joe Martin as far back as 1901. The second deed, between Carmela Catanese, et al. (the children of Giuseppa Catanese) and Maria (Di Domenico) Catanese, confirms the Joe Martin alias and references the 1901 deed:

...conveyed to Wm. Kidd and recorded in P. 259, and the said Wm. Kidd by his Deed dated the 27th day of February 1901, sold to Joe Martin of Milton [sic], Penn Township, Allegheny County, Pennsylvania. **Said Joe Martin was also known as Matteo Catanese** [emphasis added], who died March 16, 1934, intestate, leaving as his only heirs, his widow, the grantees hereof, his daughter Carmela Catanese and all the other grantors...who are children of Giuseppa Catanese Lo Schiavo, another daughter of the said Matteo Catanese who died several years ago...

Having sorted out Matteo's stateside aliases (and with solid leads about his hometown), I turned my attention to Italian records. Matteo's amended US death certificate said he was born on February 24, 1856, in Polizzi Generosa, Italy, a small town not far from Isnello, his wife's town of birth and the town listed on the couple's passenger manifests. I couldn't find a civil birth record for him in Polizzi Generosa'a regular birth registers between 1850 and 1860, nor in the second copies of these registers held in the provincial archives in Palermo. Still nothing. I also struck out searching for his baptismal and confirmation records, held in the mother church Chiesa di Santa Maria Maggiore. The state of the souls records for this town are lost, so I didn't get any help from them either.

In case he was born outside of the town limits, I checked the 1850–1860 *allegati* (supplemental) birth registers—and didn't find his records there. However, I did find a birth record for an abandoned child named Matteo Catanese in Polizzi Generosa's 1856 *atti diversi* or diverse acts register, born on 24 February 1856 to unknown parents. He had been placed without a blanket or any identifying objects (*segno*) on the *ruota* (foundling wheel) the morning after his birth. This birth record was in a slightly different format than a regular birth record and called a n*otamento di nascita* (notice of birth). His birth record also provided information on his baptism, which occurred in Chiesa di (Church of) San Giovanni Battista on February 25, 1856, also in Polizzi Generosa. The midwife stood as his godmother, a normal occurrence for an abandoned child.

Several pieces of information in this birth record provide indirect evidence that Matteo Catanese was an abandoned child:

- The administrator of the foundling wheel and midwife presented Matteo Catanese to have his birth recorded in the town hall. As we learned in chapter 7, this task was usually done by the father or the midwife who delivered the child. In the situations where the child was abandoned, the midwife was always the one to report the child's birth to the civil authorities.

- A civil records official gave him his name, which was only done if the child has been abandoned.

- The birth records of abandoned children were placed in the Diverse Acts registers in this town, but only between 1856 and 1858. No birth records for legitimate children (that is, children who were birthed within a marriage and raised by their parents) were found in these registers.

- A broad study of the 1820–1860 civil records intimated that no Catanese family resided in Polizzi Generosa in the thirty-six years before his birth.

- Two other abandoned children were given the Catanese surname in Polizzi Generosa within two years of Matteo's birth, suggesting Matteo was part of a larger system. All three of these children were found on the foundling wheel by either Gesaulda or Angela Schimmenti (a mother/daughter midwifery team that operated in the area), given names that started with an *M*, and baptized in the Church of San Giovanni.

At this point, we had pretty solid evidence that Matteo was an abandoned child. However, if he was abandoned, why were his parents listed on the US death certificate?

Some social history may be helpful here. The social stigma surrounding illegitimate births was a strong deterrent for an unwed mother to raise her own child. These women were encouraged to abandon their children because, in bearing an illegitimate child, they brought dishonor on not only themselves but also upon their families. This dishonor could even prevent her siblings from contracting good marriages. Abandoning an illegitimate child restored the honor of the mother and her family. It was uncommon (but not unheard of) for an abandoned child to be reclaimed by his natural parents. Many unwed mothers, forced to give up a child, left something with the baby (a torn picture of the Madonna, a piece of jewelry, etc.) so she could prove it was hers should she return to reclaim the child. But in Matteo's case, no such token was left with him. In fact, his mother didn't even dress him, but placed him naked on the wheel one chilly February morning in the Madonie mountains of Sicily.

Abandoned children were sometimes reclaimed by their natural parents, so I searched the 1856–1858 diverse acts registers for an Act of Recognition. Acts of Recognition allowed an abandoned child to use its birth families' surname but didn't legitimize it. Legitimizations (usually informal) were done upon the marriage of the birth parents, sometimes indicated in marriage documents. However, I couldn't find such records for Matteo.

Having learned about Matteo's birth, I wanted to investigate his marriage. We struck out with church records, as no registers for the Chiesa di San Giovanni survive within the parish archive. The diocesan archives were not very helpful either, as they didn't have any records from Polizzi Generosa. A local historian revealed the Chiesa di San Giovanni, more of a chapel than a parish during its time, was destroyed in World War II, limiting our options further. It wasn't until after World War II that Polizzi Generosa's priests saw the value of consolidating all of the older parish records within the Mother Church or Chiesa Madre.

The town of Isnello didn't hold an ecclesiastical marriage record for the couple, either, but I did find their civil marriage banns, marriage record, and marriage supplements from 1877. Their marriage banns and marriage record give Matteo's parents as Mariano *Proietto* (a designation given to abandoned children) and Maria Albert. The couple's marriage banns note Matteo was legitimized a little more than two years after his birth when his parents married on June 24, 1858, in Polizzi Generosa. His father, Mariano *Proietto*, had also been abandoned, with Mariano's 1858 marriage supplements also identifying him as *proietto*. Matteo's marriage supplements also included his extracted birth record, which stated his parents were unknown, though it was normal practice to extract the information from the record exactly as it read, whether there are any explanatory notes on other documents or not.

Moving from Matteo's marriage to potential military service, I found his *lista di leva* (draft/conscription list) in the provincial archives in Palermo, Italy. According to this document, he was born on February 24, 1856, in Polizzi Generosa. His parents were listed as *d'ignoto* (unknown) and Maria "Pompa," a new surname for Matteo's mother. (The Pompa surname can be explained by further research that showed this surname attributed to her father, Antonino Alberti, on his death record. The record also showed that the family had a double surname—*doppia cognome*—Alberti Pompa). During Matteo's military evaluation, he was determined to be able to serve physically, but, since he was the "only son of a living father," his service requirement was waived. This record contradicts itself and other records—if his father was unknown, how could they know his father was living? Also, an ancestor's military service could be waived if his father was deceased and he was the breadwinner for the family, not if his father was still living. It is likely there are two mistakes on this record: The name of Matteo's father should have been Mariano "*d'ignoto*," (meaning from unknown parents, as he was an abandoned child who was not given a surname), and his father should have been listed as deceased.

Certain town (municipal) records can also help us learn more about Matteo. As we discussed in chapter 7, each Italian town was required to keep a record of their inhabitants, showing each household and continuously following them, recording the changes to their vital statistics. In Isnello, these records were called the *registri di popolazione* (population registers) and did not begin until the 1880s. I found three undated records for Matteo Catanese, likely created before 1898 (when Maria Di Domenico and her daughters joined Matteo in America).

The first shows Matteo Catanese and his three daughters living on Via Salita San Francesco in Isnello, though no house number or population register number was given.

His date of birth is given as February 24, 1856, in Polizzi Generosa to *d'ignoti* (unknown parents). (Angela) Maria Di Domenico was listed separately, as the register was arranged alphabetically. Therefore, she was listed under her maiden name, Di Domenico, living at 16 Via Salita San Francesco, population register number 1060. Her father was named as Salvatore, which corresponds with her birth record.

The second population register was arranged by population register number and showed Matteo with his wife and surviving two daughters living at the same address. The third daughter was deceased at that time, placing the date of this record about 1888. However, the family appears to have been using the surname Librizzi—yet another surname to add to Matteo's list of aliases. Matteo "Librizzi" was born in 1857 in Polizzi Generosa, and (like Matteo Catanese) Matteo Librizzi's father's given name was Mariano, with no surname listed. The Librizzi surname might have been adopted to hide their abandoned status, as there were other Librizzi families living in Isnello.

The third population register was arranged alphabetically, and the family (still living at the same address with the same register number) again used the surname Librizzi. Matteo Librizzi's father was again given as Mariano, and (interestingly) a Mariano "Librizzi" was enumerated with Matteo and his family but resided at a separate address.

Searches for Matteo in other kinds of records, such as real property records and citizenship records, came up mostly empty. One property title in the name of his daughter, Carmela, mentions his first name and that he was deceased at that time.

So what can I do next? My research so far has kicked up a variety of records about the man with a thousand names, Matteo (or Joe) Catanese/Martin/Martino/Librizzi/Martini, though the exact reason why he had a shifting identity remains a mystery. Further lines of research could investigate records under his various aliases and records of his family members—his daughters or parents, for example. Regardless, Matteo's story is an inspiring one: a man abandoned as a child who found love and acceptance in his family, then made a name for himself as a successful entrepreneur in a new country.

MEET THE PARENTS: WORKING BACKWARD TO DISCOVER PARENTS' NAMES

Antonino Lo Schiavo didn't talk much about the family he left behind. By the time his children became adults, they knew very little about their grandparents. Most of the letters and photographs of the family in Italy had been burned when an outbuilding was sold and cleaned out. Realizing the value of what was being burned, the new owner's wife saved a few of the Schiavo family photos, but this still didn't amount to much.

As his descendants began searching for the names of Antonino's parents, they realized that, while his father's identity would be easy to find, his mother's would prove elusive.

They eventually learned her name (Maria Arrigo, the third wife of Lorenzo Lo Schiavo), but discovering this information took considerable time and effort.

Conventional resources weren't very helpful. Access to ecclesiastical records in Antonino's town of birth, Termini Imerese, has been denied researchers for many years, and immigration manifests of this time period did not always include a column for the name of a relative in the country of origin. As a result, Antonino's passenger list gave no clues as to the identity of his mother, stating only that he came from Italy in 1894. It also misspelled his surname as *Chiavo*, making it more difficult to find.

US records showed more (but still not much) promise. Five years after arriving in the United States, Antonino married a woman named Giuseppa Catanese at St. Peter's Catholic Church in Pittsburgh. The original marriage certificate, found within the families' files, misspelled the names of both the bride and groom and did not contain the names of their parents. While their civil marriage return might have included the names of his parents, the priest never filed one. And since Antonino was of legal age and didn't need a parental signature to marry, the couple's marriage license offered no evidence either.

Striking out in the initial search, I turned to Italian naming customs for hints about the given names for Antonino's parents. Antonino named his eldest daughter Maria, which (if naming customs held true) would have been his mother's first name (as we discussed in chapter 6, custom dictated the eldest daughter be named after her paternal grandmother). The same principle applies to Antonino's first-born son, Lorenzo, as naming customs would state that he was to be named after his paternal grandfather. Most—but not all—Italian families followed these customs, so I needed to find other documents to confirm or deny my theory.

With that clue in mind, I turned to other records. Antonino's WWI draft registration card logically listed his wife as his "nearest relative," not mentioning his mother's name. Antonino never naturalized, but his original alien registration booklet (and the U.S. Citizenship and Immigration Services documents he submitted) provided his birth date and place, but not his parents' names.

Antonino's death records finally gave a few clues about his father's identity, but his mother's remained a mystery. His 1948 Pennsylvania death certificate identified his father as *Lorenzo Schiavo*, and his mother is listed as "unknown." His obituary and probate records held no clues as to his parents' identities, and no siblings (nor any other extended family member) was mentioned in either record.

Then, finally, I had a breakthrough. Internal travel papers, issued so that Antonino could move freely within Italy during a visit in 1906, provide solid evidence that his parents were Lorenzo Lo Schiavo and Maria Arrigo. Issued on 31 December 1906 in the town of Termini Imerese, the travel papers give his birth date as 22 January 1876—the same date found on Antonino Lo Schiavo's US death certificate, alien registration booklet, and alien registration paperwork. Based on that, we can say with some confidence that the information here is accurate. His civil birth record, which I also found, gave the same names for his parents.

My research to this point has been pretty comprehensive, but how else could I substantiate information? Collateral research—studying records of family members who are not direct-line ancestors—can often provide the answers. I turned to Antonino's siblings: His only full-blood sister, Giuseppa, was born in 1874 in Termini Imerese to parents Lorenzo Lo Schiavo and Maria Arrigo, according to her birth record. Her marriage record backs up those names, saying she lived with her parents Lorenzo Lo Schiavo and Maria Arrigo in Caltavuturo, a small mountain town not far from Termini Imerese, just before her wedding. Giuseppa's Italian identification booklet, found later amongst the papers of her immediate family, also gives her parents as the aforementioned couple. Since this document was issued by the local *municipio* (town hall), the booklet (and the information about her parents in it) was likely taken from the official records conserved in the town hall.

How can I confirm that Antonino and Giuseppa were siblings? Lo Schiavo family papers include letters between family members that discuss the relationship between the two of them: Antonino's youngest daughter, Emily Schiavo, and her first cousin Rosaria Guercio, the daughter of Giuseppa (née Lo Schiavo) and Bartolo Guercio.

A FRANCESCO OF ALL TRADES

Francesco Catanzaro was a jack-of-all-trades, holding several different occupations over the years. Perhaps he did whatever he could to make ends meet. But regardless of his reason for frequently shifting jobs, we can learn a lot by tracking his migrations from one occupation to another.

Francesco was born about 1759, likely in Termini Imerese, Palermo province, Italy, where he married Agostina Caterina D'Ugo before 1800. When his two oldest children, Salvadore Pietro Catanzaro and Rosalia Catanzaro, each got married on the same day in 1830 (and, interestingly, to another pair of siblings), Francesco's extracted death record was included in their marriage supplements, indicating he was a sailor when he passed away in 1829. Yet his original death record indicates he was a fisherman.

Clues in records of Francesco's father (Giuseppi) and son (Salvadore) also suggest Francesco was a fisherman. In his marriage supplements, Salvadore carried the title of "Raif," which signified a master fisherman. The title was hereditary, suggesting that Francesco, too, was recognized as an elite fisherman. Likewise, Francesco's father was buried in the Church of the Annunziata of the Virgin Mary (an honor usually reserved for the rich, noble or ecclesiastical)—suggesting Giuseppi was either wealthy or an honorable

"Raif." Either case lends support to our theory that Francesco was a fisherman—he either inherited his father's title of "Raif" or had to turn to fishing/farming (lower-class professions) because he didn't inherit his father's wealth.

Furthermore, all three of Francesco's sons later became fishermen, and Francesco's only daughter married one. Indeed, Rosalia Catanzaro was well prepared to be a fisherman's wife when she married Antonino Lo Schiavo in 1830, likely having spent her childhood helping her mother with the chores associated with the fishing trade, which included weaving and fixing nets.

A "capn" (*capitano*, or captain) named Francesco Catanzaro was found in the 1815 Riveli, a census (disclosure) specific to Sicily taken to tax property and animals (see chapter 9). This Francesco Catanzaro farmed a small piece of land owned by Ignazio Felicicchia and Don Giuseppe Uglialoro in the *contrada* (district) of DoVarita, under the civil jurisdiction of Termini Imerese. I couldn't distinguish this Francesco Catanzaro and another individual with the same name, except for the fact that he was the only adult man by this name living in Termini Imerese at that time. No man by this name had been enumerated four years earlier. Might a fisherman have also farmed in order to put food on the table? Possibly. Maybe, but a fisherman's workday was long and physical.

So what do we make of his title? Francesco could have gained the "Capn" designation he'd had in 1815 from the fishing industry hierarchy...or perhaps it was a military rank, adding a third possible occupation for Francesco. After researching conscription laws from the time (see chapter 10), I discovered that the Napoleon-ruled Kingdom of Italy mandated military conscription between 1802 and 1814, a time period that lines up with a nine-year gap between the births of Francesco's second child and third children (1802–1811). Could Francesco Catanzaro have earned his "Capn" title by serving in the military during those years? Military records would help shed some light on this possibility (and whether Francesco served under French command or against Napoleon's forces), but the records for this time period have been lost.

To review our current theory: Francesco Catanzaro was in the military between 1802 and 1811 (where he earned the rank of "Captain") before becoming a farmer (by 1815) and changed to a fisherman/sailor between 1815 and his death in 1829. Is our theory correct? Only further research will tell.

14

What to Do When You Get Stuck

As you research your Italian ancestors, you will eventually encounter an ancestor who will present unique challenges and make your research even more difficult. These points in our research, when information eludes us on a particular ancestor even after trying all applicable records, are called brick wall problems.

But never fear! Tried-and-true research tactics can help you break down those brick walls. This chapter will discuss four ways to overcome research roadblocks; see the More Brick Wall-Busting Techniques sidebar for additional techniques to use in your research.

RESEARCH THE WHOLE FAMILY

Tracing other members of your ancestor's family can often provide information on the ancestor in question. Italian ancestors appeared on the genealogical records of others as parties, witnesses, or godparents. These records, while not directly about your ancestor, can provide evidence about him and perhaps help you solve a genealogical problem. Countless times, I've discovered an Italian immigrant's place of origin by researching her siblings, cousins, or other relatives.

Say, for example, that you are searching for the parents of your ancestor, but no records created about your ancestor provide this information. Researching his siblings would be a good first step toward finding the missing parents' names. A sibling's draft registration card, certificate record, naturalization record, or passport might list the town they were both born in and other key information about the family, providing you evidence on the target of your research. One might also research the ancestor's children, other relatives, or acquaintances, as their records may contain information about the parents.

More Brick Wall-Busting Techniques

- Put the research away for a few weeks and come back to it with a fresh perspective. It's amazing what we see within the records that we didn't see upon first analysis.

- Research what other resources could be used to solve the genealogical problem. Thinking beyond the standard resources may be just the answer you need!

- Consider the "who, what, when, where, why, and how" surrounding the ancestor. Who was involved, what did they do, when did they do it, where did it happen, why and how did it occur? This may involve researching collateral ancestors or the FAN club (Friends, Associates, and Neighbors) of the ancestor in question.

- Revisit your translation. A single mistranslated/misunderstood word in key records often accounts for some seemingly "brick wall" problems. For example, I recently revisited my translation of where an ancestor's father was living at the time of her marriage. Upon second inspection, I saw a second part of the hamlet name, which indicated that this hamlet was under a different municipal jurisdiction at that time. This new information directed me to the correct town, where I could find this ancestor's records.

- Map out your evidence. Simply looking at the text in records will only help so much. Creating visualizations for your ancestors' data—such as timelines, spreadsheets, genealogical compilations, or family group sheets—can help you spot important trends or gaps in your research.

- Use DNA analysis. Genetic genealogy has become increasingly popular in recent years as technology has improved and more analysis tools and testing services have become available. DNA testing is especially helpful for adoptees—a friend of mine reconnected with his twin brothers who had been put up for adoption nearly sixty years ago, all because my friend's son and brothers had their DNA tested. Use advances in technology to your advantage. Blaine T. Bettinger's book, *The Family Tree Guide to DNA Testing and Genetic Genealogy* (Family Tree Books, 2016), is a great resource to learn how to apply this type of analysis to your genealogical research. Bettinger also runs a Facebook group on DNA testing, another great resource for aspiring genetic genealogists.

- Ask for help. Have another researcher or a professional genealogist take a look at your research, as a fresh perspective can often reveal the problem. Another researcher may know of additional resources you can use to tackle your research question.

A

The records of your ancestor's siblings (like this 1955 US death certificate for my ancestor's sister) can provide valuable information about your ancestor's family.

For example, let's say I was researching for the parents of my ancestor Giuseppa (Catanese) Lo Schiavo, but none of the information or documents directly pertaining to her gave the names of her parents. I know from family lore and census records that she had only one surviving sibling, Carmela, so I should turn my attention to her since the siblings (presumably) have the same parents. Image **A** shows Carmela (Catanese) Alberti's Pennsylvania death certificate, which clearly states her parents' names as Matteo Catanese and Maria Di Domenico. (Further research proved these names to be correct.) As it turns out, the informant for this death record is Giuseppa's son, Manual Schiavo. In a similar way, Carmela (Catanese) Alberti's birth record (image **B**) from the civil records

Birth records (*atti di nascita*), like death certificates, can help you break through research brick walls. Annotations regarding the person's marriage and death may be included in the margin.

office in Isnello, Italy, not only contains the same names for her parents, but also marginal annotations that reference her date of death, the name of her second husband, and when her second marriage occurred, all of which could potentially be useful in my search for Giuseppa's parents' information.

In a similar way, researching the *lista di leva* (image) for an ancestor's brother may reveal the town of your ancestor's birth, as they may have been born in the same town.

RESEARCH THE FAN CLUB: FRIENDS, ASSOCIATES, AND NEIGHBORS

In a similar way, savvy researchers will broaden the scope of their research to include an ancestor's "FAN club" (Friends, Associates, and Neighbors). These individuals, who formed part of an ancestor's community, may have more-available records that can help you solve your research problems. Researching the people around the ancestor in

NUMERI 1	COGNOME E NOME DEGLI ISCRITTI E INDICAZIONI PER I PROVENIENTI DA LEVE ANTERIORI 2	NASCITA E RESIDENZA E VARIAZIONI ALLA LISTA DI LEVA 3	CONTRASSEGNI PERSONALI PROFESSIONE - ISTRUZIONE 4
N. d'ordine 91 all' invio della lista all' ufficio di leva)	Romano Salvatore	Figlio di Giuseppe e della Coppola Giuseppina nato addì 8 novembre 1917 nel Comune di Pompei Provincia di Napoli	Statura m. 1, Torace m. 0, Capelli { colore { forma Viso Naso
	Classi di provenienza		Mento
N. d'ordine 86, dopo la verificazio- ne definitiva)	Motivo del primo rimando	dimorante in Pompei Via Firenze 50.	Occhi Sopracciglia Fronte Colorito Bocca
		Motivo dell'aggiunzione o della cancellazione	Dentatura Segni particolari
	Motivo del secondo rimando		Arte o professione
	N. del ruolo matricolare comunale		Sa leggere? Sa scrivere? Titoli di studio

This military conscription record can be used to find place of origin/birth. In this example, Salvatore Romano was born in the town of Pompei in the Napoli province and was living in that town at 20 Via Firenze at the time of his conscription.

question can solve some of the most difficult genealogical problems, as you piece together indirect evidence to form a solid genealogical conclusion.

The FAN club is especially important for those researching immigrant ancestors, as they often did not come to this country alone. They may have had cousins, aunts, uncles, and friends make the journey before, with, or after them, and many settled within the same community in the New World. When you find your ancestor on a US census record, don't just evaluate the entries for his immediate family; you'll often find other relatives, friends, or associates living within ten households in either direction on the population schedule.

Researching a cousin, friend, or neighbor may provide information to solve a genealogical problem. The Board for Certification of Genealogists' book *Genealogy Standards* says the following about "mining" the evidence in each record:

> ...40. Evidence mining...requires attention to detail, including details that might
> initially seem insignificant. Genealogists ignore no potentially useful evidence—

including indirect and negative evidence or evidence that might conflict with or complicate a working hypothesis—and they give equal attention to direct, indirect, or negative evidence.

What about researching other Italians who settled in the same place and came from the same town? There was often some form of relationship between these individuals. And even if you can't find a relationship between your ancestor and other community members, you may learn about what might have precipitated your ancestor's emigration, what the immigration experience was like, and what his initial life was like in this country. This can go a long way towards understanding your ancestor within his historical and social context.

HIRE PROFESSIONAL RESEARCHERS

If you've hit your research limit, consider consulting professional researchers, who specialize in solving difficult genealogical problems. They can access records in a language you don't understand, research the more challenging parts of your ancestry, or help you gain access to materials only available onsite in Italy or to scholars and serious researchers. Professionals are especially helpful since some diocesan archives have placed higher restrictions on who can access their records in recent years, and credentialed (i.e., board-certified or accredited) genealogists often have the education required to access these repositories and foster relationships with the directors of the archives.

A professional has the experience in the records, language, and archives that are sometimes necessary to solve complicated problems. Qualified professionals can be found through the member directories of the Association for Professional Genealogists **<www.apgen.org>** (image **D**), the Board for Certification of Genealogists (BCG) **<www.bcgcertification.org>**, and the International Commission for the Accreditation of Genealogists (ICAPGEN) **<www.icapgen.org>**. You will also find professionals who specialize in translation or certain types of records; use these directories to determine who would be the best choice for your project. See the "Hiring a Professional" section of their website for more details on the process **<www.apgen.org/articles/hire.html>**.

Researchers in the BCG and ICAPGEN directories have had their work vetted by leaders in the field of professional genealogy. They are also required to submit work samples for subsequent evaluations every five years, showing they maintain professional standards and continue to develop their skills. Several judges give feedback on each applicant's submission, which helps the researcher grow and advance within her field.

Professional researchers will want you to provide a detailed summary of the research you've already done and any documents that pertain to your research goals. You will

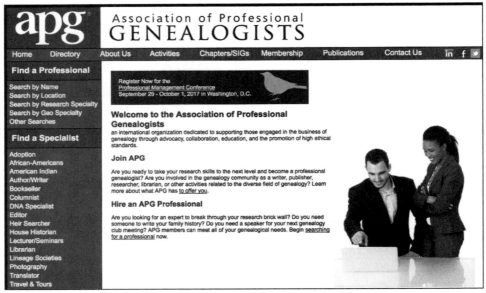

The Association of Professional Genealogists' website can connect you to for-hire genealogy researchers.

also need to tell them what you want to accomplish so they can prepare an appropriate research plan and estimate time and expenses.

You and the researcher should discuss any and all fees up front and make them clear in writing through a contract (though a professional may not require a contract for a simple document request from a civil archive). However, even in this situation, the fees involved should be made clear front. The Association of Professional Genealogists recommends that a contract between you and a professional should contain:

- Fees for various services
- The amount of hours to be worked, with agreed-upon allowances for overtime based on special circumstances
- Explanation of what the retainer (if any) covers and how it will be applied to the final payment
- Conditions for extensions to the initial agreement, such as how they would be put in writing

At this time, Italy has no professional genealogical organization. However, qualified researchers can be found in the directories previously listed. Some professionals specialize in Italian research but live in the United States and have offices in Italy, and many have other researchers who work for them and spend significant time there researching for their clients. Other professionals live and work in Italy.

TRAVEL TO THE HOMELAND

So you want to research your ancestors' records on site in Italy? Walking through your ancestors' town can be an insightful and powerful experience, and visiting your ancestral homeland can give you a new connection to and appreciation of your Italian heritage. In addition, visiting archives in person can sometimes be the only way of overcoming your research brick walls.

If you plan to visit archives during your trip, make sure you set up appointments ahead of time with the archive you wish to research in, as not all Italian archives have the staff to handle walk-in requests. Municipal archives, in particular, appreciate when a researcher makes an appointment, and diocesan archives often work only by appointment. This enables them to have the appropriate number of staff members on hand to handle your requests. If you don't speak Italian, you can make appointments via letter or e-mail—find addresses online, such as on the municipal website of a town or diocesan archives. Make sure you begin the process at least two months in advance of your trip, as setting up appointments can take time.

When making your appointment, tell the archivist exactly what you wish to research. Be as specific as possible so he can better assist you in a timely manner. Sometimes the older registers may be stored in a different building, and giving the archive a heads up about your visit will give workers time to transport your record to the appropriate building or access the record for you in the off-site storage facility.

If you are allowed access to a parish or diocesan archives, make sure you leave an offering of at least 50 to 100 euro at the end of each research day for the parish's work. Showing the proper respect for the records—and, partially through tips and donations, for the archivists who allowed you access to them—will smooth the way for a return visit and other researchers who may wish to access that archive in the future. If you forget to leave some cash behind, mail some to the parish when you get home with a brief thank you note. This will go a long way towards ensuring future access for you and other researchers.

Occasionally, you will encounter a record keeper who insists she do the research for you. In this case, be agreeable. Some archivists are a little hesitant to allow non-scholars or non-professionals to handle the valuable records. Be prepared to work with this situation and have your research objectives clearly written down. I've found that showing a family group sheet or pedigree chart with the ancestors that need to be researched can be an effective way to convey who and what you need researched.

Unfortunately, we have only ourselves to blame for some of this hesitancy to allow access to the records. I have encountered multiple situations where Americans have been allowed access to a parish archive and simply stolen the records of their ancestors, tearing them completely out of the registers. This type of behavior ruins access to these records for all researchers who follow them. The feeling of touching your ancestor's records is indescribable, but we do not own the records. They are the property of the archives in which they are conserved, so be respectful and courteous in all your actions and interactions at the archives.

KEYS TO SUCCESS

Research more broadly when records of your direct-line ancestors don't give you the information you need. Looking for records of the "FAN" (friends, associates, and neighbors) network can move your research forward, allowing you to solve difficult research problems.

Consider hiring a professional researcher if you're having trouble accessing records or don't know where to look next.

Venture to the homeland to visit archives in person and walk in your ancestors' footsteps when all else fails—or when you need an excuse to take a trip to Europe!

A

Publications and Websites

BOOKS

Research Aids

Alcuni Appunti sulle Ricerche Genea-logiche in Italia (Some Notes on Genealogy Research in Italy) by Luigi Guelfi Cama-jani (Bureau du Vème Congrès Inter-national des Sciences Généalogique et Héraldique, 1960)

Archivio di Stato di Palermo: Inventario Sommario (Ministero dell'Interno, 1950) Note: See Archivio di Stato di Palermo's website to see an updated collection.

Dizionario di Abbreviature Latine ed Italiane, 6th ed. (Dictionary of Latin and Italian Abbreviations) by Adriano Cappelli (Editore Ulrico Hoepli, 1979)

A Genealogist's Guide to Discovering Your Italian Ancestors by Lynn Nelson (Better-way Books, 1997)

Genealogy in Italy by Guelfo Guelfi Cama-jani (Istituto Genealogico Italiano, 1979)

Guida delle Regioni d'Italia (Guide of the Regions of Italy). 3 vols. (Società Italiana per lo Studio dei Problemi Reigonali, 1994/5)

Guida Generale degli Archivi di Stato Italiani (General Guide to Italian State Archives). 4 vols. (Ministero per i Beni Culturali e Ambientali, Ufficio Centrale per i Beni Archivistici, 1986)

Guida Monaci: Annuario Generale Ital-ian, 117th ed. (Italian General Directory) (Guide Monaci, 1991)

Guide to the Records of the Order of the Sons of Italy in America by John Andreozzi (Immigration History Research Center, 1989)

The Guide to Italian Libraries and Archives compiled by Rudolf J. Lewanski (Council for European Studies, 1979)

How to Find Out about Italy by F.S. Stych (Pergamon Press, 1970)

Italian Genealogical Records: How to Use Italian Civil, Ecclesiastical & Other Records in Family History Research by Trafford R. Cole (Ancestry, 1995)

Italian-American Family History: A Guide to Researching and Writing About Your Heritage by Sharon DeBartolo Carmack (Genealogical Publishing Co., 1997)

Italians to America: Lists of Passengers Arriving at U.S. Ports edited by Ira A. Glazer and P. William Filby (Scholarly Resources, Inc., 1992–present. 16 vols)

Lezioni di Paleografia (Paleography Lesson) by Giulio Battelli (Città del Vaticano, 1949)

Repertorio delle Biblioteche Italiene (Directory of Italian Libraries) by Francesco Marraro (Editoriale Cassia, 1989)

Report on the Italian American Newspaper Microfilming Project compiled by Timo Riippa (Immigration History Research Center, University of Minnesota, 1992)

Italians in America

An Album of the Italian American by Salvatore J. La Gumina (Franklin Watts, 1972)

Here in Cerchio: Letters to an Italian Immigrant by Constance Sancetta (Bordighera Press, 2014)

The Immigrant Upraised: Italian Adventurers and Colonists in an Expanding America by Andrew F. Rolle (University of Oklahoma Press, 1968)

Italian Americans: A Guide to Information Sources by Francesco Cordasco (Gale Research Co., 1978)

The Italians in America by Ronald P. Grossman (Lerner Publications, 1975)

The Italians in America, 1492–1972 by Anthony F. LoGatto (Oceana Publications, 1973)

The Italians in America before the Civil War by Giovanni Ermenegildo Schiavo (Vigo Press, 1934)

A Portrait of the Italians in America by Vincenza Scarpaci (Scribner's Sons, 1983)

La Storia: Five Centuries of the Italian American Experience by Jerre Mangione and Ben Morreale (Harper Collins, 1992)

Italian Local History

Casteldaccia nella Storia della Sicilia (Casteldaccia in the History of Sicily) by Rocco Russo (Edizioni Arti Grafiche "Battaglia," 1961)

I Sette Re di Agrigento (The Seven Kings of Agrigento) by Francesco Bilello (Editore A. Quartararo, 1975)

Il Monte Erice, Oggi, San Giuliano: Paesaggio, Storia e Costumi (Mount Erice, Today, San Giuliano: Landscape, History and Costumes) by Domenico Giannitrapani (Zanichelli, 1892)

Storia della Puglia (History of Puglia). 2 vols. edited by Giosue Musca (Mario Adda Editore, 1979)

Italian Surnames

Dizionario dei Cagnomi Italiani (Dictionary of Italian Surnames) by Emidio DeFelice (Arnoldo Mondadori, 1978)

I Cognomi degli Ebrai d'Italia (The Surnames of the Jews of Italy) by Samuele Schaert (Casa Editrice Israel, 1925)

Our Italian Surnames by Joseph G. Fucilla (Genealogical Publishing Company, 1996)

Maps and Gazetteers

Allgemeines Geografisch-Statistisches Lexikon aller Osterreichischen Staaten by Franz Raffelsperger (Zehnter Thell Sopacz bis Tir., 1854). Other years available

Annuario Cattolico d'Italia (Catholic Dictionary of Italy) (Editoriale Italiana, 1978–79). Published yearly

Annuario delle Diocesi d'Italia (Annals of the Dioceses of Italy) (Marietti Editori, Ltd., 1951)

Annuario Generale, Comuni e Frazioni d'Italia (General Directory, Municipalities and Regions of Italy) (Touring Club Italiano, 1968). Published every five years

Euro-Atlas: ITALY (American Map Corporation, 1998)

Grande Carta Topografica del Regno d'Italia (Great Topographic Paper of the Kingdom of the Italy) (Istituo Geografico Militare, 1882). Updated periodically

Guida della Regioni d'Italia (Guide of the Italian Regions). 3 vols. (Società Italiana per lo Studio dei Problemi Regionali, 1994/5). Published annually

Nuovo Dizzionario dei Comuni e Frazioni di Comuni (New Dictionary of Towns and Comunes) (Società Editrice Dizionario Voghera dei Comuni, 1977). Published periodically

WEBSITES

Census Records

Archivi di Stato Census Holdings
<media.regesta.com/dm_0/ASNA/ xdamsProgettareFuturo/allegati%20/IT/ ASNA/CATA/LOGO/0002367/IT.ASNA. CATA.LOGO.0002367.0001.pdf>

Census Holdings in Venice State Archives
<www.archiviodistatovenezia.it/siasve/cgi-bin/pagina. pl?Tipo=inventari&Lettera=5>

University of Bologna
<www.archiviostorico.unibo.it/it/?LN=IT#>

Vatican Secret Archives
<asv.vatican.va/content/ archiviosegretovaticano/en.html>

Church Records

Eastern Orthodoxy
<benedett.provincia.venezia.it/comenius/ multicult/benedetti/en/enortodossia.html>

Guida degli Archivi diocesani d'Italia (Guide to the Diocesan Archives of Italy) by Vincenzo Monachino
Volume I **<www.archivi.beniculturali. it/dga/uploads/documents/Quaderni/ Quaderno_61.pdf>**
Volume II **<www.archivi.beniculturali. it/dga/uploads/documents/Quaderni/ Quaderno_74_II.pdf>**

Italian Catholic Church
<www.webdiocesi.chiesacattolica.it>

Italian-Jewish Genealogy
<www.jewishgen.org/infofiles/italy/italian.htm>

La Memoria dei Sacramenti
<www.registriparrocchiali.weebly.com>

Orthodox Archdiocese of Italy and Malta
<win.ortodossia.it/The%20Holy%20
Orthodox%20Archdiocese%20of%20
Italy%20ed%20Malta.htm>

Parish and Church Boundaries
<www.italia.indettaglio.it>

Parish Search
<www.parrocchie.it>

Waldensian (Valdese)
<www.chiesavaldese.org/eng/indexen.php>

Waldensian Families Research Website
<www.waldensian.info>

Directories

PagineBianche
<www.paginebiance.it>

PagineGialle
<www.paginegialle.it>

Pronto
<www.pronto.it>

DNA

Italy DNA Project
<www.familytreedna.com/groups/italy/
about/background>

The Sicilian DNA-Genealogy Project
<www.familytreedna.com/public/
Sicily?iframe=yresults>

Messina Sicily DNA Project
<www.familytreedna.com/groups/
messina-provinceof-sicily/about/
background>

Forums/Groups

Gente di Mare
<www.gentedimaregenealogy.com>

ItalianGenealogy.com
<www.italiangenealogy.com/forum>

Italian Heritage Forums
<www.abruzzoforum.com>

Italian Roots Forum
<disc.yourwebapps.com/Indices/104917.
html>

ValdoGen: Genealogy in Valle d'Aosta (in
French)
<valdogen.leforum.eu/index.php>

Geography and Maps

Comuni-Italiani.it
<www.comuni-italiani.it>

David Rumsey Map Collection
<www.davidrumsey.com>

Edmaps
<www.edmaps.com>

Geoplan
<www.geoplan.it>

Google Earth
<www.google.com/earth>

Italian Town Database in One Step
<www.rootsweb.ancestry.com/~itappcnc/
pipcntown.htm>

Mapquest
<www.mapquest.com>

Perry-Castañeda Library Map Collection
<www.lib.utexas.edu/maps/italy.html>

Wikipedia Atlas of Italy
<commons.wikimedia.org/wiki/
Atlas_of_Italy>

Language Tools

ITALIAN

FamilySearch Genealogical Word List
<www.familysearch.org/learn/wiki/en/
Italian_Genealogical_Word_List>

Italian handwriting: Brigham Young
University
<www.script.byu.edu/Pages/Italian/en/
handwriting.aspx>

LATIN

FamilySearch Genealogical Word List
<www.familysearch.org/learn/wiki/en/
Latin_Genealogical_Word_List>

*An Introduction to Greek and Latin Pale-
ography* by Sir Edward Maunde Thompson (Clarendon Press, 1912)
<www.archive.org/details/
greeklatin00thomuoft>

The Latin Library
<www.thelatinlibrary.com>

Tutorial for Beginning Latin
<www.nationalarchives.gov.uk/latin/
beginners>

Military Records

Archivio Centrale dello Stato in Roma
<acs.beniculturali.it>

Italian Ministry of Defense
<www.difesa.it/Ministro/Commissari-
ato_Generale_per_le_Onoranze_ai_Caduti_
in_Guerra/Pagine/default.aspx>

Military Digitization Projects
<www.antenati.san.beniculturali.it/link>

Military Documents
<www.antenati.san.beniculturali.it/
Le-fonti-degli-Archivi-di-Stato>

Military Terms
<www.antenati.san.beniculturali.it/
glossario>

Names

D'Addezio.com First Name Translator
<www.daddazio.com/genealogy/italian/
names.html>

Italian Names and English Equivalent
<www.oocities.org/irishkenj/givename.
html >

Sicilian and Italian Given Names
<www.conigliofamily.com/
SicilianAndItalianGivenNames.htm>

Newspapers

Corriere della Sera
<www.archivio.corriere.it/Archivio/
interface.landing.html>

Euro Docs
<www.eudocs.lib.byu.edu/index.php/
Italy:_Historical_Collections>

La Gazetta del Mezzogiorno
<www.archivio.lagazzettadelmezzogiorno.
it/gazzettadelmezzogiorno/archive/archive.
jsp?>

La Repubblica
<www.repubblica.it>

La Stampa
<www.lastampa.it/archivio-storico/index.
jpp>

B

Italian Provinces and Archives

Agrigento

ARCHIVIO DI STATO DI AGRIGENTO

Via G. Mazzini, 185 - 92100 Agrigento

Website <**www.provincia.agrigento.it/ flex/cm/pages/ServeBLOB.php/L/IT/ IDPagina/428**>

Access instructions <**www.asagrigento. beniculturali.it**>

ARCHIVIO DI STATO DI AGRIGENTO. SEZIONE DI SCIACCA

Via Figuli, 28 - 92019 Sciacca

Access instructions <**www.asagrigento. beniculturali.it/index.php?it/147/ sezione-di-archivio-di-stato-di-sciacca**>

Alessandria

ARCHIVIO DI STATO DI ALESSANDRIA

Via G. Solero, 43 - 15121 Alessandria

Website <**www.provincia.alessandria.gov.it**>

Access instructions <**www.asalessandria. beniculturali.it**>

Ancona

ARCHIVIO DI STATO DI ANCONA

Via A. Maggini, 80 - 60127 Ancona

Website <**www.provincia.ancona.it/Engine/ RAServePG.php**>

Access instructions <**www.asancona. beniculturali.it**>

Aosta

Website <www.regione.vda.it>

Arezzo

ARCHIVIO DI STATO DI AREZZO

Piazza del Commissario, 1 - 52100 Arezzo

Website <www.provincia.arezzo.it>

Access instructions <www.archiviostato.arezzo.it>

Ascoli Piceno

ARCHIVIO DI STATO DI ASCOLI PICENO

Via San Serafino da Montegranaro, 8/c - 63100 Ascoli Piceno

Website <www.provincia.ap.it>
Access instructions <www.archiviodistatoap.it>

Asti

ARCHIVIO DI STATO DI ASTI

Via G. Govone, 9 - 14100 Asti

Website <www.provincia.asti.gov.it>

Access instructions <www.archiviodistatoasti.beniculturali.it>

Avellino

ARCHIVIO DI STATO DI AVELLINO

Via G. Verdi, 15/17 - 83100 Avellino

Website <www.provincia.avellino.it>

Access instructions <www.asavellino.beniculturali.it/index.php/en>

Bari

ARCHIVIO DI STATO DI BARI

Via Pietro Oreste, 45 - 70123 Bari

Website <www.cittametropolitana.ba.it/provinciaba/s2magazine/index1.jsp?idPagina=2>

Access instructions <www.archiviodistatodibari.beniculturali.it>

Barletta-Andria-Trani

ARCHIVIO DI STATO DI BARI. SEZIONE DI BARLETTA

Via Ferdinando d'Aragona, 132 - 76121 Baletta

Website <www.provincia.barletta-andria-trani.it>

Access instructions <www.archiviodistatodibari.beniculturali.it/index.php?it/109/sezione-di-barletta>

ARCHIVIO DI STATO DI BARI. SEZIONE DI TRANI

Piazza Sacra Regia Udienza, 3 - 76125 Trani

Access instructions <www.archiviodistatodibari.beniculturali.it/index.php?it/156/sezione-di-trani>

Belluno

ARCHIVIO DI STATO DI BELLUNO

Via Santa Maria dei Battuti, 3 - 32100 Belluno

Website <www.provincia.belluno.it/nqcontent.cfm?a_id=1>

Access instructions <www.asbelluno.beniculturali.it>

Benevento

ARCHIVIO DI STATO DI BENEVENTO

Via G. de Vita, 3 - 82100 Benevento

Website <www.provincia.benevento.it>

Access instructions
<archiviodistatobenevento.beniculturali.it>

Bergamo

ARCHIVIO DI STATO DI BERGAMO

Via F.lli Bronzetti, 24/26/30 - 24124
Bergamo

Website <www.provincia.bergamo.it/
Provpor/portalProcess.jsp>

Access instructions <www.asbergamo.
beniculturali.it>

Biella

ARCHIVIO DI STATO DI BIELLA

Via G. Arnulfo, 15/a - 13900 Biella

Website <www.provincia.biella.it/on-line/
Home.html>

Access instructions <www.asbi.it>

Bologna

ARCHIVIO DI STATO DI BOLOGNA

Piazza de' Celestini, 4 - 40123 Bologna

Website <www.cittametropolitana.bo.it/
portale>

Access instructions <www.
archiviodistatobologna.it>

**ARCHIVIO DI STATO DI BOLOGNA.
SEZIONE DI IMOLA**

Via G. Verdi, 6 - 40026 Imola

Access instructions <www.
archiviodistatobologna.it/it/imola>

Bolzano (South Tyrol)

ARCHIVIO DI STATO DI BOLZANO

Via A. Diaz, 8 - 39100 Bolzano

Website <www.provincia.bz.it/it/default.
asp>

Access instructions <www.asbolzano.
beniculturali.it>

Brescia

ARCHIVIO DI STATO DI BRESCIA

Via G. Galilei, 42/44 - 25123 Brescia

Website <www.provincia.brescia.it>

Access instructions <www.asbrescia.
beniculturali.it>

Brindisi

ARCHIVIO DI STATO DI BRINDISI

Piazza Santa Teresa, 4 - 72100 Brindisi

Website <www.provincia.brindisi.it>

Access instructions <www.asbrindisi.
beniculturali.it>

Cagliari

ARCHIVIO DI STATO DI CAGLIARI

Via Gallura, 2 - 09125 Cagliari

Website <www.provincia.cagliari.it/
ProvinciaCa>

Access instructions <www.
archiviostatocagliari.it>

Caltanissetta

ARCHIVIO DI STATO DI CALTANISSETTA

Via P. Borsellino, 2/2a - 93100 Caltanissetta

Website **<www.provincia.caltanissetta. it/010>**

Access instructions **<www.ascaltanissetta. beniculturali.it>**

Campobasso

ARCHIVIO DI STATO DI CAMPOBASSO

Via degli Orefici, 43 - 86100 Campobasso

Website **<www3.provincia.campobasso. it/flex/cm/pages/ServeBLOB.php/L/IT/ IDPagina/1>**

Access instructions **<www.ascampobasso. beniculturali.it>**

Carbonia-Iglesias

Website **<www.provincia.carboniaiglesias.it>**

Caserta

ARCHIVIO DI STATO DI CASERTA

Viale dei Bersaglieri, 9 – 81100 Caserta

Website **<www.provincia.caserta.it/it/web/ il-sito-istituzionale/home>**

Access instructions **<www.ascaserta. beniculturali.it>**

Catania

ARCHIVIO DI STATO DI CATANIA

Via Vittorio Emanuele, 156 - 95131 Catania

Website **<www.cittametropolitana.ct.it>**

Access instructions **<www.ascatania. beniculturali.it>**

ARCHIVIO DI STATO DI CATANIA. SEZIONE DI CALTAGIRONE

Via S. Maria di Gesù, 90 - 95041 Caltagirone

Access instructions **<www.ascatania. beniculturali.it/index.php?it/196/ sezione-di-archivio-di-stato-di-caltagirone>**

Catanzaro

ARCHIVIO DI STATO DI CATANZARO

Piazza Rosario, 6 - 88100 Catanzaro

Website **<www.provincia.catanzaro.it>**

Access instructions **<www.ascatanzaro. beniculturali.it>**

ARCHIVIO DI STATO DI CATANZARO. SEZIONE DI LAMEZIA TERME

Via A. Moro, 40, Palazzo Gigliotti - 88046 Lamezia Terme

Access instructions **<www.ascatanzaro. beniculturali.it/index.php?it/143/sezione- di-archivio-di-stato-di-lamezia-terme>**

Chieti

ARCHIVIO DI STATO DI CHIETI

Via F. Ferri, 25/27 - 66100 Chieti

Website **<www.provincia.chieti.it/flex/cm/ pages/ServeBLOB.php/L/IT/IDPagina/1>**

Access instructions **<www.aschieti. beniculturali.it>**

ARCHIVIO DI STATO DI CHIETI. SEZIONE DI LANCIANO

Viale Cappuccini, 131 - 66034 Lanciano (CH)

Access instructions **<www.aschieti. beniculturali.it/index.php?it/97/ sezione-di-archivio-di-stato-di-lanciano>**

Como

ARCHIVIO DI STATO DI COMO

Via Briantea, 8 - 22100 Como

Website <www.provincia.como.it>
Access instructions <www.ascomo.beniculturali.it>

Cosenza

ARCHIVIO DI STATO DI COSENZA

Via G. V. Gravina, 12, zona Paparelle (ex Caserma)

Website <www.provincia.cosenza.it/portale>

Access instructions <www.archiviodistatocosenza.beniculturali.it>

ARCHIVIO DI STATO DI COSENZA. SEZIONE DI CASTROVILLARI

Via Porta della Catena, - 87012 Castrovillari

Access instructions <www.archiviodistatocosenza.beniculturali.it/index.php?it/130/sezione-di-archivio-di-stato-di-castrovillari>

Cremona

ARCHIVIO DI STATO DI CREMONA

Via Antica Porta Tintoria, 2 - 26100 Cremona

Website <www.provincia.cremona.it>

Access instructions <www.archiviodistatocremona.beniculturali.it>

Cuneo

ARCHIVIO DI STATO DI CUNEO

Corso Marcello Soleri, 6 - 12100 Cuneo

Website <www.provincia.cuneo.gov.it>

Access instructions <www.ascuneo.beniculturali.it>

Enna

ARCHIVIO DI STATO DI ENNA

Via A. Tranchida, contrada S.Lucia, - 94100 Enna

Website <www.provincia.enna.it>

Access instructions <www.asenna.beniculturali.it>

Fermo

ARCHIVIO DI STATO DI FERMO

Via A.Saffi, 5 - 63023 Fermo

Website <www.provincia.fermo.it>

Access instructions <www.asfermo.beniculturali.it>

Ferrara

ARCHIVIO DI STATO DI FERRARA

Corso della Giovecca, 146 - 44100 Ferrara

Website <www.provincia.fe.it>

Access instructions <www.asferrara.beniculturali.it>

Firenze

ARCHIVIO DI STATO DI FIRENZE

Viale Giovine Italia, 6 - 50122 Firenze

Website <www.cittametropolitana.fi.it>

Access instructions <www.archiviodistato.firenze.it/asfi/index.php?id=2>

Foggia

ARCHIVIO DI STATO DI FOGGIA

Piazza XX Settembre, 3 - 71121 Foggia

Website <www.provincia.foggia.it>

Access instructions <www.archiviodistatofoggia.beniculturali.it>

ARCHIVIO DI STATO DI FOGGIA. SEZIONE DI LUCERA

Via dei Saraceni, 1 - 71036 Lucera

Access instructions <www.archiviodistatofoggia.beniculturali.it/index.php?it/3/le-sedi-ed-i-servizi-dellarchivio-di-stato-di-foggia>

Forlì-Cesena

ARCHIVIO DI STATO DI FORLÌ

Via dei Gerolimini, 6 - 47121 Forlì

Website <web.provincia.fc.it>

Access instructions <www.asforli.beniculturali.it>

ARCHIVIO DI STATO DI FORLÌ. SEZIONE DI CESENA

Via Montalti, 4 - 47521 Cesena

Access instructions <www.asfo.beniculturali.it>

Frosinone

ARCHIVIO DI STATO DI FROSINONE

Piazza De Matthaeis, 41 - 03100 Frosinone

Website <www.provincia.fr.it>

Access instructions <www.asfrosinone.beniculturali.it>

ARCHIVIO DI STATO DI FROSINONE. SEZIONE DI ANAGNI-GUARCINO

Via del Monastero, 71 - 03012 Anagni

Access instructions <www.asfrosinone.beniculturali.it/index.php?it/148/archivio-di-stato-di-frosinone-sezione-di-anagni-guarcino>

Genova

ARCHIVIO DI STATO DI GENOVA

Piazza S. Maria in Via Lata, 7 - 16128 Genova

Website <www.cittametropolitana.genova.it>

Access instructions <www.asgenova.beniculturali.it>

Gorizia

ARCHIVIO DI STATO DI GORIZIA

Via dell'Ospitale, 2 - 34170 Gorizia

Website <www.provincia.gorizia.it/custom/home.php>

Access instructions <www.archiviodistatogorizia.beniculturali.it>

Grosseto

ARCHIVIO DI STATO DI GROSSETO

Piazza E. Socci, 3 - 58100 Grosseto

Website <www.provincia.grosseto.it/#&panel1-1>

Access instructions <www.asgrosseto.beniculturali.it>

Imperia

ARCHIVIO DI STATO DI IMPERIA

Viale G. Matteotti, 105 - 18100 Imperia

Website <www.provincia.imperia.it>

Access instructions <www.asimperia.beniculturali.it>

ARCHIVIO DI STATO DI IMPERIA. SEZIONE DI SAN REMO

Corso F. Cavallotti, 362 - 18038 San Remo

Access instructions <www.asimperia.beniculturali.it/index.php?it/152/sezione-di-san-remo>

ARCHIVIO DI STATO DI IMPERIA. SEZIONE DI VENTIMIGLIA

Via Hanbury, 12 - 18039 Ventimiglia

Access instructions <www.asimperia.beniculturali.it/index.php?it/153/sezione-di-ventimiglia>

Isernia

ARCHIVIO DI STATO DI ISERNIA

Corso Risorgimento, centro commerciale 2, palazzo INPDAP, - 86170 Isernia

Website <www.provincia.isernia.it>
Access instructions <www.asisernia.beniculturali.it>

L'Aquila

ARCHIVIO DI STATO DELL'AQUILA

Bazzano, zona industriale, via Galileo Galilei, 2 - 67100 L'Aquila

Website <www.provincialaquila.info>

Access instructions <www.archiviodistatolaquila.beniculturali.it>

ARCHIVIO DI STATO DELL'AQUILA. SEZIONE DI AVEZZANO

Piazza Torlonia, 36 - 67051 Avezzano

Access instructions <www.archiviodistatolaquila.beniculturali.it/index.php?it/121/sezione-di-avezzano>

ARCHIVIO DI STATO DELL'AQUILA. SEZIONE DI SULMONA

Viale Sant'Antonio, 30 - 67039 Sulmona

Access instructions <www.archiviodistatolaquila.beniculturali.it/index.php?it/120/sezione-di-sulmona>

La Spezia

ARCHIVIO DI STATO DI LA SPEZIA

Via L. Galvani, 21 - 19124 La Spezia

Website <www.provincia.sp.it/flex/cm/pages/ServeBLOB.php/L/IT/IDPagina/1>

Access instructions <archiviodistatolaspezia.beniculturali.it>

Latina

ARCHIVIO DI STATO DI LATINA

Address: via dei Piceni, 24 - 04100 Latina

Website <www.provincia.latina.it/flex/cm/pages/ServeBLOB.php/L/IT/IDPagina/1>

Access instructions <www.archiviodistatolatina.beniculturali.it>

Lecce

ARCHIVIO DI STATO DI LECCE

Via Sozy Carafa, 15 - 73100 Lecce

Website <www.provincia.le.it/web/provincialecce;jsessionid=7482D1C13535D579760D1E4EB482B21B>

Access instructions <www.archiviodistatolecce.beniculturali.it>

Livorno

ARCHIVIO DI STATO DI LIVORNO

Via Fiume, 40 - 57123 Livorno

Website <www.provincia.livorno.it>

Access instructions <www.aslivorno.beniculturali.it>

Lucca

ARCHIVIO DI STATO DI LUCCA

Sede Centrale: Piazza G. Guidiccioni, 8 55100 Lucca

Sede Sussidiaria: Via dei Pubblici Macelli, 155 - 55100 Lucca

Website <www.provincia.lucca.it>

Access instructions <www. archiviodistatoinlucca.beniculturali.it/ index.php?id=46>

Macerata

ARCHIVIO DI STATO DI MACERATA

Corso Fratelli Cairoli, 175 - 62100 Macerata

Website <www.provincia.mc.it>

Access instructions <www. archiviodistatomacerata.beniculturali.it>

ARCHIVIO DI STATO DI MACERATA. SEZIONE DI CAMERINO

Via Viviano Venanzi, 20 - 62032 Camerino

Access instructions <www. archiviodistatomacerata.beniculturali.it/ index.php?it/148/sezione-di-camerino>

Mantova

ARCHIVIO DI STATO DI MANTOVA

Via Ardigò, 11 - 46100 Mantova

Website <www.provincia.mantova.it>

Access instructions <www.asmantova. beniculturali.it>

Massa-Carrara

ARCHIVIO DI STATO DI MASSA

Via G. Sforza, 3 - 54100 Massa

Website <portale.provincia.ms.it>

Access instructions <www.asmassa. beniculturali.it>

ARCHIVIO DI STATO DI MASSA. SEZIONE DI PONTREMOLI

Via Nazionale, ex Convento SS. Annunziata, - 54027 Pontremoli

Access instructions <www.asmassa. beniculturali.it/index.php?it/165/ sezione-di-pontremoli>

Matera

ARCHIVIO DI STATO DI MATERA

Via T. Stigliani, 25 - 75100 Matera

Website <www.provincia.matera.it/ Provincia>

Access instructions <www.asmatera. beniculturali.it>

Messina

ARCHIVIO DI STATO DI MESSINA

Via Giuseppe La Farina, 293 - 98124 Messina

Website <www.cittametropolitana.me.it>

Access instructions <www.asmessina. beniculturali.it>

Milano

ARCHIVIO DI STATO DI MILANO

Via Senato, 10 - 20121 Milano

Website <www.cittametropolitana.mi.it>

Access instructions <www.asmilano. beniculturali.it>

Modena

ARCHIVIO DI STATO DI MODENA

Corso C. Cavour, 21 - 41121 Modena

Website <www.provincia.modena.it>

Access instructions <www.asmo.beniculturali.it>

Napoli

ARCHIVIO DI STATO DI NAPOLI

Piazzetta del Grande Archivio, 5 - 80138 Napoli

Website <www.cittametropolitana.na.it>

Access instructions <www.archiviodistatonapoli.it>

Novara

ARCHIVIO DI STATO DI NOVARA

Via dell'Archivio, 2 - 28100 Novara

Website <www.provincia.novara.it>
Access instructions <www.asnovara.beniculturali.it>

Nuoro

ARCHIVIO DI STATO DI NUORO

Via A. Mereu, 49 - 08100 Nuoro

Website <www.provincia.nuoro.gov.it/index.asp>

Access instructions <www.archiviodistatonuoro.beniculturali.it>

Ogliastra

Website <www.provinciaogliastra.gov.it/provincia>

Olbia-Tempio

Website <www.provincia.olbia-tempio.it/joomla15/index.php>

Oristano

ARCHIVIO DI STATO DI ORISTANO

Piazza Ungheria, 9 - 09170 Oristano

Website <www.provincia.or.it/it/index.html>

Access instructions <www.archiviodistatooristano.beniculturali.it>

Padova

ARCHIVIO DI STATO DI PADOVA

Via dei Colli, 24 - 35143 Padova

Website <www.provincia.pd.it>

Access instructions <www.aspd.beniculturali.it>

Palermo

ARCHIVIO DI STATO DI PALERMO

Sede centrale: Corso Vittorio Emanuele, 31

Sede della Gancia: 1° Cortile Gancia, - 90133

Website <www.cittametropolitana.pa.it/provpa/provincia_di_palermo/00003757_Home_Page.html>

Access instructions <www.archiviodistatodipalermo.it>

ARCHIVIO DI STATO DI PALERMO. SEZIONE DI TERMINI IMERESE

Via Stesicoro, 242 - 90018 Termini Imerese

Access instructions <www.archiviodistatodipalermo.it/pagina.php?id=28>

Parma

ARCHIVIO DI STATO DI PARMA

Strada M. d'Azeglio, 45 (*sede sussidiaria*: via La Spezia 46) - 43125 ParmaWebsite <www.provincia.parma.it>

Access instructions <www.asparma.beniculturali.it>

Pavia

ARCHIVIO DI STATO DI PAVIA

Via G. Cardano, 45 - 27100 Pavia

Website **<www.provincia.pv.it/index. php?lang=it>**

Access instructions **<www. archiviodistatopavia.beniculturali.it>**

Perugia

ARCHIVIO DI STATO DI PERUGIA

Piazza Giordano Bruno, 10 - 06100 Perugia

Website **<www.provincia.perugia.it/home>**

Access instructions **<www. archiviodistatoperugia.it>**

ARCHIVIO DI STATO DI PERUGIA. SEZIONE DI ASSISI

Corso G. Mazzini, 10 - 06081 Assisi

Access instructions **<www. archiviodistatoperugia.it/listituto/le-sedi/ assisi>**

ARCHIVIO DI STATO DI PERUGIA. SEZIONE DI FOLIGNO

Piazza del Grano, 1 - 06034 Foligno

Access instructions **<www. archiviodistatoperugia.it/listituto/le-sedi/ foligno>**

ARCHIVIO DI STATO DI PERUGIA. SEZIONE DI GUBBIO

Piazza XL Martiri, 1 - 06024 Gubbio

Access instructions **<www.archivio- distatoperugia.it/L%27Istituto/Le%20sedi/ Gubbio>**

ARCHIVIO DI STATO DI PERUGIA. SEZIONE DI SPOLETO

Largo G. Ermini, 1 - 06049 Spoleto

Access instructions **<www. archiviodistatoperugia.it/listituto/le-sedi/ spoleto>**

Pesaro e Urbino

ARCHIVIO DI STATO DI PESARO

Via della Neviera, 44 - 61100 Pesaro

Website **<www.provincia.pu.it>**
Access instructions **<aspesaro. beniculturali.it>**

ARCHIVIO DI STATO DI PESARO. SEZIONE DI FANO

Via C. Castracane, 1 - 61032 Fano

Access instructions **<aspesaro. beniculturali.it/?it/151/sezione-di-fano>**

ARCHIVIO DI STATO DI PESARO. SEZIONE DI URBINO

Via Piano Santa Lucia, 11 - 61029 Urbino

Access instructions **<aspesaro. beniculturali.it/?it/152/sezione-di-urbino>**

Pescara

ARCHIVIO DI STATO DI PESCARA

Via C. De Titta, 1 - 65129 Pescara

Website **<www.provincia.pescara.it>**

Access instructions **<www. archiviodistatopescara.beniculturali.it>**

Piacenza

ARCHIVIO DI STATO DI PIACENZA

Piazza Cittadella, 29 - 29121 Piacenza

Website **<www.provincia.piacenza.it>**

Access instructions **<www. archiviodistatopiacenza.beniculturali.it>**

Pisa

ARCHIVIO DI STATO DI PISA

Lungarno Mediceo, 30 - 56100 Pisa

Website <www.provincia.pisa.it>

Access instructions <www.aspisa.beniculturali.it>

Pistoia

ARCHIVIO DI STATO DI PISTOIA

Piazzetta Scuole Normali, 2 - 51100 Pistoia

Website <www.provincia.pistoia.it>

Access instructions <www.aspistoia.beniculturali.it>

ARCHIVIO DI STATO DI PISTOIA. SEZIONE DI PESCIA

Piazza XX Settembre, 3 - 51017 Pescia

Access instructions <www.aspistoia.beniculturali.it/index.php?it/164/sezione-di-archivio-di-stato-di-pescia>

Pordenone

ARCHIVIO DI STATO DI PORDENONE

Via Montereale, 7 - 33170 Pordenone

Website <www.provincia.pordenone.it>

Access instructions <www.aspordenone.beniculturali.it>

Potenza

ARCHIVIO DI STATO DI POTENZA

Via N. Sauro, 1 - 85100 Potenza

Website <www.provincia.potenza.it/provincia/home.jsp>

Access instructions <archiviodistatopotenza.beniculturali.it/aspz/Startup.do>

Prato

ARCHIVIO DI STATO DI PRATO

Via Ser Lapo Mazzei, 41 - 59100 Prato

Website <www.provincia.prato.it>

Access instructions <www.archiviodistato.prato.it>

Ragusa

ARCHIVIO DI STATO DI RAGUSA

Viale del Fante, 7 - 97100 Ragusa

Website <www.provincia.ragusa.it>

Access instructions <www.asragusa.beniculturali.it>

ARCHIVIO DI STATO DI RAGUSA. SEZIONE DI MODICA

Via Liceo Convitto, 33 - 97015 Modica

Access instructions <www.asragusa.beniculturali.it/index.php?it/193/sezione-di-archivio-di-stato-di-modica>

Ravenna

ARCHIVIO DI STATO DI RAVENNA

Piazzetta dell'Esarcato, 1 - 48121 Ravenna

Website <www.provincia.ra.it>

Access instructions <www.asravenna.beniculturali.it>

ARCHIVIO DI STATO DI RAVENNA. SEZIONE DI FAENZA

Via Manfredi, 14 - 48018 Faenza

Access instructions <www.asravenna.beniculturali.it/index.php?it/144/larchivio>

Reggio Calabria

ARCHIVIO DI STATO DI REGGIO CALABRIA

Via L. Casalotto - 89122 Reggio Calabria

Website <www.provincia.rc.it>

Access instructions
<archiviodistatoreggiocalabria.beniculturali.it>

ARCHIVIO DI STATO DI REGGIO CALABRIA. SEZIONE DI LOCRI

Via G. Matteotti, 356 - 89044 Locri

ARCHIVIO DI STATO DI REGGIO CALABRIA. SEZIONE DI PALMI

Via Carbone, 3 - 89015 Palmi

Reggio Emilia

ARCHIVIO DI STATO DI REGGIO EMILIA

Corso Cairoli, 6 - 42122 Reggio Emilia

Website <www.provincia.re.it>

Access instructions <www.
archiviodistatoreggioemilia.beniculturali.it>

Rieti

ARCHIVIO DI STATO DI RIETI

Viale L. Canali, 7 - 02100 Rieti

Website <www.provincia.rieti.it>

Access instructions <www.asrieti.it>

Rimini

ARCHIVIO DI STATO DI RIMINI

Piazzetta San Bernardino, 1 - 47900 Rimini

Website <www.provincia.rimini.it>

Access instructions <www.
archiviodistatorimini.beniculturali.it>

Roma

ARCHIVIO DI STATO DI ROMA

Website <www.cittametropolitanaroma.gov.it>

Sede di Sant'Ivo alla Sapienza:

Corso del Rinascimento, 40 - 00186 Roma

Access instructions <www.
archiviodistatoroma.beniculturali.it>

Sede di via Galla Placidia:

Via di Galla Placidia, 93 - 00159 Roma

Access instructions <www.
archiviodistatoroma.beniculturali.it>

Rovigo

ARCHIVIO DI STATO DI ROVIGO

Via Sichirollo, 9-11 - 45100 Rovigo

Website <provincia.rovigo.it/web/provro>

Access instructions <www.
archiviodistatorovigo.beniculturali.it>

Salerno

ARCHIVIO DI STATO DI SALERNO

Piazza Abate Conforti, 7- 84121 Salerno

Website <www.provincia.salerno.it>

Access instructions <www.
archiviodistatosalerno.beniculturali.it>

Sassari

ARCHIVIO DI STATO DI SASSARI

Via G. M. Angioy, 1/A - 07100 Sassari

Website <www.provincia.sassari.it>

Access instructions <www.assassari.beniculturali.it>

Savona

ARCHIVIO DI STATO DI SAVONA

Address: Via Valletta San Cristoforo, 15R - 17100 Savona

Website <www.provincia.savona.it>

Access instructions <www.assavona.beniculturali.it>

Siena

ARCHIVIO DI STATO DI SIENA

Via Banchi di Sotto, 52 - 53100 Siena

Website <www.provincia.siena.it>

Access instructions <www.archiviodistato.siena.it>

Siracusa

ARCHIVIO DI STATO DI SIRACUSA

Via Turchia, 4/s - 96100 Siracusa

Website <www.provincia.siracusa.it>

Access instructions <www.assiracusa.beniculturali.it>

ARCHIVIO DI STATO DI SIRACUSA. SEZIONE DI NOTO

Via S. Impellizzeri, 2 - 96017 Noto

Access instructions <www.assiracusa.beniculturali.it/index.php?it/100/sezione-di-archivio-di-stato-di-noto>

Sondrio

ARCHIVIO DI STATO DI SONDRIO

Via Dante/via Perego, - 23100 Sondrio

Website <www.provincia.so.it>

Access instructions <www.assondrio.beniculturali.it>

Taranto

ARCHIVIO DI STATO DI TARANTO

Via F. di Palma, 4 - 74123 Taranto

Website <www.provincia.taranto.it>

Access instructions <www.astaranto.beniculturali.it>

Teramo

ARCHIVIO DI STATO DI TERAMO

Sede Sant'Agostino: Via C. Battisti, 55

Sede San Domenico: Corso Porta Romana, 68-64100 Teramo

Website <www.provincia.teramo.it>

Access instructions <www.archiviodistatoteramo.beniculturali.it/index.php?it/1/home>

Terni

ARCHIVIO DI STATO DI TERNI

Via C. Cavour, 28 - 05100 Terni

Access instructions <www.asterni.beniculturali.it>

ARCHIVIO DI STATO DI TERNI. SEZIONE DI ORVIETO

Piazza del Duomo, 31- 05018 Orvieto

Access instructions <www.asterni.beniculturali.it/index.php?it/144/sezione-di-archivio-di-stato-di-orvieto>

Torino

ARCHIVIO DI STATO DI TORINO

Sezione Corte: Piazza Castello, 209 - 10124 Torino

Sezioni Riunite: Via Piave, 21 - 10122 Torino

Website **<www.cittametropolitana.torino.it/cms/index.php>**

Access instructions **<archiviodistatotorino.beniculturali.it>**

Trapani

ARCHIVIO DI STATO DI TRAPANI

Via Libertà, 35; piazzetta Sant'Anna - 91100 Trapani

Website **<www.provincia.trapani.it/hh/index.php>**

Access instructions **<www.astrapani.beniculturali.it>**

Trento

ARCHIVIO DI STATO DI TRENTO

Via Maestri del Lavoro, 4 - 38121 Trento

Website **<www.provincia.tn.it>**

Access instructions **<www.astrento.beniculturali.it>**

Treviso

ARCHIVIO DI STATO DI TREVISO

Via Pietro di Dante, 11 - 31100 Treviso

Website **<www.provincia.treviso.it>**

Access instructions **<www.archiviodistatotreviso.beniculturali.it>**

Trieste

ARCHIVIO DI STATO DI TRIESTE

Via A. La Marmora, 17 - 34139 Trieste

Website **<www.provincia.trieste.it/opencms/opencms/it>**

Access instructions **<www.archiviodistatotrieste.it/web/index.php/it>**

Udine

ARCHIVIO DI STATO DI UDINE

Via F. Urbanis, 1 - 33100 Udine

Website **<www.provincia.udine.it>**

Access instructions **<www.archiviodistatoudine.beniculturali.it>**

Varese

ARCHIVIO DI STATO DI VARESE

Via Col di Lana, 5 - 21100 Varese

Website **<www.provincia.va.it>**

Access instructions **<www.archiviodistatovarese.beniculturali.it>**

Venezia

ARCHIVIO DI STATO DI VENEZIA

Campo dei Frari, 3002 San Polo - 30125 Venezia

Website **<www.cittametropolitana.ve.it>**

Access instructions **<www.archiviodistatovenezia.it/web>**

Verbano-Cusio-Ossola

ARCHIVIO DI STATO DI VERBANIA

Via L. Cadorna, 37 - 28922 Verbania

Website <www.provincia.verbano-cusio-ossola.it>

Access instructions <www.asverbania.beniculturali.it>

Vercelli

ARCHIVIO DI STATO DI VERCELLI

Via A. Manzoni, 11 - 13100 Vercelli

Website <www.provincia.vercelli.it>

Access instructions <www.asvercelli.beniculturali.it>

ARCHIVIO DI STATO DI VERCELLI. SEZIONE DI VARALLO

Via T. Rossi, 9 - 13019 Varallo

Access instructions <www.asvercelli.beniculturali.it>

Verona

ARCHIVIO DI STATO DI VERONA

Via S. Teresa, 6 - 37135 Verona

Website <portale.provincia.vr.it>

Access instructions <www.archiviodistatoverona.beniculturali.it/index.php?it/1/home>

Vibo Valentia

ARCHIVIO DI STATO DI VIBO VALENTIA

Via J. Palach, 46 - 89900 Vibo Valentia

Website <www.provincia.vibovalentia.it>

Access instructions <www.asvibo.beniculturali.it>

Vicenza

ARCHIVIO DI STATO DI VICENZA

Borgo Casale, 91 - 36100 Vicenza

Website <www.provincia.vicenza.it>

Access instructions <www.archiviodistatovicenza.beniculturali.it>

ARCHIVIO DI STATO DI VICENZA. SEZIONE DI BASSANO DEL GRAPPA

Via Beata Giovanna, 58 - 36061 Bassano del Grappa

Access instructions <www.archiviodistatovicenza.beniculturali.it/index.php?it/171/archivio-di-stato-sezione-di-bassano>

Vitterbo

ARCHIVIO DI STATO DI VITERBO

Via V. Cardarelli, 18 - 01100 Viterbo

Website <www.provincia.viterbo.gov.it>

Access instructions <www.archiviodistatoviterbo.beniculturali.it>

Sample Letters to Request Records

While more and more records are being made available to researchers online, you'll still want to contact an individual *parrocchia* (parish), *archivio di stato* (state archive), or *ufficio stato civile* (town civil office) to conduct research and request copies of records. Researchers planning to travel to the homeland might also want to set up an appointment at an archive or office, opening up new avenues for your research. But how do you request that information or set up an appointment if you don't speak Italian?

This section contains sample letters you can use when requesting information or scheduling an appointment from a records repository. Each includes sample text to include in your correspondence (whether by mail or e-mail), plus a set of instructions and a translation on the opposite page. Simply follow the instructions and plug in the appropriate information to craft a mail-ready request letter to an Italian archive.

If you'd like to see more sample text (e.g., if you have a more specific request to make of an archive), check out the FamilySearch Wiki's Italy letter writing guide <www.familysearch.org/wiki/en/Italy_Letter_Writing_Guide>.

REQUEST FOR RECORD

1. Decide which archive(s) you want to request records from. Use this book's information on record types to determine what resources you'd like to find and where those documents are held for your ancestor's place of origin. It's wise to order no more than two documents at a time, as the archive is more likely to process a quick request.

2. Find the appropriate address and/or e-mail address for the archive, usually on the organization's website. Simply search for your ancestor's town/parish (e.g., *Comune di Agrigento*), or consult the list of provinces/archives in appendix B.

3. Copy the template below into an e-mail or word-processing program.

4. Replace the [Name,] [Date], and [Address] fields with the current date and the archive/parish/office's name and contact information at the top right of your message. Be sure to format the address correctly. Keep in mind that most European countries (including Italy) use the date-month-year format for dates, and Italians use a period instead of a

---

SAMPLE LETTER

[Date]
[Name of archive]
[Address of archive]

Spett.le,

Mi chiamo [your name, surname first]. Sto svolgendo una ricerca sui miei antenati, ed avrei bisogno di informazioni dal Vostro Archivio, circa l'atto di [type of record] di [ancestor's name], nato [place of birth] il [date of event—DD.MM.YYYY].

Resto in attesa di una Vostra risposta al riguardo, anche per quanto riguarda i costi per i suddetti atti.

Vi ringrazio per la Vostra attenzione e collaborazione.

Distinti saluti,
[Your name, surname first]
[Your signature]
[Your address]
[Your e-mail address]

slash between the day, month, and year. (For example, December 8, 2017, would be written as *08.12.2017*). If you spell out the name of a month, be sure to write it in Italian.

5. Add your name, address, e-mail address, the type of record you're requesting, and your ancestor's name and birth/marriage/death information in the appropriate spaces. Be as specific as possible. Again: The easier it is for the employees to find, the more apt they are to timely process your request.

6. Consider including additional information to your request based on the record you're searching for. For example, add your ancestor's death date (and, if you know it, place) if you're seeking a civil death record, and add *per uso cittadinanza* if the document is needed for dual citizenship purposes. Use the word lists in appendix D to help.

7. Sign your name, add your address, and include your e-mail address, in case they wish to correspond with you about postal fees owed for the request or with questions.

TRANSLATION

[Date]
[Name of archive]
[Address of archive]

Dear Sirs,

My name is [your name, surname first]. I am conducting research on my ancestors, and I need information from your archive about the [type of record] act for [ancestor's name], born in [birth place] on [DD/MM/YYYY].

I am waiting for your response to this, even with regard to the costs for these acts.

Thank you for your attention and collaboration.

Best regards,
[Your name, surname first]
[Your signature]
[Your address]
[Your e-mail address]

REQUEST FOR RESEARCH APPOINTMENT

1. Determine when you will be in Italy and what days you are available to research. Most archives operate on the 9 a.m. to 1 p.m. schedule, though state archives have different hours.

2. Decide which archive(s) you want to visit. Use this book's chapters on individual records to determine what resources you'd like to find and where those documents are held for your ancestor's place of residence.

3. Find the appropriate address and/or e-mail address for the archive, usually on the town/parish/archive website. Look at the bottom of a town's website for the address. Simply search for your ancestor's town/parish, or consult the list of provinces/archives in appendix B.

SAMPLE LETTER

[Date]
[Name of archive]
[Address of archive]

Spett.le,

Mi chiamo [your name], e sto svolgendo una ricerca sui miei antenati. Avrei bisogno di alcune informazioni dal Vostra Archivio. Al riguardo, vorrei chiederVi se é possibile avere un appuntamento per effettuare una ricerca, riguardante la famiglia [surname, dates].

Resto in attesa di una Vostra risposta in merito.

Vi ringrazio per la Vostra attenzione e collaborazione.

Distinti saluti,
[Your name/signature]
[Your address]
[Your e-mail address]

4. Replace the name, date, and address fields with the current date and the archive/parish/office's contact information at the top right of your message. Be sure to format the address correctly, and keep in mind that most European countries (including Italy) use the date-month-year (DD.MM.YYYY) format for dates. If you spell out the name of a month, be sure to write it in Italian.

5. Add your name and the dates of your visit in the appropriate spaces. (Again, keep in mind that most Europeans use the DD.MM.YYYY format). Also add the names of the record type, the family surname you're researching, and what years you would like to search between (e.g., 1845–1890) in the respective spaces.

6. Sign your name, add your address, and include your e-mail address, in case the archive wishes to correspond with you about your request.

TRANSLATION

[Date]
[Name of archive]
[Address of archive]

Dear Sirs,

My name is [your name], and I'm doing research on my ancestors. I need some information from your archive. In this regard, I would like to ask you if it is possible to have an appointment to carry out a family search [surname, dates].

I am waiting for your answer.

Thank you for your attention and collaboration.

Best regards,
[Your name/signature]
[Your address]
[Your e-mail address]

D

Italian Genealogical Word Lists

As we discussed in chapter 6, Italian researchers don't need to speak Italian to understand genealogy records from the homeland. Rather, aspiring Italian genealogists need only learn a handful of vocabulary that is likely to appear in records. In this section, we'll share some of these useful terms in both Italian and Latin.

DAYS OF THE WEEK

English	Italian	Latin
Sunday	domenica	dominica, dies dominuca, dominicus, dies Solis, feria prima
Monday	lunedì	feria secunda, dies Lunae
Tuesday	martedì	eria tertia, dies Martis
Wednesday	mercoledì	feria quarta, dies Mercurii
Thursday	giovedì	feria quinta, dies Jovis
Friday	venerdì	feria sexta, dies Veneris
Saturday	sabato	feria septima, sabbatum, dies sabbatinus, dies Saturni

MONTHS OF THE YEAR

English	Italian	Latin
January	gennaio	Januarius
February	febbraio	Februarius
March	marzo	Martius
April	aprile	Aprilis
May	maggio	Maius
June	giugno	Junius
July	luglio	Julius/Quintilis
August	agosto	Augustus/Sextilis
September (7bre)	settembre	September, Septembris
October (8bre)	ottobre	October, Octobris
November (9bre)	novembre	November, Novembris
December (10bre or Xbre)	dicembre	December, Decembris

NUMBERS

English	Italian		Latin	
	Cardinal (one, two, ...)	Ordinal (first, second, ...)	Cardinal (one, two, ...)	Ordinal (first, second, ...)
0	zero		nihil, nulla	
1	uno	primo(a)	unus (I)	primus
2	due	secondo(a)	duo (II)	secundus
3	tre	terzo(a)	tres (III)	tertius
4	quattro	quarto(a)	quattuor (IV)	quartus
5	cinque	quinto(a)	quinque (V)	quintus
6	sei	sesto(a)	sex (VI)	sextus
7	sette	settimo(a)	septem (VII)	septimus
8	otto	ottavo(a)	octo (VIII)	octavus
9	nove	nono(a)	novem (IX)	nonus
10	dieci	decimo(a)	decem (X)	decimus

English	Italian		Latin	
	Cardinal (one, two, …)	Ordinal (first, second, …)	Cardinal (one, two, …)	Ordinal (first, second, …)
11	undici	undicesimo(a)	undecim (XI)	undecimus
12	dodici	dodicesimo(a)	duodecim (XII)	duodecimus
13	tredici	tredicesimo(a)	tredecim (XIII)	tertius decimus
14	quattordici	quattordicesimo(a)	quattuordecim (XIV)	quartus decimus
15	quindici	quindicesimo(a)	quindecim (XV)	quintus decimus
16	sedici	sedicesimo(a)	sedecim (XVI)	sextus decimus
17	diciassette	diciassettesimo(a)	septendecim (XVII)	septimus decimus
18	diciotto	diciottesimo(a)	duodeviginti (XVIII)	duodevicesimus
19	diciannove	diciannovesimo(a)	undeviginti (XIX)	undevicesimus
20	venti	ventesimo(a)	viginti (XX)	vicesimus, vigesimus
21	ventuno	ventunesimo(a)	viginti unus (XXI)	vicesimus primus
22	ventidue	ventiduesimo(a)	viginti duo (XXII)	vicesimus secundus
23	ventitre	ventitreesimo(a)	viginti tres (XXIII)	vicesimus tertius
24	ventiquattro	ventiquattresimo(a)	viginti quattuor (XXIV)	vicesimus quartus
25	venticinque	venticinquesimo(a)	viginti quinque (XXV)	vicesimus quintus
26	ventisei	ventiseiesimo(a)	viginti sex (XXVI)	vicesimus sextus
27	ventisette	ventisettesimo(a)	viginti septem (XXVII)	vicesimus septimus
28	ventotto	ventottesimo(a)	duodetriginta/Viginti octo (XXVIII)	vicesimus octavus
29	ventinove	ventinovesimo(a)	undetriginta/viginti novem (XXIX)	vicesimus nonus
30	trenta	trentesimo(a)	triginta (XXX)	tricesimus
31	trentuno	trentunesimo(a)	triginta unus (XXXI)	triginta primus
40	quaranta	quarantesimo(a)	quadraginta (XL)	quadragesimus
50	cinquanta	cinquantesimo(a)	quinquaginta (L)	quinquagesimus
60	sessanta	sessantesimo(a)	sexaginta (LX)	sexagesimus
70	settanta	settantesimo(a)	septuaginta (LXX)	septuagesimus
80	ottanta	ottantesimo(a)	octoginta (LXXX)	octogesimus
90	novanta	novantesimo(a)	nonaginta (XC)	nonagesimus
100	cento	centesimo(a)	centum (C)	centesimus

FAMILY RELATIONSHIPS

Italian	Latin	English
bisnonna	proavia	great-grandmother
bisnonno	proavus	great-grandfather
cugino	amitinus, consobrina (f)/ consobrinus (m), matruelis (on mother's side), patruelis (on father's side)	cousin
figlia	filia	daughter
figliastro(a)	privigna (f), privignus (m)	stepchild
figlio	filius	son
figlioccio(a)	ejusque	godchild
fratello	frater	brother
genitori	parentes, genitores	parents
madre	mater	mother
madrina	commater, matrina, patrina, susceptorix	godmother
matrigna	noverca	stepmother
marito	maritus, sponsus, conjux, vir	husband
moglie	uxor, marita, conjux, sponsa, mulier, femina, consors	wife
neonato, neonata, infante, bambino	infans, filius (f)/filia (m), puer, proles	child
nipotina, nipote	neptis	granddaughter, niece
nipotino, nipote	nepos, nepotis	grandson, nephew
nonna	ava, avia	grandmother
nonni	avi	grandparents
nonno	avus	grandfather
padre	pater	father
padrini	susceptores, patrini, spirituales	godparents
padrino	compater, patrinus	godfather
patrigno	vitricus	stepfather
sorella	soror	sister
sposa	nupta, sponsa,	bride
sposo	cameranius, sponsus	bridegroom
vedovo(a)	vidua (f), viduus (m), relicta (f), relictus (m)	widower, widow
zia	amita (father's sister), matertera (mother's sister)	aunt
zio	avunculus (mother's brother), patruus (father's brother)	uncle

VITAL EVENTS

Italian	Latin	English
battesimo	baptismi, baptizatus, renatus, plutus, lautus, purgatus, ablutus, lustratio, battezzato	baptism
matrimonio	matrimonium, copulatio, copulati, conjuncti, intronizati, nupti, sponsati, ligati, mariti	marriage
morte	mortuus, defunctus, obitus, peritus, mors, mortis, obiit, decessit	death
nascita, nati	nati, natus, genitus, natales	birth
seppellimento, sepultura. sepulture, supoltura	sepulti, sepultus, humatus	burial

OTHER GENEALOGICAL TERMS

Italian	Latin	English
anno	anno, annus	year
certificato di stato di famiglia	libellum familiae statum	certificate of family status/state of the family certificate
cimitero	cimeterium, coemeterium	cemetery
cognome	cognomen	surname
giorno	feria, dies	day
indice	index, registrum, repertorium,	index
mese	mense, mensis	month
nome	nomen	name
nome da ragazza	virgo nomen	maiden name
occupazione	occupatio, megotium, capio, obcupatio	occupation
parrocchia	parochia, pariochialis	parish
passaporto	singraphus	passport
prenome	nomen	given name/first name
stato di famiglia storico	quisque statum familiae historia	historical state of the family certificate

INDEX

PHOTO CREDITS

COVER

Map: Courtesy the David Rumsey Map Collection
<www.davidrumsey.com>

Wedding: Courtesy the author

Woman: From the New York Public
Library <digitalcollections.nypl.org/
items/510d47da-dc88-a3d9-e040-e00a18064a99>

INTRODUCTION

p. 6 (left): Courtesy Getty Images

p. 6 (right): Courtesy the author

p. 7 (left): Courtesy Getty Images

p. 7 (right): Courtesy Getty Images

CHAPTER 1

Image A: Courtesy the author

International Immigration sidebar: Courtesy
Getty Images

Image B: Courtesy Ancestry.com <www.ancestry.
com>

Image C: Courtesy the author

Image D: Courtesy the author

CHAPTER 3

Image A: Courtesy Melissa Picceri Croad

Image B: Courtesy the author

Image C: Courtesy the author

Image D: Courtesy Ancestry.com <www.ancestry.com>

Image E: Courtesy Ancestry.com <www.ancestry.com>

Image F: Courtesy Ancestry.com <www.ancestry.com>

PHOTO CREDITS

CHAPTER 4

Image A: Courtesy Wikimedia Commons

Image B: Courtesy the Basilica di Santa Maria Assunta, Clusone, Italy

Image C: Courtesy the author

Image D: Courtesy of iStock <**www.istockphoto.com**>, owner: GeorgiosArt, used under extended license

Image E: Courtesy the author. Map out of copyright.

Image F: Courtesy Ron Venezie

CHAPTER 5

Image A: Courtesy the *Family Tree Magazine* archive

Image B: Illustration created by Cuccia Creative. Used with permission

Image C: Courtesy the Motore di Ricerca Parrocchie <**www.parrocchie.it**>

Image D: Courtesy the author

CHAPTER 6

Image A: Courtesy the Archivio di Stato di Palermo, Palermo, Italy

Image B: Courtesy the Tribunale di Potenza, Potenza, Italy

Image C: Courtesy the Archivio di Stato di Bergamo, Bergamo, Italy

Image D: Courtesy the author

CHAPTER 7

Image A: Courtesy the Archivio di Stato di Pescara, Pescara, Italy

Image B: Courtesy the Archivio di Stato di Palermo, Palermo, Italy

Image C: Courtesy the Archivio di Stato di Palermo, Palermo, Italy

CHAPTER 8

Image A: By User:Wento (chiesacattolica.it) [CC BY 2.5 (http://creativecommons.org/licenses/by/2.5)], via Wikimedia Commons

Image B: Courtesy the author

Image C: Courtesy the Parrocchia di Natività di Maria Santissima, Bogliasco, Italy

Image D: Courtesy the Parrocchia di Natività di Maria Santissima, Bogliasco, Italy

Image E: Courtesy the Parrocchia di Natività di Maria Santissima, Bogliasco, Italy

CHAPTER 9

Image A: Courtesy Archivio di Stato di Venezia, Venezia, Italy

Image B: Courtesy the Archivio di Stato di Avellino, Avellino, Italy

Image C: Courtesy the Sistema Informativo degli Archivi di Stato <**www.archivi-sias.it**>

Image D: Courtesy the Archivio Generale del Comune di Trieste, Trieste, Italy

Image E: Courtesy the Archivio di Stato di Palermo, Palermo, Italy

PHOTO CREDITS

CHAPTER 10

Image A: Courtesy the Archivio di Stato di Torino, Torino, Italy

Image B: Courtesy the Archivio di Stato di Torino, Torino, Italy

Image C: Courtesy the Archivio di Stato di Torino, Torino, Italy

Image D: Courtesy the Family History Library <www.familysearch.org>

Image E: Courtesy Conservatoria.it <**conservatoria.it**>

Image F: Courtesy the author

Image G: Courtesy the Agenzia Entrate <**www.agenziaentrate.gov.it**>

Image H: Courtesy Catasto.it <**www. catasto.it**>

CHAPTER 11

Image A: Courtesy the Family History Library <**www.familysearch.org**>

Image B: Courtesy the Archivio di Stato di Torino, Torino, Italy

Image C: Courtesy the Archivio di Stato di Napoli, Napoli, Italy

Image D: Courtesy the Archivio di Stato di Torino, Torino, Italy

Image E: Courtesy the Archivio di Stato di Torino, Torino, Italy

Image F: Courtesy the author

Image G: Courtesy Margaret R. Fortier

CHAPTER 12

Image A: Courtesy GenealogyBank <**www. genealogybank.com**>

Image B: Courtesy the Family History Library <**www.familysearch.org**>

Image C: Courtesy PagineBlanche <**www. paginebianche.it**>

Image D: Courtesy the Università di Bologna <**www.archiviostorico.unibo.it/ it/?LN=IT#**>

Image E: Courtesy the author

Image F: Courtesy the author

Image G: Courtesy the Archivio Generale del Comune di Trieste, Trieste, Italy

Image H: Courtesy the author

Image I: Courtesy the Covi family

CHAPTER 13

Image A: Courtesy the author

Image B: Courtesy the author

CHAPTER 14

Image A: Courtesy Ancestry.com <**www. ancestry.com**>

Image B: Courtesy of the Archivio di Stato di Palermo, Palermo, Italy

Image C: Courtesy of the Archivio di Stato di Napoli, Napoli, Italy

Image D: Courtesy the Association of Professional Genealogists <**www.apgen.org**>

ACKNOWLEDGEMENTS

My deepest thanks go to my patient and supportive husband and daughter who are my greatest fans. If not for them, I wouldn't be where I am today.

My sincere appreciation goes to my co-workers Corey Oiesen, Cathy Granatino Gill, and Michele Giove who aided me in pulling the contents of this book together. I am grateful to Suzanne Russo Adams for her help on the Italian military records chapter.

Thank you to all of the Italian archival staff for their help during this process. If it wasn't for their work in indexing, cataloguing, and conserving these records, the research on our ancestors would be so much harder. Appreciation also goes to FamilySearch, whose microfilming and digitization initiatives have made millions of Italian records accessible to all.

ABOUT THE AUTHOR

Melanie D. Holtz, CG is a full-time professional genealogist and owner of Lo Schiavo Genealogica **<www.italyancestry.com>**, an international business that maintains offices in both the United States and Italy. She travels frequently to Italy, expanding her skills in genealogy, history, and language. In 2010, Melanie became a board-certified genealogist and has worked as a professional genealogist for fourteen years. Her love of travel and the Italian language played a large part in the vocation she chose.

Melanie lectures and writes on Italian genealogy, dual citizenship, professional development, and genealogical standards. She's written courses for the Virtual Institute of Genealogical Research, Family Tree University, and the National Institute of Genealogical Studies. Melanie lectures around the country to various Italian organizations, historical societies, or at genealogical conferences.

As a former board member for the Association of Professional Genealogists (APG) and chair of APG's Professional Development Committee, she was an advocate for professionalism within the field of genealogy, mentorship, and expanded educational offerings within the organization. Melanie is also a co-administrator of the Virtual Institute of Genealogical Research **<www.vigrgenealogy.com>**, a business that offers Institute quality genealogical education using a virtual platform.

DEDICATION

To my descendants...I hope this book bring you a deeper understanding of yourself and the generations that came before you.

To my Italian immigrant ancestors, Antonino Lo Schiavo, Giuseppa Catanese, Matteo Catanese, and Maria Di Domenico...I am grateful for the sacrifices you made so that we might have and enjoy the life we have now.

To my Lord, whose love and grace get me through each day.

ISBN: 978-1-4403-4905-8

Other Family Tree Books are available from your local bookstore and online suppliers. For more genealogy resources, visit **<www. familytreemagazine.com/store>**.

21 20 19 18 17   5 4 3 2 1

DISTRIBUTED IN CANADA BY FRASER DIRECT
100 Armstrong Avenue
Georgetown, Ontario, Canada L7G 5S4
Tel: (905) 877-4411

DISTRIBUTED IN THE U.K. AND EUROPE BY
F&W Media International, LTD
Brunel House, Forde Close,
Newton Abbot, TQ12 4PU, UK
Tel: (+44) 1626 323200,
Fax (+44) 1626 323319
E-mail: enquiries@fwmedia.com

a content + ecommerce company

PUBLISHER AND COMMUNITY LEADER: Allison Dolan
EDITOR: Andrew Koch
DESIGNER: Julie Barnett
PRODUCTION COORDINATOR: Debbie Thomas

4 FREE

FAMILY TREE templates

- decorative family tree posters
- five-generation ancestor chart
- family group sheet
- bonus relationship chart
- type and save, or print and fill out

Download at <www.familytreemagazine.com/familytreefreebies>

MORE GREAT GENEALOGY RESOURCES

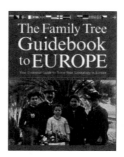
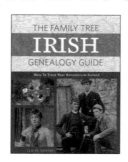
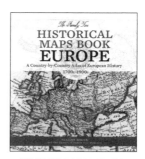